LAS RARAS

LAS RARAS

Feminine Style, Intellectual Networks, and Women Writers during Spanish-American Modernismo

Sarah Moody

VANDERBILT UNIVERSITY PRESS
Nashville, Tennessee

Copyright 2024 Vanderbilt University Press
All rights reserved
First printing 2024

This book will be made open access within three years of publication thanks to Path to Open, a program developed in partnership between JSTOR, the American Council of Learned Societies (ACLS), University of Michigan Press, and the University of North Carolina Press to bring about equitable access and impact for the entire scholarly community, including authors, researchers, libraries, and university presses around the world. Learn more at https://about.jstor.org/path-to-open/.

Library of Congress Cataloging-in-Publication Data
Names: Moody, Sarah, 1978- author.
Title: Las raras : feminine style, intellectual networks, and women writers during Spanish-American Modernismo / Sarah Moody.
Description: Nashville, Tennessee : Vanderbilt University Press, 2024. | Includes bibliographical references and index.
Identifiers: LCCN 2024011360 (print) | LCCN 2024011361 (ebook) | ISBN 9780826506887 (paperback) | ISBN 9780826506894 (hardcover) | ISBN 9780826506900 (epub) | ISBN 9780826506917 (pdf)
Subjects: LCSH: Spanish American literature--Women authors--History and criticism. | Modernism (Literature)--Latin America. | Women and literature--Latin America. | Latin America--Intellectual life--20th century. | LCGFT: Literary criticism.
Classification: LCC PQ7081.5 .M66 2024 (print) | LCC PQ7081.5 (ebook) | DDC 860.9/8287098--dc23/eng/20240511
LC record available at https://lccn.loc.gov/2024011360
LC ebook record available at https://lccn.loc.gov/2024011361

Front cover image: Portrait of Zoila Aurora Cáceres by Daniel Hernández, courtesy of Sistema de Biblioteca Colecciones Especiales, Pontificia Universidad Católica del Perú

For Will, Wyatt, and Elena

CONTENTS

Acknowledgments ix

INTRODUCTION. The Missing Women of Modernismo 1

1 The Feminine Aesthetic of Modernismo 17

2 *Crónicas de París*: Darío and Gómez Carrillo on the Feminine Modern 46

3 Alternative Modernities: Exile and the Re-invention of Clorinda Matto de Turner 76

4 *Rareza*: María Eugenia Vaz Ferreira and Montevideo's "Generation of 1900" 103

5 Souvenirs: Aurora Cáceres and the *Álbum personal* as Collection 134

CONCLUSION 157

Notes 163
Bibliography 191
Index 211

ACKNOWLEDGMENTS

The first sparks of this project started during my graduate studies at the University of California, Berkeley, a formative time that continues to fuel my work. I am unendingly grateful to Francine Masiello for her guidance, her inspiring example, and the title of this book. To many other professors there, including Gwen Kirkpatrick, José Luis Passos, Natalia Brizuela, Mark Healey, Ignacio Navarrete, Estelle Tarica, and Michael Iarocci, I send my gratitude. I thank the Tinker Foundation and, at UC Berkeley, the Department of Spanish and Portuguese and Verónica López, the Graduate Division, the Center for Latin American Studies, and the Center for Race and Gender for their support of my work. Thank you, Joanna O'Connell, for pointing the way to Berkeley.

For her friendship, support, and boundless energy, my deepest gratitude to Ana Corbalán. I greatly appreciate my wonderful colleagues at the University of Alabama, including Connie Janiga-Perkins, Bill Worden, Mike Schnepf, Erin O'Rourke, and Micah McKay. I thank Cheryl Toman, Doug Lightfoot, Tom Fox, and the UA Research Grants Committee, as well as Tricia McElroy, Robert Olin, and Joseph Messina in the College of Arts and Sciences for supporting this project. Riley Doyle's assistance was helpful and appreciated. Thank you to Claudia Cabello Hutt, Mónica González García, George Thompson, and Luisa Campuzano Sentí. My appreciation for access to materials goes to Cristina Echevarría in Uruguay and to Cristina Saori Almeida and Francesca Denegri in Peru, as well as to the Rubén Darío Collection with the digital *Archivo IIAC*, housed at Argentina's Universidad Tres de Febrero.

I am grateful to friends near and far: Rachel Stephens, Holly Grout, Jenny Shaw, Jolene Hubbs, Mercedes López Rodríguez, Mayra Bottaro, Nancy LaGreca, Ainai Morales Pino, Alejandra Aguilar Dornelles, Ronald Briggs, Andrew Reynolds, Vanesa Miseres, Carlos Abreu Mendoza, Aurélie Vialette, and Anna Hiller. Thank you for friendship, support, and all kinds of exciting ideas.

Francine, Gwen, and Bill were generous to read and offer suggestions on a draft of this book: thank you! I am grateful to Zack Gresham, who reached out and was patient with my slow process, as well as to the incomparable Gianna Mosser and her excellent staff at the Vanderbilt University Press, including Patrick Samuel, Joell Smith-Borne, and Alissa Faden. My deepest gratitude to the anonymous reviewers of *Las Raras*, whose suggestions made the book significantly better. Thank you to Silvia Benvenuto for her expert indexing assistance.

This book cover reproduces a portrait of Zoila Aurora Cáceres by the Peruvian artist Daniel Hernández. I found it in the *Álbum personal* of Cáceres, which is held by the Special Collections of the libraries of the Pontificia Universidad Católica del Perú (PUCP), and I thank them for granting me permission to use the image. Elements of the Introduction reflect part of my article published by *Chasqui*, "Radical Metrics and Feminist Rebellions: Agustini Rewrites Darío's *Prosas profanas*" (2014). Parts of Chapter 2 draw on material in my article "Women of Paris, World Literature, and a Counter-Mythology of the Metropolis in Manuel Ugarte's Early Literary Work," published by the *Bulletin of Hispanic Studies* (2016). Chapter 3 dialogues closely with the arguments presented in my book chapters "Clorinda Matto de Turner en la Cosmópolis moderna: Espacio urbano y comunidad intelectual en Buenos Aires" (in *Clorinda Matto en el siglo XIX*, edited by Ana Peluffo and Francesca Denegri, Fondo Editorial de la PUCP, 2022), and "Clorinda's Cosmopolis: Crisis, Reinvention, and the Birth of *Búcaro Americano*" (in the *Palgrave Handbook of Transnational Women's Writing in the Long Nineteenth Century*, edited by Claire Emilie Martin and Clorinda Donato, Palgrave Macmillan, 2024). I thank these presses and editors for their generous permission to continue publishing my work on these materials.

Thank you to my family and especially my parents, who allowed me to miss a year of high school and experience Argentina as a Rotary Exchange student. My gratitude also to the Rotary Clubs of Willmar, Minnesota, and Mercedes, Buenos Aires; to Alberto Rocca and Mark Morris; to my *compañeros* at the Escuela Normal of Mercedes; and to my beloved Argentine families, the Altieris, Zuninos, Bonets, Luchinis, and Finocchios.

For love and companionship on adventures of all sorts, I thank Will, Wyatt, and Elena.

INTRODUCTION
The Missing Women of Modernismo

In 1907, in her first book publication, a young Uruguayan poet named Delmira Agustini (1886–1914) presented an audacious critique of Modernismo, then a fashionable literary current. One example of the challenge she presented is found in the poem "El poeta y la ilusión" (The poet and illusion), which deconstructs the passive and beautiful muse: it describes a *princesita* (little princess) knocking on the poet's door late one night and, with the crystalline voice of a flute, offering her services as a muse. Sculpted as if in porcelain, with turquoise eyes and "a rose-pink soul," this archetypal Modernista muse finds herself swept into an overwhelming embrace, amid musical metaphors that signify the poet's new productivity. Although the princess-muse speaks within the frame of dialogue, Agustini writes in the first-person and from the position of the poet who opens the door. In this way she claims the central position of creative subjectivity traditionally occupied by male poetic voices:

> La princesita hipsipilo, la vibrátil filigrana,
> —Princesita ojos turquesas esculpida en porcelana—
> Llamó una noche a mi puerta con sus manitas de lis.
> Vibró el cristal de su voz como una flauta galana.
>
> —Yo sé que tu vida es gris.
> Yo tengo el alma de rosa, frescuras de flor temprana,
> Vengo de un bello país
> A ser tu musa y tu hermana!—

The little princess butterfly, the vibratile filigree
—Turquoise-eyed little princess, sculpted in porcelain—
Called one night at my door with her little lily hands.[1]
The crystal of her voice trembled like a triumphant flute.[2]

—I know that your life is gray.
I have a rose-pink soul, freshness of early flowers,
I come from a beautiful country
To be your muse and your sister!—[3]

Agustini's images and diction comment unmistakably on Modernismo and in particular on the work of Rubén Darío, who lived in the River Plate region during a key period of Modernista group identity formation. She echoes Darío's metrical experimentation, using a sixteen-syllable verse with octosyllabic hemistiches, or what could be considered a variation on his trademark alexandrine verses of fourteen syllables. The poem goes on to describe an "abrazo de alabastro" (alabaster embrace), a meta-poetic metaphor of a sexual encounter representing poetic productivity, as can be found often in Darío's work and in Modernismo more broadly. Agustini also uses her diction to suggest that her work belongs within the poetic tradition of Modernismo (as with *hipsipilo*, "filigree," "alabaster," etc.). At the same time, however—and this is the most important point for the moment—she destabilizes that recognizable style by emptying three verses of their first hemistich. These voids appear within the muse's dialogue, interrupting the melodious rhythm with a disconcerting silence, precisely in the moment when inspiration should peak. Her poem closes with a surprise when, the morning after the little princess's visit, the poet awakens to find the floor strewn with "Un falso rubí muy rojo y un falso rizo muy rubio!" (a false ruby, so red, and a false curl, so golden!), casting doubt on the muse's sincerity. We can even interpret her nighttime house visit as suggestive of sex work; in this reading, "El poeta y la ilusión" parodically mocks Modernista tradition.

The muse is the central image for women's place in poetry, and within the logic of Modernismo she was constantly on duty as an erotic metaphor of the poetic productivity of men. If the muse is untrustworthy and perhaps a deception, as Agustini's sonnet suggests, then what space remains for women in poetry? What, moreover, is Agustini saying about Modernismo's space for women as poets, that is, in the active role of creation, rather than in the passive role of inspiration? In "El poeta y la ilusión," Agustini invites us to read her sonnet as a parody of Darío's style, giving us a *princesita* instead of a *princesa*, and pointing to his obsession with feminine beauty and with his own productivity. Most importantly, she frames the Modernista muse as fake and uses the voided hemistiches of the muse's dialogue to trace the outline of women's absence in that literary movement. Summarizing, we could say that "El poeta y la ilusión" ironically deconstructs the emptiness of a woman's role as the muse in Modernismo.[4]

Agustini saw problems with women's roles in Modernista literary conventions that were not merely abstract. She had personally experienced the hostility of a cultural milieu that subverted her cultural authority as a poet, and instead infantilized, romanticized, or otherwise diminished her confrontational work. Feminist scholarship has allowed us to interpret the vampires and other violent women evoked in Agustini's imagery as a rejection of cultural expectations that demanded women's passivity and dominance by men. This book picks up that observation and carries it forward into a broader reading of the gendered system of Modernismo and the literary work of women on its margins. It builds on recent developments within queer studies that invite us to *queer the archive*, that is, to bring to the archive a sensitivity to non-normative experiences of gender and an openness to sometimes coded expressions of resistant gender identity. Claudia Cabello Hutt defines queer subjects expansively as those who "lived their creative and intellectual lives outside normative parameters of marriage, reproduction, family, patriarchal bodily control, and economic dependence."[5] As a divorcée who continued to have contact with her ex-husband after their separation, Agustini certainly meets this definition of a queer subject, as do (to varying degrees) the other women writers whose work this book considers in depth.[6] I point out the possibility of a queer reading of writers and their work from the turn of the twentieth century to cast into sharper relief the challenge they presented to their social environment, as well as to highlight the interplay between aesthetics and social positions in the literary field in which they operated.

The point here is not that Modernismo or Modernistas were queer, although that argument could be made elsewhere, but rather that considering a queer reading allows us to peer past the limits of normativity and better see the women working on the edges of that field. This book is thus a starting point for a queer reading of Modernismo. It seeks to understand the discourse of gendered style that supported that movement's development, circulation, and systems of self-recognition, alongside a consideration of the women writing on its margins, including their critiques of that discourse and the alternative paths they charted to build their careers.

One of the key proposals in this book is that a shared approach to gender contributed to the development of Modernismo as both an aesthetic tendency and an intellectual network. At the level of individual authors, this generalization applies in different ways. To continue with our example of Agustini, while her family supported her career, her contemporaries misread her work because their reading of her was skewed by the fact of her sex; they tended to deflect her aesthetic challenge and comment instead on her youth, her prettiness, and the novelty of a woman treating erotic themes. In this they demonstrated what Cabello Hutt calls a "misreading of queer archives," or a "failure of normative, dichotomic imagination [that] functions as a form of denial."[7] Building on the work of Cabello Hutt, Pierce, and others, in what follows I examine gendered discourses and styles as foundational to Modernismo in a way that both provided mechanisms of self-recognition for those who would be included, and—in its simultaneous effect of demarcating what would be excluded—made Agustini's misreading inevitable.

Indeed, cultural gatekeepers demonstrated the illegibility of Agustini's work at every stage of her career. One example can be found in her first book, *El libro blanco (Frágil)* (The White Book [Fragile]), in which "El poeta y la ilusión" appears. The volume includes a prologue by Manuel Medina Betancourt, author and director of the magazine *La Alborada* (The Dawn), that introduces her poetry as the opposite of an intellectual or aesthetic project. It is "gorjeos en vez de palabras" (twittering instead of words), the sound of a baby or a bird; her visit to the magazine writing room is "algo que fuera como un milagro, o como un prodigio, o como un sortilegio, algo extraño y divino, a la vez que fuera una figura hecha con carne y sangre de rosas, con rayos de sol en cabellera, y con gotas de cielo celeste que tuvieran pupilas" (something that seemed like a miracle, or like a marvel, or like a spell, something strange and divine, at the same time that she seemed a figure made of flesh and blood of roses, with rays of sunshine in her hair, and with drops of blue sky for pupils); she is an angel with five-petaled lilies for hands; although she is over the age of twenty when the book is published, he infantilizes both her person and her work, which he considers "rebelde por inexperiencia" (rebellious due to inexperience).[8] Medina Betancourt's frequent reference to miracles and mysticism frames Agustini's talent as supernatural, adopting an awe-struck or bewildered tone common among her earliest audiences.[9] Many other commentators also performed and taught others to perform a misreading of her work. As a result, *El libro blanco (Frágil)*, a book that offered enormous potential to Modernismo by pushing forward the reach for aesthetic innovation, was instead tamed by these opening pages and received as the work of *La Nena* (The Baby), Agustini's harmless public persona.

If the sonnet "El poeta y la ilusión" points to the lack of space given to women as artists in Agustini's time and place, other poems in *El libro blanco (Frágil)* and her later work would expand and sharpen this insight. The irony, of course, is that the radical aspects of the poet and her work—and specifically her accusation of Modernismo's traditionalism and myopia in some areas, amid its claims of innovation—were rendered illegible by the very object of her critique, that is, by the normative sexism of her environment. She nonetheless continued writing challenging poetry for about seven more years, resulting in the books *Los cantos de la mañana* (Songs of the Morning, 1910), *Los cálices vacíos* (1913), and the posthumous *El rosario de Eros* (The Rosary of Eros, 1924). At the age of twenty-seven her life was cut tragically short when her ex-husband, Enrique Job Reyes, murdered her about a month after their divorce was granted. Newspapers swooped in to cover the story in spectacular fashion, with gruesome photographs published alongside lurid speculation about the nature of the couple's relationship, rendering public what had been private.[10] This is to say that Agustini was silenced not only discursively through the misreading of her work; she was also silenced in a literal sense by intimate partner violence.

Without considering the two equivalent, we can nonetheless situate both instances—the discursive violence of the literary field and the physical violence enacted by Job Reyes—on a spectrum of silencing responses to a voice that challenged normative sex roles and rejected limits on gender expression. Considering the two gestures together allows us to better understand them both. It clarifies the high stakes of one woman's disruption of normative gender roles in her closest personal relationships and in her work. As this book re-reads canonical and less-known texts and writers from Modernismo to trace the idea of a *gendered aesthetic* as a mechanism of the movement's self-recognition, it also inquires into the lived experience of women writers who worked alongside Modernistas, yet found themselves to be excluded. We will see how Modernismo's re-semantization of femininity as a style belonging to that movement had the paradoxical effect of blocking women's participation as writers. Understanding that context is necessary to understanding Agustini's inferior status in the eyes of both her literary counterparts and her murderer. Listening to the women writers like Agustini is the precondition for charting the path of this critique, which will shed light both on their writing and lives in their own terms, and on Modernismo as an intellectual network and as a literary style.

Today, more than a century later, the circumstances of Agustini's death prompt questions of continuing relevance. What subject positions, for example, are authorized in the productive work of poetry, and what is the role of women in high-prestige intellectual networks, in which taste and aesthetic value are themselves understood as gendered?[11] Focusing more narrowly on Modernismo, what relationships emerge between the idea of a *gendered aesthetics* proper to that movement and its mechanisms of inclusion and exclusion as a literary field? More specifically still, how did women writers, made partially illegible by the sexism that shaped their social environment, respond to their exclusion, and how did they respond to Modernismo and its discourses of femininity? When considering the particularly transnational nature of Modernismo, its mainstream reach through the newspaper chronicle, and its importance for shaping perceptions of modernity for a trans-Hispanic readership, what broad consequences can we trace for this rhetoric of feminine style, especially as it intersected with ideas about the would-be periphery coming into contact with hegemonic modernities?[12]

Although this book does not delve deeply into Agustini's work, because scholarship in that area has grown impressively in recent years and many excellent sources are available, it does inquire into the gendered rhetorical systems and aesthetics that shaped the literary field in which she operated.[13] Sylvia Molloy has proposed that Modernismo "produced persuasive icons of femininity.... These stereotypes legitimated by *modernismo* were not limited moreover to literature; they were applied to all aspects of life, became ways of viewing women inside and outside texts, and, quite specifically, became ways of viewing—and controlling—women writers themselves."[14] This book interrogates ideas of feminine style and a feminine modernity as contributors to this historical reality. In particular, I am concerned with femininity or feminine style as a foundational discourse for Modernismo, and I propose that understanding this discourse better will help to explain why so few (or perhaps no) women were considered participants in that literary movement. In what follows, I trace the gendered systems of recognition and consecration of Modernismo as a literary field that rendered women's writing illegible within that field. Within a global panorama of competing styles of modernity, I also examine the idea of a "feminine" literary style that influential Modernistas associated with a preferable modernity, that is, a sort of protection for their values of spirituality and beauty against growing cultures of industrialism and an ostensibly "masculine" modernity emanating from the United States, which increasingly threatened Latin America with invasion and destabilization. Femininity was a sort of shorthand for the anti-utilitarian values that undergirded Modernista style, along with beauty, *ensueño* (daydream or illusion), exoticism, and a poetic *reino interior* (interior realm), and as such it was inextricably a part of that movement's identity and the broader search for a trans-Hispanic role in modernity.

LOS RAROS, LAS RARAS

Agustini's *El libro blanco (Frágil)* emerged in a literary field shaped by the work and personality of Rubén Darío, who had lived just across the River Plate in Buenos Aires between 1893 and 1898, marking an important moment of Modernista group identity formation. In 1896 Darío published two influential books in the Argentine capital. The second of these was the poetry volume *Prosas profanas y otros poemas* (Profane Proses and Other Poems), a tour de force for Darío's metrical genius and vision for poetry as an idealist phenomenon, which inspired important poems by many writers, including Agustini. His first book of that year, *Los raros* (The Strange Ones), was similarly innovative but appeared in prose: it introduced groundbreaking world literature to a trans-Hispanic readership by collecting twenty-one profiles of writers from around the world, with most of the pieces originally appearing in the modern daily *La Nación*.[15] A majority of the authors profiled in *Los raros* wrote in French (including Jean Moréas, Leconte de Lisle, Paul Verlaine, Paul Adam), and only one was from Latin America (José Martí); he included Edgar Allan Poe, Henrik Ibsen, and Eugenio de Castro as well. Many were enthusiasts of Symbolism or Decadentism, a challenging literary movement that questioned bourgeois utilitarianism and evoked dreams, mysticism, and poetic reverie to reject naturalism and realism, seeking deeper meaning in an increasingly industrialized and commercialized world. Darío is nonetheless clear that his label of *raro* (strange or eccentric) and an author's inclusion in *Los raros* reflected primarily his own interest and sense of inspiration: the book includes "los principales poetas que entonces me parecieron raros, o fuera de lo común" (the principal poets who then struck me as strange, or out of the ordinary).[16] Defined by strangeness, the authors of this group were accused of "decadentism" and even "neurasthenia," but their lines of flight from bourgeois discipline were precisely the sort of innovation that interested Darío. He called his critics "ocas normales" (normal geese), associating normalcy with mindless cacophony and sloppiness, in opposition to the self-conscious refinement and innovations that were the imprint of *rareza* (strangeness).[17]

The cohesion of *Los raros* thus comes from the echoes Darío traced among his varied objects of study, the intertextualities and cross-references built from his own critical perceptions.[18] He considers them aristocrats of the spirit, suggesting a class of poets defined by a finely-tuned sensibility: "A la poesía la logran hombres de especial capacidad para percibir y expresarse; semigenios, genios. Genio es el que crea, el que ahonda más en lo divino y misterioso.... Aún la locura puede servir a la poesía" (Poetry is achieved by men of special capacity to perceive and express themselves; semi-geniuses, geniuses. The genius is someone who creates, who goes deeper into the divine and mysterious. Even insanity can serve poetry).[19] Although Spanish grammar allows us to read the masculine form of *los raros* as a neutral intention, this book proposes that for Darío and for Modernismo, the literary movement that he represented, women played a vanishingly small role as writers of consequence. Darío includes one woman, Rachilde, a pseudonym for the Frenchwoman Marguerite Vallette-Eymery, in *Los raros*; with rare exceptions—rarer even than Rachilde's inclusion would suggest—his *hombres de especial capacidad* were indeed men.

Today, trans-Hispanic literature is still in the thrall of Modernismo and its ideology of innovation, of radical departures. If the alexandrine verses of Darío have fallen out of favor, what has remained strong through the *vanguardias* (avant-gardes) of the 1920s and '30s, the Boom of the 1960s, and up to today, is his praxis of vision and reinvention on the basis of an aesthetic, that is, a literary style that is unmistakably individual, even as it communicates a sense of collective identity and situates its readership as a transnational community, an *us*. Modernismo has been studied extensively by scholars for more than a century. Rather than summarize or repeat that work, this book proposes something new: that discourses of femininity were foundational to Modernismo, apparent in many ways in the myriad production associated with the movement; and that this discourse contributed to an even greater exclusion of women writers than can be found in earlier, parallel, and later literary movements. After defining what I mean by Modernismo and by discourses of femininity, this book will examine particular uses of that concept by influential Modernistas, with the goal not of an exhaustive treatment, but of an interpretive framework that readers can apply more broadly. I also consider how discourses of femininity influenced the formation of intellectual networks and, ultimately, made the idea of a woman Modernista all but impossible. I leave aside many important Modernistas and can manage only a partial treatment of others, because I am committed to examining seriously the responses of women writers to the Modernista discourse of femininity and its consequences. To that end, I dedicate three chapters to the work of women who wrote professionally around the turn of the twentieth century, but only on the edges of Modernismo and occasionally in direct opposition to that movement, in effect studying the discourse both from within and from outside Modernismo.

I hope that this book helps us to understand Modernismo better and that it helps to answer the persistent question of why that literary movement admitted—depending on one's definition of Modernismo—arguably no women writers.

In this sense, the title of the present book, *Las Raras*, riffs on Darío's foundational *Los raros* and challenges scholars to account for the women ignored by a literary field, an archive, and a canon. It asks how we might better train ourselves to see women, understand their realities, and not take their absence for granted. With this framing I emphasize the mutually constitutive workings of power between cultural productivity, intellectual networks of prestige, and the more material consequences of misogyny on women's day to day existence. In this I suggest a continuity between these issues both historically and today, as well as a continuity among various points on a spectrum of misogyny, without considering them all equally violent or violent in the same way. The paradox of course is that the women writers whose work I examine expanded the possibilities of the Spanish language as much as male Modernistas did—perhaps the most important aesthetic criteria for defining Modernista work—but their illegibility as writers within the framework of Modernismo meant that they were largely lost in the twentieth-century process of the consolidation and narrowing of a critical field of Modernista studies. These women operated in double opposition to societal expectations, first by writing and sharing their work publicly when their milieu marked that activity as the territory of men, and second by pursuing their own literary innovations and ambitions and developing, each in her own way, a style and a proposal for a different vision of modern life and the art that would respond to it. In other words, in their iconoclasm they marked the limit of the Modernista challenge: their difference built from and toward a different modernity and a different modernism, even as they critiqued the established intellectual network known as Modernismo.[20]

Las Raras begins by tracing the Modernista rhetoric of feminine style that undergirds the movement's particularly misogynistic understanding of literary creation. Chapter 1 considers varied approaches to femininity as a stylistic question in the work of three influential Modernistas. It examines the erotic metaphors of Rubén Darío, particularly in his early work, in which the female object of discourse provides a reproductive metaphor for poetic productivity; Manuel Gutiérrez Nájera's varied approaches to the muse, his cultivation of an intimate tone modeled on a chat among girlfriends, and his linking of the instability wrought by modernity to newly destabilized gender roles; and Amado Nervo's ventriloquism of women or gendered poses in an early newspaper series, within the broader scope of his work. Chapter

2 turns to the particular associations of femininity with Paris around the turn of the century, especially in the journalistic work of Darío and Enrique Gómez Carrillo, and the discourses of feminine modernity that these writers presented as appropriate for Latin America's own future, a modernity that in their view operated in opposition to the industrialism and threatening expansionism of the United States. Focusing on both literary writing (such as poetry) and journalistic work, these two chapters provide a framework and focused examples of the Modernista ideology of feminine style.

I next turn to the writing and lives of three women who worked on the edges of Modernismo's intellectual network—Clorinda Matto de Turner, María Eugenia Vaz Ferreira, and Zoila Aurora Cáceres—each of whom I consider within a particular literary field defined by time and space, in roughly chronological order. We study Matto during her professional reinvention as she began a lengthy exile in Buenos Aires, when she founded the literary magazine *Búcaro Americano* (American Vase) and coincided with Darío residing in that city. Vaz Ferreira, in contrast, was a university professor and an idiosyncratic and secretive poet who struggled with illness and considered the social roles of woman and of artist-poet to be irreconcilable, choosing the latter. Cáceres lived longer than Vaz Ferreira and did marry, albeit briefly, and built an international name for herself in journalism, literature, and feminist campaigns, even as she experienced the othering of Modernismo and found that a literary career was incompatible with her married life. The texts examined in these chapters vary significantly in genre, as they include poetry, periodical articles and editorial choices, personal correspondence, speeches, a scrapbook, and glimpses of a novel. In quite different ways, these chapters delve into women's strategies for building a career, which each defines differently, and for preserving a memory of their work. Probing the exterior of Modernismo, I examine the critiques that Matto de Turner, Vaz Ferreira, and Cáceres presented of the literary movement, and with their insight gain new clarity about its foundational discourse of feminine style. These chapters also explore their projects to develop alternative styles and networks on the fringes of Modernismo.

The account presented by this book is anything but exhaustive, even regarding authors who are the primary focus of a chapter. One limiting factor is my attention primarily to the intellectual network that developed around Rubén Darío and Enrique Gómez Carrillo in particular geographies of Modernista activity: the River Plate region and Paris figure prominently, with significant attention also to Lima and Mexico City. However, the broad reach of trans-Hispanic Modernismo necessitates a selection among many possible participants, and readers will certainly think of additional examples

I could have included, or complementary approaches to the Modernista feminine that I have been unable to treat. The lives and careers of Julián del Casal and José Asunción Silva, for example, would provide ample material for analysis within my framework; José Enrique Rodó and José Martí both merit substantial studies on this topic; and much more could be written about the authors that I do include. Rather than provide a comprehensive treatment of a narrow topic, my object has been instead to demonstrate a kind of reading, a way of unpacking texts and linking them together in the context of the literary field, that provides new insight on both the workings of trans-Hispanic Modernismo and the literary careers of women writers in the same period. I outline the emergence and circulation of a particular discourse on modern femininity in the work of some of the movement's key figures, then examine that same discourse from the perspective of those that it excluded from Modernismo. I ask what women writers wrote about that rhetoric, and how they worked to build careers outside the intellectual network and the system of prestige that we call Modernismo. My goal is to develop our understanding of the work of women writers in their relation to Modernismo, and to provide a partial answer to the question of why that movement admitted no women writers unconditionally.

My selection criteria stem from a specific definition of this movement that may differ from other scholars' usage of the term, which sometimes refers simply to literature produced in Spanish around the turn of the twentieth century. For me, in contrast, periodicity, intellectual networks, and literary style all factor into use of the label. Here, *Modernismo* refers to trans-Hispanic literature (including literary journalism) from approximately 1885 to 1916, with a style defined by self-conscious innovation, cosmopolitan influences, and an urgent concern with Latin America's place in the world.[21] What I mean by *style* is a recognizably individual arrangement of the art's most basic materials, or, in literature, the images, sounds, and rhythms created with words, punctuation, sentence length, and similar elements, that create the effect of an individual voice; it is no coincidence that Modernismo had a heightened sensitivity to style and to the expectation that expression be individualized, two characteristics that go hand in hand in Modernista thought. My use of the phrase *intellectual network* is a specifically transnational reference to a community of writers who saw themselves as participants in a shared cultural cause and who were in direct, largely continuous contact with each other, in person via travel or mediated through the circulation of letters and periodicals, sometimes across great distances. What made this a "Modernista" network was their mutual belief—although it might vary somewhat over time and among people—that, against traditionalism or the utilitarianism they observed in their modernizing countries, they shared a commitment to the cause of literary innovation and of forging a new aesthetic for the trans-Hispanic world that would respond to cultural and geopolitical upheaval.

In the case of Modernismo, participants' self-identification and group consciousness were facilitated by their shared sense of alienation from mainstream culture, which struck them as increasingly commercialized, industrialized, and indifferent to the special social position of the artist. Rubén Darío anchored the intellectual network and was the most prominent voice publicizing Modernismo, providing a direct mechanism of network formation with his extensive travels and international publication. At early dates cohesion is hard to find, and authors such as José Martí, Manuel Gutiérrez Nájera, and Julián del Casal had less of a synergistic cohort than can be found later, particularly starting with the early to mid-1890s in Buenos Aires. I propose that a foundational rhetoric of feminine style and *rareza*, or strangeness, inspired by their reading of innovative authors in other languages, allowed Modernistas to recognize each other and eventually to develop a degree of group consciousness. This is true in part because this rhetoric provided a metaphor of subject positions that mediated participants' encounters with hegemonic modernities, as with their experiences in Paris, but it also contributed significantly to the exclusion of women writers as participants in Modernismo. Why this is the case, and how women writers responded, will be my main concerns in this book.

Another point on which I disagree with some scholars is the very idea of women Modernistas. Scholarly discussions of "las poetas modernistas" (Modernista women poets) and "las escritoras modernistas" (Modernista women writers) are not uncommon in the field of literary studies in Spanish, and many of these have made essential contributions to our understanding of women writers and their work. That scholarship's importance cannot be overstated as a necessary foundation for this book, because it attends to many misogynistic elements of Modernismo and allows us to see both the brilliance of these women's work and the challenges they faced in establishing literary careers. Writing *during* Modernismo, however, is not the same as writing *as a part of* Modernismo. Here I push back on the notion that these women writers are Modernistas at all, to ask what is at stake in that label. What criteria do we use when applying this category, and what responsibility do we have to account for exclusionary circumstances that the authors faced during their lifetimes? If it is true, as I propose, that their exclusion was real, and that it resulted in part from the discourse, foundational in Modernismo, of women's objectification and non-subjectivity, then discussing these women writers as Modernistas does an injustice to that history and to that experience. Indeed, it fails to recognize elements of their work that draw attention to and criticize the misogynistic mechanisms of Modernista rhetoric, minimizing their radical bravery and mainstreaming their particularity. I also resist phrasing common in our field, especially in Spanish, of "escritura femenina" (feminine writing) to refer to writing by women, because it conflates writing by women with writing characterized by a style that is itself feminine. To state the obvious, literary style bears no connection to biological sex, and we must approach discourses of gendered aesthetics as relational metaphors. In order to create semantic space for the consideration of gendered style (and specifically feminine style), I avoid phrasing that connects feminine writing to female writers, drawing instead from a vocabulary of gender as expression or gender as performance.

Throughout this study I make use of vocabulary developed by Pierre Bourdieu, particularly his notion of *field* as the social space or environment in which people operate and compete within hierarchies, an approach that allows for both individual agency and structural controls. When I refer to the *literary field*, what I mean is the social milieu of writers of different genres and varied prestige, some with greater experience and renown than others, a milieu that situates individuals within a hierarchy shaped by institutions, practices, rituals, rules, etc. Also important is Bourdieu's notion of capital—such as *symbolic capital*, *social capital*, and *cultural capital*—which refers to the hierarchies of prestige and power that condition interactions within the field and beyond. This lexicon has been broadly adopted in Latin American studies, in part because similar frameworks have emerged from within, simultaneously or even prior to Bourdieu's proposals, from scholars including Ángel Rama and Rafael Gutiérrez Girardot.[22] Because the evidence of intellectual networks' influence can be found in canonization, periodicity, and other organizing structures of literary history as a field, the study of networks and their mechanisms of formation helps us to glimpse alternative organizations of the field. Indeed, it is often only in retrospect that past junctures of contingency, precarity, and instability take on the appearance of the definite or the monumental. Moreover, to study Latin American literature of the nineteenth century is often to study periodicals, which can be read as manifestations of intellectual networks, and certainly their study encourages a sensitivity to the formation of intellectual networks. This is to say that a "networked," field-based approach has long been a part of Latin American literary studies focusing on the period under examination here. Recent work continues to develop these comparisons and the relative merits of the various frameworks.[23]

The turn of the twentieth century was a moment of increasing professionalization among Latin American writers as the field shifted away from older economic models based on patronage. One measure of this change is increasing associationism, in which writers paid greater attention to the norms defining professionalism by founding and joining *ateneos* (athenaems), clubs, associations, and other coteries. For Claudio Maíz and Álvaro Fernández Bravo, "es durante el momento finisecular cuando las redes culturales alcanzan una articulación madura en Latinoamérica" (it is around turn of the twentieth century when cultural networks reach a mature degree of articulation in Latin America).[24] Montevideo between 1902 and 1908 offers examples that both parodied this associative impulse and took it very seriously; in one case, the literary coterie Consistorio del Gay Saber (Consistory of Gay Wisdom) was a synergistic hothouse for the production of innovative poetry, a small group of poets whose bohemian tastes flouted bourgeois norms of the day, and who assumed titles emulating ecclesiastic ranks, both reflecting a desire for institutionalization and poking fun at that same desire. The period's literary clubbishness is important to the issue of women writers' participation in the literary field, as increasing differentiation of the field tended to isolate them from the highest-prestige organizations. This helps to explain why higher numbers of women writers did not mean broader acceptance of them or admiration for their work: they could establish women's magazines or other associations in less-proscribed realms, but they could not participate in the nighttime sociability of cafés and expect to be taken seriously as writers. Similarly, they were not invited as members of the Real Academia Española (Royal Spanish Academy), which marked the apex of prestige and tradition in Spanish literature, as is clear in the furor surrounding Emilia Pardo Bazán's repeated rejection (in 1889, 1892, and 1912).[25] To account for both women's exclusion and their success, it is important to attend to associations and other institutions of quasi-professional sociability at a variety of positions on a scale of social and aesthetic prestige.[26]

Maíz and Fernández Bravo are right to ask, "¿Qué ideas, experiencias, vivencias tienen su origen en *la lógica de enlace* de la red, sin la cual una idea, experiencia o vivencia no habría sido viable?" (What ideas, experiences, lifeways have their origin in the network's *logic of connection*, without which an idea, an experience, or a lifeway would not have been viable?).[27] This book builds on their question to ask another, related one: what ideas, experiences, and lifeways originate in the network's *logic of exclusion*, without which they would never have developed, but which also conditioned their circulation and limited their reach? In what follows, I consider how the core values of Modernismo created obstacles to the circulation of certain *excluded* ideas, experiences, and lifeways, and what that exclusion can tell us today about Modernismo. I examine Modernista networks but also their refractions: their definition by participants and their evaluation by those marginalized. Importantly, we will also glimpse alternative networks, such as that of exiled Peruvians in Buenos Aires in 1895, or a genealogy of women writers dedicated to preserving memory across generations, or alternative transnational relationships forged by women artists whose work was very modernist in aesthetic terms, but who are not generally recognized as participants in Modernist coteries. The study of Modernismo as an intellectual network thus opens new understandings of how power intersected with literary production among Latin Americans in a trans-Hispanic, globalized cultural space.

CHAPTER 1

THE FEMININE AESTHETIC OF MODERNISMO

The introduction to this book began by considering Delmira Agustini's critique of the place of women in Modernismo. We discovered textual voids and a revelation of artifice in "El poeta y la ilusión," a sonnet about a sexual encounter between poet and muse, and traced references to the emerging Modernista tradition. One of her inspirations and targets, given its echoes in her work, seems to have been "Sonatina," by Rubén Darío. When that poem was published in *Prosas profanas*, in July of 1896, Agustini was a mere ten years old, but we can surmise that she read it and Darío's earlier volume, *Azul...* (Blue..., 1888), not long after. She included "El poeta y la ilusión" in her own first book, published about a decade after *Prosas profanas*, already exhibiting the forceful response to his work that other scholars have noted for a later point in her career.

Agustini was exceptional in many ways, but not in her access to Darío's work. Indeed, in his prologue to the first edition of *Azul . . .*, Eduardo de la Barra addresses his readers as women and girls, suggesting that Darío's early poetry was considered particularly appropriate for young women. De la Barra imagines himself presenting a conference before a rapt female audience of "lindas curiosas" (curious, pretty ladies), a "muchacha coqueta" (coquettish girl), and even "bellas ninfas, adoradoras del arte" (beautiful nymphs, adorers of art).[1] Although it is not broadly remembered by scholars today, the female readership of Modernismo has been noted, including by José María Martínez who considers it "una característica esencial del *movimiento*" (an essencial characteristic of the *movement*).[2] De la Barra also discusses femininity as defining the style of Darío's book—"Qué libro! Todo luz, todo perfume, todo juventud y amor" (What a book! All light, all perfume, all youth and love)—and associates this new aesthetic with sensitivity, idealism, and fine taste.[3] He even personifies the volume as a woman when discussing what he considers its defects: "Qué diríais de la muchacha que untara de bermellón sus mejillas frescas y rozagantes? Qué, de la niña que vistiera perpétuamente de baile por parecer mejor? . . . El poeta [Darío] tiene su flaco: esmalta y enflora demasiado sus bellísimos conceptos, abusa del colorete, del polvo de oro, de las perlas irisadas, . . . y sin necesidad" (What would you say of the girl who smears her fresh and healthy cheeks with rouge? What, of the girl who always wears ballgowns, to look better? . . . The poet [Darío] has his weak point: he covers his very beautiful concepts with too much enamel and flowers, he uses too much blush, gold powder, and irridescent pearls, . . . and needlessly).[4] De la Barra's prologue proposes that with a perhaps exaggerated delicacy and sensitivity to self-conscious artificiality, *Azul* . . . reached beyond the commerce and utilitarianism that seemed to define the historical moment, seeking beauty and an artistic ideal associated with femininity.

Early Modernista uses of a feminine aesthetic often critiqued a utilitarian, bourgeois logic of productivity in a market economy, positing the value of art for art's sake alone. This is apparent in Darío's stories in *Azul* . . ., "El pájaro azul" (The blue bird) and "El velo de la reina Mab" (The veil of Queen Mab), for example, in which writers and artists—all men—find themselves trapped in an uncomprehending, utilitarian world and long for an escape that is associated with or offered by a feminine figure. Modernistas' extension of that concept to literary form, including a self-conscious attention to artifice and beauty, rejects utilitarian use of language; at the same time, they were prolific journalists who educated and responded to their own readership in newspaper *crónicas* (chronicles). This is to say that Modernismo's relationship to a mass-market readership is complex, including a whole-hearted rejection of bourgeois mentality on a symbolic level, particularly at early stages of the movement, as well as an engagement with and dependence on their own "buyers" in a journalistic marketplace.[5] Although this dynamic would change in later years of Modernismo's productivity— some illustrated magazines of later Modernismo, such as *Mundial Magazine* (Worldwide Magazine) and *Elegancias* (Elegances), evince a fuller embrace of modern commerce—what I consider in this chapter is the early Modernista obsession with femininity in both journalism and poetry, when the movement was gaining cohesion and renown. I will do this by examining the work of Rubén Darío, Manuel Gutiérrez Nájera, and Amado Nervo, three writers whose influence was significant across broad temporal and geographic spans.[6]

Trans-Hispanic writers around the time of Modernismo were keenly attuned to style approaches articulated through gender. They were invested in the idea that writing could have a feminine or a masculine aesthetic, and they described their own, individual style in these terms, as well as that of their aesthetic coteries and even their national literary production. José Martí was one of many who considered Latin American culture to be "feminine" in contrast with the "masculine" culture of North America; to him, these terms meant artistic and spiritual, as opposed to utilitarian or materialistic, respectively. For example, he wrote in 1881 of the United States that "aquella gran tierra está vacía de espíritu" (that great land is empty of spirit), while he identified Latin American culture with an "espíritu femenil" (feminine spirit) that was "origen del sentido artístico y complemento del ser nacional" (origin of artistic sense and complement to national identity).[7] Another example that associates national character with gendered style can be found in Spanish *enfrentismo*, a twentieth-century paradigm in which, according to Richard Cardwell, "historians privileged an invented Generation of 1898 as robust, virile, nationalistic and serious in comparison with the *modernistas* who were presented as effeminate, neurotic, cosmopolitan and frivolous."[8] The debate responded to Spain's 1898 loss of its last colonies and its last imperialist hopes, as artists and writers throughout independent Spanish America turned increasingly to France and other countries for their inspiration. Thus the accusations in Spain against Modernismo's feminine aesthetic and its *afrancesamiento*, or exaggerated French influence, can be read as nearly synonymous insults within a Spanish nationalist framework, which favored the Generation of 1898 as Modernismo's perceived opposite.[9]

Returning again to Darío's *Azul . . .*, this backdrop of gender metaphors and aesthetic nationalism helps us to understand the replacement of de la Barra's prologue with one by Juan Valera for the book's second edition, which circulated significantly more and is now considered definitive. (The first edition of *Azul . . .* had a print run of only twenty, and de la Barra's prologue was nearly forgotten for over a century.) The approbation of Valera, a senior diplomat, author, and critic, provided the volume with valuable symbolic capital, and his Spanish nationality suggested Darío's consecration even in that aesthetically conservative corner of the trans-Hispanic literary space. The book's title refers to a Victor Hugo quote that establishes Darío's aesthetic idealism—"L'Art c'est l'azur" (Art is the azure)—and Valera wryly commented that "no hay autor en castellano más francés que usted" (there is no author in Castilian more French than you), which he postulated was a result of Nicaragua's lack of literary tradition.[10] It is within the context of colonial history—according to which Spaniards tended to believe firmly that Spain established the pinnacle of trans-Hispanic literary production—that the import of Valera's approval of *Azul . . .* and Darío's aesthetic project becomes clear.

Outside the literary field of Spain, accusations of *afrancesamiento* and even literary femininity caused less offense and could be assumed with pride, particularly when a writer openly rejected or aimed to move beyond recent Spanish tradition. This is especially true at a later stage of Modernismo, as the movement became well-known and broadly associated with the literary entry of the Spanish-speaking world into a cosmopolitan modernity. In this way the discourse of the "feminizing" of literary style became code for experimentation and contributed to the systems of recognition and cohesion for Modernismo as a literary movement. The task of this chapter is to examine varied approaches to the idea of a feminine literary style in the work of three influential Modernistas, providing a sense of the contours of this discourse as it appeared in poetry and prose, with an emphasis on the earlier years of Modernista productivity, particularly between 1883 and 1898. We will see that Rubén Darío, Manuel Gutiérrez Nájera, and Amado Nervo deployed the idea differently, but for all of them femininity was a conceptual cornerstone to their expansion of possibilities for the Spanish language and for trans-Hispanic literature. Nájera was the oldest of these three, and Nervo became well-known only around the time of Nájera's death. Meanwhile, Darío's period of productivity spans both their careers, although this chapter focuses primarily on the first half of his productive years. In what follows, I ask what it meant for these writers to designate reading and writing as "feminine" activities; what was at stake in the feminine pose with which some writers shaped their relationship with readers; and what purposes femininity served as an aesthetic concept for the writers under examination. Although the notion of feminine style emerges differently for each, the chapter concludes by proposing that authors of Modernismo obsessively referenced femininity as resonant with their own aesthetic innovations and as a cipher of a culturally appropriate modernity for trans-Hispanic and Latin American readers.

Let us first consider the work of other scholars on women's roles in trans-Hispanic Modernismo. While it is true that many define the movement broadly and as a result see no contradiction in discussing women writers as participants, it is also true that I am not the first to observe Modernismo's particular exclusion of women and to suggest a relationship between that exclusion and women's imagery, which was often referenced and broadly understood by most participants in the movement. Readers might recall Manuel Gutiérrez Nájera's "Hija del Aire" (Daughter of the Air), a child acrobat who represents extreme vulnerability and inspires an ethical conflict in the writer, or José Asunción Silva's mythically beautiful and elusive Helena in *De sobremesa* (After-Dinner Conversation), as two ciphers of the feminine in Modernismo.[11] The femme fatale appears often and is, according to Nancy Saporta Sternbach, the most common image of women in Modernismo; also frequent is the dead beloved and the languishing *enferma* (sick woman), which Ana Peluffo has examined.[12] Many of these images circulated beyond Modernismo in the period, as authors drew on representations common in Naturalism and in European Romanticism as well. What emerges as a particularly Modernista representation of women is a heightened interest in her potential as a symbol of literature or language, or as an opportunity to reformulate the writer's own position in relation to the text and to readers. Women's role representing representation itself has been noted; for example, Gwen Kirkpatrick traces a Modernista interest in decoration of visual space, of language, and of women's bodies, proposing that "the female figure in *modernismo* is an object almost at one with the language, heavily decorated, distant and elusive."[13]

A few scholars have considered the effects of this imagery on the lives of women. In this vein, Tina Escaja proposes that "en esta amplia y sincrética propuesta [del modernismo] la mujer no tiene cabida más que como objeto decorativo y fetiche del ideario spiritual, político y estético" (in this broad and syncretic proposal [of Modernismo] woman has no more space than as decorative object and fetich of spiritual, political, and aesthetic ideology).[14] Laura Kanost agrees and extends Escaja's proposal on women to consider women writers specifically, asserting that "the *modernista* canon cast women as aesthetic objects imbued with meaning by male artists, leaving no clear position for a woman writer to participate in the movement."[15] Sylvia Molloy had earlier suggested something similar; she points out that Rubén Darío pays homage to the Cuban poet Juana Borrero on the occasion of her death "less as a literary *author* than as a literary *creature*," an observation that could apply to Darío's treatment of other women writers as well.[16] For example, we have seen that he considered Agustini to be a "delicious muse," assigning her the role of inspirer rather than creator of poetry; in Chapter 5 of this book I discuss his similar comments in reference to Aurora Cáceres.[17] There is little doubt that for Modernismo, woman is the object, not the creative subject, of literary discourse.

As early as 1984, Molloy discussed shifting ideas about women's interventions in society as a "threat" to Modernista systems of representation, which produced fetishizing representations of women.[18] She has been especially attentive to the exclusionary consequences of Modernismo's obsession with femininity, summarizing the image of women in the movement succinctly:

> *Modernismo* sees woman exclusively as subject matter: it focuses on her as the passive recipient of its multiple desires, as a commodity that is alternately (or at times simultaneously) worshipped in the spirit and coveted in the flesh. A movement that prizes the crafting and collecting of precious objects, *modernismo* makes woman the most valuable piece in its museum. Yet within this brotherhood, there are no women poets, which should, on closer look, not come as a surprise.[19]

In this framing, the objectification of women in literary discourse was not disconnected from the intellectual network ("brotherhood") of Modernismo, and Molloy attends to its real effects on the opportunities available to women writers within the movement's systems of prestige and recognition. I draw on her approach when I agree with Thomas Ward's statement that "se podría llegar a la conclusión de que no había autoras en esta escuela" (one could come to the conclusion that there were no women authors in this school). Ward contrasts Modernismo with earlier literary currents: "El modernismo, en este sentido, es diferente del romanticismo cuando una miríada de autoras publicaban sus obras" (Modernismo, in this sense, is different from Romanticism, when a myriad of women authors published their work).[20] Modernismo's exclusion of women was greater than in Romanticism, and it differed from simultaneous currents as well.[21] This is to say that the illegibility of women writers within a Modernista way of understanding literature must not be oversimplified as true of all trans-Hispanic literature prior to the levels of women's professionalization that emerge later in the twentieth century. The implicit question of Ward, Molloy, and others—why are there no women writers in trans-Hispanic Modernismo?—inspires this book.

Martínez has studied the construction of a stereotyped feminine reader in Modernismo—historical, implied, or fictional—with special attention to the work of Manuel Gutiérrez Nájera and Amado Nervo. In Nájera's case, he notes "la identificación del público dominante de sus crónicas y cuentos con las mujeres de las élites del Porfiriato" (the identification of their chronicles' and stories' predominant public with elite women of the Porfiriato), proposing that the author's concept of women's reading relates to "notas como pasividad, sentimentalismo, melancolía, esteticismo o capacidad evocadora" (notes such as passivity, sentimentalism, melancholy, aestheticism, or evocative capacity).[22] In the case of Nervo, in contrast, Martínez writes that "los datos que confirman su lectura e intercambios con esa audiencia femenina son realmente abrumadores, tienen muy diversa procedencia, y no hacen sino justificar algunas afirmaciones del poeta que presentarían a ese público femenino como un sector bien definido" (data that confirms his reading by and interchanges with this group of women is truly overwhelming and of very diverse provenance, and it does nothing but justify a few of the poet's affirmations, which present that female public as a well-defined sector).[23] His study provides an important context for the proposal of this chapter, which examines the uses of femininity in the writings of these authors and of Darío. We will consider the conceptual uses of femininity in their work, including as a metaphor for modernity and for a writing style, and their recourse to feminine poses as an opportunity to expand the expressive capacities of the Spanish language in its encounter with globalizing modernity. While Noël Valis proposes of the broader *fin de siglo* that "the artist fetishizes the feminine into a trope of ambivalent values," this chapter will consider a particularly Modernista construction of the feminine that is sufficiently cohesive as to suggest one of the movement's discourses of self-recognition.[24]

DARÍO'S EROTIC FEMININE AS METAPOETICS

Introductory remarks have considered the work of the Nicaraguan poet and journalist Rubén Darío (1867–1916), a writer of unparalleled influence and who continues to be shape trans-Hispanic literature today. Here we will more deeply consider the theme of femininity in a few of his early pieces, before turning to the same topic in the work of other Modernista authors. When Darío arrived in Chile in June of 1886, he was not yet twenty years old and his writing had circulated little, but by the time he moved to Buenos Aires in 1893 he had built a name for himself as an innovator. The primary reason for this shift was his 1888 book *Azul . . .*, published in Valparaíso, with a prologue by Eduardo de la Barra that we considered earlier. This book combined short stories with poetry, including the fourteen-syllable alexandrine that would become his signature innovation, developed with his friend Francisco Gavidia in preceding years. Early Darío criticism identified in *Azul . . .* an eroticism that would continue in his later work as well, and which Mapes associates with a "Parisian" influence.[25] At this early stage, we can already see Darío's use of female characters as objects of poetic discourse and focal points to facilitate the articulation of a poetic "yo."

Included in the second edition of *Azul...*, the sonnet "De invierno" (In winter) describes a luxurious home in Paris, cozy and calm in contrast with the snow falling outside, and a languid woman named Carolina, who dozes with her cat and awaits the arrival of the poetic voice. The opening verse includes a command directed at the reader, "mirad a Carolina" (look at Carolina), which establishes the poetic voice as active and authoritative, and emphasizes Carolina's passivity and status as object of the male gaze. The first two stanzas describe her toilette and the surrounding space, replete with luxury products from around the world. Lounging in a sable wrap, Carolina is herself an expensive bibelot; she is a pet like her cat, the "fino angora blanco" (fine, white angora) that nuzzles her skirt as she dozes, a comparison underscored by the rhyme of "marta cibelina" (sable) with "Carolina." The sensual textures and play of light—as with her lace skirt or a silk screen from Japan—parallel the poetic voice's savoring of sound and rhythm, presenting an emphasis on pleasure that would become a mainstay of Darío's work and of Modernismo more broadly. The sonnet uses fourteen-syllable alexandrine verses, the form that became Darío's signature, and is powered by a series of oppositions: wakefulness/sleep, inside/outside, male/female, black/white, translucent/solid, with a transition between these taking place in the ninth and tenth verses.

The only movement in the poem occurs in the tercets, verses nine through fourteen:

> Con sus sutiles filtros la invade un dulce sueño;
> entro, sin hacer ruido; dejo mi abrigo gris:
> voy a besar su rostro, rosado y halagüeño
>   como una rosa roja que fuera flor de lis.
> Abre los ojos, mírame con su mirar risueño,
> y en tanto cae la nieve del cielo de París.

> With its subtle filters, a sweet dream invades her;
> enter, not making a sound; I set down my gray overcoat:
> I go to kiss her face, rosy and promising
>   like a red rose or a fleur de lis.
> She opens her eyes, gazes at me with her happy gaze,
> and meanwhile snow falls from the heavens of Paris.[26]

Here the poetic voice transitions between exterior and interior spaces, leaving behind the cold city outside and shedding his gray overcoat, perhaps signaling the end of a workday. In response, Carolina transitions from sleep to wakefulness and smiles at him. Movement, voice, and agency are associated with the arriving man, whose gaze and visual description drive the poem, as is typical in Darío's work more broadly. In "De invierno" the feminine represents passivity and dreams, luxurious sensuality, and the languorous pleasures of the interior sanctuary, reflecting both a home and an early version of the poet's "reino interior" (interior realm) that Darío would continue to develop.[27] If de la Barra's earlier prologue develops a discourse of femininity by addressing a figured female reader, this sonnet adds another meditation on femininity as associated with a female passivity and sensuality.

Darío's next volume of poetry, *Prosas profanas*, saw a first edition published in Buenos Aires in 1896 and an expanded, second edition in Paris in 1901. This book cemented his position as the visionary spokesman for Modernismo, developing his metrical experiments and claiming his role as leader of "los nuevos de América" (the new ones of America), although he is adamant that the new movement not be considered homogenous, and that participants pursue their own style. In *Prosas profanas*, Darío shows increased confidence and commitment to announcing his program, and he uses metaphors of literary creation enough that they become almost obsessive. Women appear as personifications of inspiration, beauty, and pleasure, and are associated with the fundamental Modernista value of *ensueño* and the aesthetic, in opposition to bourgeois values or utilitarianism. Explicitly or implicitly, these muses are vessels of inspiration for the creativity of Darío or the male poetic voice, such that writing and developing a poetic voice are figured as activities of men only. This begins with the opening text, "Palabras liminares" (Liminal Words), which repeatedly grounds Darío's insistence on an individual style—"mi literatura es *mía* en mí" (my literature is *mine* in me)—in an assertion of his own masculinity. He figures literary creation as reproduction, and the closing words of the "Palabras liminares" emphasize fertility as a primary structuring metaphor for the book: "Y la primera ley, creador: crear. Bufe el eunuco. Cuando una musa te dé un hijo, queden las otro ocho encinta" (And the first law, creator: to create. Let the eunuch seethe. When a muse gives you a child, may the other eight remain pregnant).[28]

In the "Palabras liminares," Darío's poetic metaphors link his poetry both to French tradition and to something else, related to a "tú" (you): "mi órgano es un viejo clavicordio pompadour, al son del cual danzaron sus gavotas alegres abuelos; y el perfume de tu pecho es mi perfume, eterno incensario de carne, Varona inmortal, flor de mi costilla. Hombre soy" (my organ is an old pompadour clavichord, to the sound of which happy grandfathers danced their gavottes; and the perfume of your breast is my perfume, eternal censer of flesh, immortal Lady, flower of my rib. I am a man).[29] Here the materiality of the female body provides a "perfume" representing inspiration that Darío claims as his own, with the explanation that the woman is "flower" of his own rib. This reference to the Biblical story of Adam and Eve posits that women derive from men and exist to complement and accompany them. By naming the "tú" *Varona*, Darío uses an antiquated address for a young lady, as he also reinforces the idea that man is the origin of woman, strengthening his claim to her body as his own: she is a vessel of his inspiration, an *eterno incensario de carne* that produces his perfume. The closing statement of the passage—*Hombre soy*—insists on the poet's own masculinity, but its superfluousness points to an anxiety about possible doubt. Darío reprises this connection between the poetic voice's masculinity and his inspiration and poetic productivity frequently throughout the volume.

In the rest of *Prosas profanas*, Darío often writes about muses as occasion to highlight the poetic voice's skill and productivity. For example, "Sonatina," included in the first edition, seems for all but the last of its eight stanzas to describe a passive and frustrated princess who longs to escape her luxurious but confining life. Readers realize in the closing stanza, however, that she serves as metaphor for Spanish-language poetry, and her main purpose is to characterize the need for Darío himself, as the "feliz caballero" (happy knight) to arrive, rescue her with his "beso de amor" (kiss of love), and revivify her.[30] The news of his impending arrival comes from her fairy godmother, who hushes her despite her silence—"calla, calla, princesa" (hush, hush, princess)–, complete since the second verse, when she emitted mere whispers. With the princess representing Spanish-language poetry, lackluster and stagnant, her savior is clearly Darío himself, whose name of Félix reflects the knight's description as "feliz." The closing twist is that he has, of course, already arrived: we can see his revivifying influence in the verse before us. His rhymes dazzle, his images inspire, his rhythms demonstrate metrical skill and originality. Here as elsewhere in *Prosas profanas*, Darío finds in the muse a productive archetype for his meta-poetics and a stage upon which the poetic voice develops a performance of virtuosity.

Another alexandrine sonnet in *Prosas profanas*, "Ite, Missa Est," also begins with an active statement by the poetic voice that situates the woman-muse as his passive object of discourse. This poem has a strong note of eroticism, and Darío approaches the sex-poetry metaphor through language of spirituality and ritual:

> Yo adoro a una sonámbula con alma de Eloísa,
> virgen como la nieve y honda como la mar

su espíritu es la hostia de mi amorosa misa
y alzo al són de una dulce lira crepuscular.

    I adore a sonambulant woman with the soul of Heloise,
Virgin like the snow and deep like the sea
Her spirit is the heavenly host of my loving mass,
and I lift up to the sound of a sweet twilight lyre.[31]

The sonnet's tercets shift to a future tense to describe, as we have seen also with "Sonatina," the impending change to be initiated by the poetic voice:

    Y he de besarla un día con rojo beso ardiente;
apoyada en mi brazo como convaleciente,
me mirará asombrada con íntimo pavor;
    la enamorada esfinge quedará estupefacta,
apagaré la llama de la vestal intacta,
¡y la faunesa antigua me rugirá de amor!

    and I shall kiss her one day with a red, burning kiss;
draped on my arm like a convalescent,
she will look at me stunned with intimate terror;
    the sphinx in love will be left stupefied,
I will quench the flame of the intact vestal,
and the ancient girl-fawn will bellow with love!

Somnambulant and convalescent, Eloísa reflects the nineteenth-century fashion of the beautiful, ill woman, or even the Ophelia whose dead body is fetishized, as Ana Peluffo has studied for other Modernista works.[32] She will experience a moment of terror before her rape, but will manage to protest only through her horrified gaze. In Greek mythology, the sphinx was a guardian monster who prevented travelers from entering or leaving Thebes, devouring all who could not solve a riddle; here the reference to a sphinx situates Eloísa as the gatekeeper who would block the poetic voice's passage. Her passivity is overcome by his strength, however, and her deflowering releases, from beneath her passive surface, an ancient "faunesa," the female fawn, in a reference to sexuality and lust in Roman mythology. Here Darío associates sexual desire with voice, and Eloísa-as-faunesa will roar with love in the final verse. Thus, similarities between "Ite, Missa Est" and "Sonatina" abound: the poetic voice focuses on a passive and mute woman, describing her in the present but promising a future of revivification and erotic experience; the reanimating influence of the erotic mirrors an innovation in poetry as well; and the poetic persona of Darío's "yo" is undoubtedly the source of all innovation and movement.

Octavio Paz was one of the earliest critics to comment on Darío's use of eroticism to fuel poetic innovation. He interprets Darío's "Yo persigo una forma" (I Pursue a Foem), the alexandrine sonnet that closes the second edition of *Prosas profanas*, as a search for what he calls "una hermosura que está más allá de la belleza.... Más ritmo que cuerpo, esa forma es femenina. Es la naturaleza y es la mujer" (a beauty that is beyond beauty.... More rhythm than flesh, that form is feminine. It is nature and it is woman).[33] Paz points out what he considers the "virile" nature of Darío's poetry, marking in this way Darío's difference from Verlaine, who was homosexual.[34] Molloy interprets Paz's gesture as analogous to the Modernistas' own logic when they adapted European decadentism by erasing "las marcas del desvío" (the signs of diversion), that is, by evading suggestions of homosexuality; she relates their anxiety to the exclusion of women by Modernismo, which she considers "el movimiento más claramente homosocial de Hispanoamérica" (the most clearly homosocial movement in Spanish America).[35] This is to say that Darío used desire and sexuality as a metaphor of poetic subjectivity, a metaphor that scholars of his work would later depend on as well, but that such formulations depended upon the figured passivity of women and the coding of femininity as always the object and never the subject of poetic discourse. These few but telling examples suggest how Darío used images of women as a part of his discourse of a feminine aesthetic in Modernismo. The next sections will consider two other Modernistas, Gutiérrez Nájera and Nervo, whose different uses of the concept will allow us to trace a broader Modernista rhetoric of modern, feminine style. Later chapters of this book will circle back on Modernismo's exclusion of women as writers, in order to consider how the literary field translated this aesthetic into a lived reality of exclusion.

GUTIÉRREZ NÁJERA'S FEMININE MODERNISMO

Manuel Gutiérrez Nájera (1859–1895) was a poet and prolific journalist in Mexico City between the 1870s and his early death. Although he began writing before Darío, it is primarily in the second half of his career that we see a developing Modernista style, in part before that moniker was in use. Nájera wrote during Mexico's conservative Porfiriato defined by the oligarchic president Porfirio Díaz, when modernization projects and economic development coincided with increasing inequality and eventually led to the Mexican Revolution of 1910. He was influential during his lifetime and has been well known ever since as an early Modernista or a precursor of Modernismo, thanks to his innovations in both poetry and prose. Although he never left Mexico, he found inspiration abroad, particularly in French Symbolists and the Romantics Alfred de Musset and Théophile Gautier, and his numerous translations from French informed his own work. Nájera used many pseudonyms, including "el Duque Job" (The Duke Job), and throughout his career he often wrote about reading and writing as feminine activities, and personified literature itself as a woman. This section examines Nájera's discourse of femininity in two poems and two chronicles that include some of the first traces of what would eventually be called trans-Hispanic Modernismo. His work established some of the earliest characteristics of the movement around 1884 and continued through the consolidation of a Modernista practice in Mexico with the *Revista Azul* (Azure Magazine) ten years later.

The title of Nájera's best-known poem, "La Duquesa Job" (The Duchess Job, 1884), refers to his frequent pseudonym of el Duque Job, and describes his wife, a young and beautiful working woman of Mexico's new middle class. The poem opens with a narrative frame portraying a scene of abundance and leisure, in which the poetic voice promises his friend a portrait of the lovely lady, and the verses that follow are heavily visual in their description. The initial scene communicates intense pleasure and homosocial intimacy, as the two friends chat: "En dulce charla de sobremesa / mientras devoro fresa tras fresa / y abajo ronca tu perro Bob" (in sweet conversation after dinner / as I devour strawberry after strawberry / and at our feet, your dog Bob snores).[36] The men relish the delicious strawberries as much as the conversation, and the English-named dog suggests their cosmopolitan education and tastes. Following this opening frame, the rest of the poem describes la Duquesa Job also in terms of pleasure and consumption: she is a beauty with a mischievous personality, but she lacks the gentlemen's cultural knowledge of global fashions. A constant point of comparison and reference is the beauty of consumer culture in a globalized Mexico City, which she reflects and surpasses, refracting cosmopolitan influences in her own characterization thanks to the cultural knowledge of the poetic voice. This is to say that Nájera defines her as much by what she is *not* as by what she *is*: she does not know the latest dance from abroad or attend horse races or afternoon tea, as a wealthier young woman of the time might, and she is not a part of the aristocracy or landed elite.

The Duquesa Job is instead "Mimí Pinsón" and the *grisette* of Paul de

Kock, references to the mythical bohemian lifestyle of artists in Paris; her eyes dance the tango; her beauty transcends France. The Duquesa's body is a Modernista collage of loveliness from around the world, with her

> pie de andaluza, boca de guinda,
> esprit rociado de Veuve Clicquot,
> talle de avispa, cutis de ala,
> ojos traviesos de colegiala
> como los ojos de Louise Théo.

> foot of an Andalucian lady, mouth like a berry
> esprit sprinkled with Veuve Clicquot,
> waist of a wasp, skin soft like a wing,
> mischievous eyes like a schoolgirl
> like the eyes of Louise Théo.

As the poetic voice reminds us in the memorable refrain, "no hay española, yanqui o francesa, / ni más bonita ni más traviesa / que la duquesa del duque Job" (No Spanish, Yankee, or Frenchwoman / is prettier or more mischievous / than the duchess of Duke Job).[37] A working girl enjoying city life and seemingly unencumbered by traditional women's roles, the Duquesa enjoys singing in a bubble bath and skipping church to sleep late, a scene that the poetic voice imagines with pleasure as well. This male *imagining* of a woman is the poem's foundation, as the poetic voice has experienced only through imagination some of the moments he describes. For example, he was outside the room with the bubble bath rather than a direct witness, as we realize in the following stanza: "Toco; se viste; me abre; almorzamos . . . ." (I knock; she dresses; opens the door; we lunch . . .).[38] In this poem, space and voice are firmly segregated according to gender, with the feminine object of poetry absent from the scene of poetry's production, that is, the men enjoying strawberries and chatting after dinner.

Similarly to what we have seen with Darío's "Sonatina," in "La Duquesa Job," the duchess can be read as a personification of Nájera's verse in this poem, defined by beauty, playfulness, and sensuality. In metrical terms, he uses a ten-syllable verse with regular, five-syllable hemistiches and consonant rhyme. He incorporates surprising rhymes using calques from different languages, clearly having fun with new sound combinations: "corsé de crac" (whale-bone corset) pairs with "como el coñac" (like cognac), for example, and he savors the unusual mouthfeel of words like "Veuve Clicquot" (a champagne) and "Louise Théo" (a French actress). Nájera even relies on onomatopoeia to express the ineffable, when he can't resist bragging that the duchess "tiene un cuerpo tan v'lan, tan pschutt . . . " (she has a body so v'lan, so pschutt . . .; ellipsis original). The poem's approach to innovative beauty and cosmopolitanism make it an early example of Modernista verse, and it can be considered one of the pieces that gained recognition and eventually made that style identifiable. Like the literary production of that movement, the duchess is beautiful and embodies cosmopolitan influences; she is modern in her productive role as a wage-earner and her comfort on the fashionable streets of a modernized city; however she sticks close to women's traditional roles in the spheres of education and creativity, i.e., she is naïve of the cosmopolitan comparisons that the poetic voice assigns her, and nowhere is there a hint that this muse might be a poet or artist herself. Her description and the poem's homosocial frame mark a developing split that would become foundational to Modernista thought, in which women reflect the modernity of globalized consumer culture, but are framed as always the object and never the subject of poetic discourse.

Another poem written about six years later, "Mis enlutadas" (My mournful ladies, 1890), maintains the feminine personification of poetry and again genders the poet as a man, but its anxious, melancholic tone could not be more different from that of "La Duquesa Job." In "Mis enlutadas" the title figures come to represent the author's anxieties, which fuel his work as a poet. I quote from its opening:

> Descienden taciturnas las tristezas
> al fondo de mi alma,
> y entumecidas, haraposas, brujas,
> con uñas negras
> mi vida escarban
>
> The sadnesses descend taciturn
> to the depths of my soul,
> and numb, raggedy, witchy,
> with black fingernails
> they scratch my life.[39]

These silent, dirty daughters, with tears of snow and pupils the color of blood, are born of the poet's sadness and dredge up secrets he has pushed aside, demanding that he return home with them to write. He longs for them but also fears them, describing them as violent and threatening, "hambrientas lobas" (hungry she-wolves), fishers of tears and divers for black shells in the icy depths, in an image that resonates with nineteenth-century discussions of the unconscious.[40] Nájera seeks to escape these "enlutadas" (women in mourning) but eventually resigns himself to togetherness. He associates them with family relationships and a domestic space, in which social patterns, even when oppressive or violent, are familiar and strangely comforting. Their interaction, moreover, inspires conversation as a stand-in for poetic productivity, suggesting that the "tristezas" are a motor of poetry's production. The poem closes:

> Venid y habladme de las cosas idas,
> de las tumbas que callan,
> de muertos buenos y de ingratos vivos . . .
> Voy con vosotras,
> vamos a casa. (ellipses original)
>
> Come and speak to me of things gone,
> of the tombs that hush,
> of dead good people and of living ingrates...
> I go with you, ladies,
> let's go home.[41]

Here the persistent rhythms of family life are unavoidably entwined with the poet's anxieties and perhaps depression, spurring him like nagging daughters to speak and write.

In the traditional representation of a muse, similar to that described in "La Duquesa Job," she shares an erotic relationship with the male poet that results in the "birth" of poetry, a formula that we have considered in the work of Darío as well. In "Mis enlutadas," in contrast, poetry results from their unhealthy, tortured relationship, and the muses are anything but beautiful and joyful. The production of verse results from their incessant, horrifying nagging, rather than from their love. Najera's metrical pattern here is regular but unusual, and his originality in this regard constitutes one of the most typically Modernista aspects of the poem. Each stanza has verses of 11, 7, 11, 5, and 5 syllables, combining assonant rhyme with blank verse, which has no rhyme, and creating an effect of restless anxiety. As would other Modernistas, especially Darío, here Nájera crafts an original poetic structure to create an emotional effect in consonance with the poem's theme.

The sensuous language and meta-poetic philosophies of Gutiérrez Nájera's poetry condition his prose as well. Toward the end of a prolific journalistic career, he co-founded a literary magazine, the *Revista Azul*, with fellow journalist Carlos Díaz Dufóo on May 6, 1894. After years of developing his idea of literature as a social space for women readers, he made this idea concrete in his presentation of the new magazine. His editor's note to the first issue, "Al pie de la escalera" (At the foot of the stairs), uses the metaphor of a personal residence to introduce the magazine as a self-consciously private space that was appropriate for women, tastefully decorated, and respectful of good manners. Nájera opens the doors of his magazine-home to the visits of chatty friends like the reader, a "curiosa señorita" (curious young lady), and announces his plan to visit to their homes also in the form of a weekly magazine delivery.[42] When calling on his reader, he promises to follow etiquette to the letter: "Nos proponemos no llegar jamás á casa, á esta casa que es vuestra, con las manos vacías: traeremos ya la novela, ya la poesía, ya la acuarela, ya el grabado, ya el wals para la señora, ya el juguete para el niño" (We propose never to arrive at this, your house, with empty hands: we will bring perhaps a novel, perhaps poetry, perhaps a watercolor, perhaps a print, perhaps a waltz for the lady, perhaps a toy for the child).[43] The entertaining variety available in the magazine will thus be regulated by a careful regard for refinement and courtesy, and Gutiérrez Nájera affirms that "á esta casa no llegarán los envidiosos, los mal educados, los que al pisar alfombras las enlodan, los que no saben conversar con una dama" (those who will never arrive to this house are the envious or rude people, those who muddy the rugs when they step, those who know not how to chat with a lady).[44]

Importantly, this magazine-home is a space of aesthetic innovation and literary craft. Within the *Revista Azul*, Nájera writes, "galanteamos la frase, repujamos el estilo, quisiéramos, como diestros batihojas, convertir el metal sonoro de la lengua, en tréboles vibrantes y en sutiles hojuelas lanceoladas" (we romance the phrase, we emboss style, we wish, like expert goldbeaters, to convert the sonorous metal of language into quivering clovers and subtle, small, lanceolate leaves), representing the innovations and craft of Modernista writing as the fine metalwork of cutting-edge Art Nouveau.[45] The metaphor of the magazine-as-home extends to personify this new aesthetic style as "la loca de la casa" (the crazy lady of the house), a beautiful woman who recites poetry in French.[46] Despite this reflection on the magazine's nature, Nájera goes on to resist the expectation that a new periodical present its purpose in its first issue. He insists that "nuestro programa se reduce a no tener ninguno. No hoy como ayer y mañana como hoy . . . y siempre igual. . . . Hoy, como hoy; mañana de otro modo; y siempre de manera diferente" (our program boils down to not having one. Not today as yesterday and tomorrow as today . . . and always the same. . . . Today as today; tomorrow in another way; and always in a different way).[47] With the exception of his commitment to the discipline of good manners, Nájera insists that a fixed program is unnecessary, preferring instead flexibility, innovation, and sensitivity to changing circumstances. This gesture anticipates Rubén Darío's defense of an "estética acrática" (anarchistic aesthetic) in "Palabras liminares," which would be published one year later.[48] Nájera's note establishes that *Revista Azul* would be a space for playfulness and variety, which he associates with women and literary innovation defined by femininity.

Although Nájera worked on the magazine for only nine months before his death, many of his contributions in that interim built on his idea of Modernismo and literature more broadly as a feminine affair. He returned to the question of a modern literary aesthetic in a later piece, dated July 22, 1894. Fronting the twelfth issue of *Revista Azul* and titled "La vida artificial" (The artificial life), the chronicle associates modernity with artificiality, a lack of sobriety, and disconcerting upheaval in relation to gender. In contrast with the campesino and his milieu, which he considers timeless, Nájera deems urban modernity "artificial," characterizing it as "una inquietud nerviosa, una excitación febril, un deseo de brincar y de gritar, que no pueden ser naturales" (a nervous restlessness, a feverish excitement, a desire to jump and shout, which cannot be natural).[49] These symptoms recall the markedly woman-associated malaise of hysteria—identified occasionally in men as well, although for them it was more often called neurasthenia—and prefigure a definition of modernity as an experience of radical flux and instability, which Marshall Berman would offer almost one hundred years later.[50] Nájera's identification of modern experience with nervous energy resonates also with José Martí's earlier work, which interpreted modernity as an experience of anxiety stemming from vulnerability and uncertainty.[51] The profound disquiet of the modern subject inspires a search for novelty in artistic responses, and in literature new literary styles stretched the reach of a language's possibilities. Nájera finds inspiration in the "circus" of French literature in the throes of this historical shift: "¡Qué kaleidoscopia de palabras y qué descoyuntura de ideas! Diríase que la literatura francesa es ahora un admirable circo en el que hay atletas, trapecistas, *ecuyères*, *clowns*, arlequines, gimnastas que hacen extraordinarios juegos malabares" (What a kaleidoscope of words, what a twisting of ideas! One might say that French literature is now an admirable circus with athletes, trapeze artists, horseback riders, clowns, harlequins, gymnasts who do extraordinary juggling games).[52] Similarly, Darío insisted in 1901 that "un intelectual no encontrará en la tarea periodística sino una gimnasia que le robustece" (an intellectual will not find in journalistic work anything but a gym that strengthens him).[53] In this way, the demands of modern experience force literary style into new rhythms and sounds, stretching its reach toward ever more spectacular performances of innovation.

Although this new literary style challenges past assumptions about tone, formal integrity, and topic choice, Nájera insists that the disorientation it produces is pleasurable and accurately reflects modern experience. "Leo los versos de Verlaine, y me pregunto ¿qué he leído? No son versos ... unos no tienen rima ... otros no tienen metro ... el pensamiento está en algunos tan enharinado, que no acierto á distinguir sus facciones. ... Me gustan porque acaso yo también padezco de esta vida moderna ... pero ¿qué son?" (I read Verlaine's verses, and I ask myself, what have I read? They're not verses ... some have no rhyme ... others have no meter ... the thought in some is so over-powdered, that I can't make out their features. ... I like them because I also might suffer from this modern life ... but what are they?).[54] Indeed, this unfamiliar aesthetic reflects everyday life in Mexico, strange even as it is commonplace: "Yo lo entiendo porque todos estamos hablando en una lengua extraña, artificial y que no tiene nombre. Pero ¿lo entenderán nuestros descendientes?" (I understand it because we are all speaking a strange language, artificial and unnamed. But will our descendants understand it?).[55] Here Nájera points to the shared experience of modernity's profound uncertainty about the future, suggesting that global synchronicity—in which news from abroad is transmitted and received almost instantaneously (as with the new technology of the telegraph)—has overtaken diachronous transmission of culture. As a result, his readers might have more in common with their contemporaries in France than with their own children and grandchildren. Modernity thus comes into focus as a crisis of language and of sign systems more broadly, of the heightened temporality of language and experience, which change according to worldwide trends, rather than reflecting a stable local reality or a national identity lasting beyond the lifetime of a generation.

Nájera likens the instability produced by this crisis to inebriation and a robbed sense of individual agency, a generalized disorientation that he sees manifested in gender roles. "Ya no hay hombres ni mujeres, propiamente hablando," he writes, "sino muñecos movidos por alcohol ó por morfina ... somos autómatas" (There are no longer men and women, properly speaking, but rather dolls made to move by alcohol or by morphine ... we are automatons).[56] He condemns this change in life and in literature as a shrinking of the human personality: "en la vida moderna la personalidad humana se ha empequeñecido ... o somos títeres, ó somos autómatas; pero ya no somos hombres" (in modern life the human personality has shrunk ... we're either puppets or automatons, but we are no longer men).[57] He closes the article by summarizing, "hay mucho alcohol, mucha morfina y mucho éter en la vida moderna" (there is much alcohol, much morphine, and much ether in modern life).[58] This article posits modernity as an experience of instability, nervous excitement, and dizzying flux that unmoors modern subjectivity from core identity factors such as gender, agency, and a sense of belonging in a community that would make communication or continuity possible among generations.

We have seen that in the poems "La Duquesa Job" and "Mis enlutadas," Gutiérrez Nájera explores the feminine as a powerful concept in the writer's toolkit, as variously a metaphor for poetry, a way of situating the relationship between the poetic voice and the reader, and a defining factor of historical change in the city that the writer observed. The two chronicles we have also examined were written five to ten years later and reveal an author sharpening his critique of modernity as a fundamental restructuring of social roles. In "La vida artificial" this disturbing crisis destabilizes everything from gender identities to the possibility of intergenerational communication. The crisis of modernity, however, also offers the writer opportunities to explore new authorial positions, and in "Al pie de la escalera" Nájera plays with a feminine pose as an opportunity to chat with his reader, a "curiosa señorita," and to build a relationship with her based on affection and mutuality. What unites all the Nájera pieces examined here is that femininity functions as a cipher of the modern and of aesthetic innovation, making poetry possible and highlighting the novelty of Modernista expression. His narrator's pose in "Al pie de la escalera" as hostess in the house of Modernismo, and her foil, the male poetic voice who describes his girlfriend as he guides us through modern urban space in "La Duquesa Job," are the key images to remember as we compare his foundational work with that of other Modernistas.

NERVO'S MINUTIAE OF FEMININE SENSIBILITY

Amado Nervo (1870–1919) in some senses picked up where Manuel Gutiérrez Nájera left off. Nervo participated in a later generation of Modernismo and was just arriving in Mexico City at the time of Gutiérrez Nájera's premature death. Born in Tépic, Jalisco (today Nayarit), Nervo studied briefly in Michoacán before dedicating himself to journalism in Mazatlán. His arrival in Mexico City in July of 1894 put him in immediate contact with the cohort of the *Revista Azul*, founded in May of that year. Much like Gutiérrez Nájera, Nervo was an assiduous contributor to Mexico City newspapers, including *El Mundo* and *El Nacional*, but unlike Nájera he did eventually live abroad. In 1900 he traveled to Paris to cover the World Exhibition there, putting him in sustained contact with Rubén Darío, Enrique Gómez Carrillo, Manuel Ugarte, and other important contributors to Modernismo, which by this time was becoming well-known throughout the Spanish-speaking world. He stayed until 1903 and in this period met Ana Cecilia Luisa Dailliez, the love of his life. Back in Mexico in 1904, he began co-directing the *Revista Moderna de México* with José Valenzuela, and in 1905 he became a diplomat, living thereafter principally in Madrid. Soon after Dailliez's death from typhoid fever in 1912, he wrote *La amada inmóvil* (The Immobile Beloved), though the volume would not be published until 1922, after his death. This section will offer a brief overview of Nervo's approach to femininity, followed by a deeper consideration of "Cartas de mujeres" (Letters from women), a newspaper series that has gone almost unnoticed by scholars.

Many scholars have examined Nervo's complex treatment of women, sexuality, and gender roles. Adela Pineda Franco observes that misogynistic comments "proliferan en la revista" (proliferate in the magazine), the *Revista Moderna de Mexico*, during his co-directorship.[59] Robert McKee Irwin calls attention to biological sex as "a troubling theme for Nervo. He seems comfortable with neither heterosexuality nor homosexuality and prefers to obliterate sexual difference in any way possible."[60] Nervo's novella *El Bachiller* (The Graduate, 1895)—published shortly after he moved to Mexico City, and the beginning of his fame—features a startling scene of the protagonist's self-castration, which Ignacio Sánchez Prado interprets not as a gesture of feminization, but rather as a means to achieving a desired homosociability by excluding a potential suitor, Asunción, from the protagonist's theologically oriented future: "El rol de Asunción como objeto de deseo ... introduce el desorden en el camino al espíritu. Por ello, solo un acto de violencia, un acto sacrificial como la castración permite el restablecimiento del orden" (The role of Asunción as object of desire ... introduces disorder in the path of the spirit. For this reason, only an act of violence, a sacrificial act such as castration, permits the restoration of order).[61] For Nervo, femininity is not simply about representation of women or girls or an associated sensibility. Rather, it functions as an abstract system of representation that allowed him to explore different narrative voices, nonhegemonic subjectivities, and even a veiled critique of the social mores of the Porfiriato.

The fact that Nervo wrote to or for women was widely recognized during his lifetime, and in *Amado Nervo y las lectoras del Modernismo* (Amado Nervo and the Female Readers of Modernismo), José María Martínez considers the different types of female narratees, recipients, and figured readers that appear in his writing. What Martínez calls the "especial sintonía de Nervo con sus lectoras" (special harmony of Nervo with his female readers) extended to include an intense "epistolario cargado de una cursi sentimentalidad y con unas lectoras que consideraban a Nervo una especie de director espiritual" (epistolary charged with a sentimental tackiness, and with some female readers who considered Nervo to be a sort of spiritual director).[62] A tone of intimacy with these women readers is noteworthy in much of his literary writing as well, as if the text reflected a chat among dear friends attending to the details and emotional complexity of daily life. Martínez observes that "la sensibilidad específica de sus textos se identificará en parte con lo que él entendería como propio de *la sensibilidad femenina* en general, o, al menos, del conjunto de sus lectoras contemporáneas" (the specific sensibility of his texts will be identified in part with what he would understand as proper to *the feminine sensibility* in general, or at least the group of his contemporary female readers).[63] This sensibility of delicacy and feelings is the pathos Molloy has identified as important throughout Nervo's writing, a pathos that today has partially lost its original gendering: "En el momento en el que escribe Nervo, [este patetismo] se lo asocia con lo femenino; es decir, con cierta construcción de lo femenino, basado en la emoción, la sensibilidad y cierta delicadeza amenazada por el desorden. . . . Postulo que lo femenino se da en Nervo como categoría deshabitada, disponible" (At the time when Nervo writes, [this pathos] is associated with the feminine; that is, with a certain construction of the feminine based on emotion, sensitivity, and a certain delicacy threatened by disorder. . . . I postulate that the feminine appears in Nervo as an empty, available category).[64] The feminine sensibility as a writerly position and a tone of intimacy, emotion, and delicacy is definitive in Nervo's work and relates to his ideas on Modernismo as well.

In another early novella by Nervo, *El donador de almas* (The Donor of Souls, 1899), the protagonist, Rafael Antigas, falls in love with Alda, a feminine spirit who ends up trapped within his own mind, prompting him to ask his friend, Esteves, for help. This premise allows Nervo to spin a series of gender-bending fantasies, including the possibility of harboring a woman's spirit or a dualistic masculine-feminine spirit in a male body; a solipsistic eroticism of self-pleasure; and the idea of a fully subservient sex slave whose paranormal abilities open new possibilities of mystical union with the universe. As Christopher Conway points out, however, *El donador* is also clearly positioned against any freedom for women (or, more precisely, for the enslaved Alda):

> the desire to penetrate mystery by crossing the dividing line between man and woman results in despair, madness and the marshalling of male forces

(Esteves) against the invasion of the feminine. Cultural anxieties about [Rafael's] mediumistic experience and Alda's fate underline that women are desirable as long as they are chaperoned by men; free to control their own bodies and be like 'men' literally or figuratively, women are a menace to the integrity of masculinity itself.[65]

Rather than a representation of a transgender subjectivity ahead of his time, Rafael and Alda can be read as a thought experiment on homosocial bonding, in which femininity is an idea that supports relationships among men. Conway points out moreover that a fear of female sexuality is a recurring theme in Nervo's work: "the transaction between the masculine and the feminine in Nervo's supernatural fiction is always mediated by the anxiety over losing control of the feminine."[66]

El donador de almas was likely written around the same time that Nervo authored "Cartas de mujeres," a column that appeared 49 times between November of 1898 and April of 1899, and signed with the pseudonym of Prevostito (Little Prévost).[67] Presented as found letters penned by women, the column evidently draws inspiration from the work of Marcel Prévost, a French novelist and best-seller of the nineteenth century known as the great "novelist of the feminine soul." At least some of Prévost's "Lettres de femmes" (Letters From Women) had appeared in the *Revista Azul* in 1894, translated into Spanish as "Cartas de mujeres," possibly by Gutiérrez Nájera. The pseudonym of Prevostito has been attributed posthumously to Amado Nervo, whom critics have described similarly as a "profundo conocedor del alma femenino" (deep knower of the feminine soul).[68] The variety of fictional women represented in the series is mostly bourgeois, ranging from ingénues worried about their boyfriends, to newlyweds traveling abroad, to separated spouses disputing the visitation of a sick child; a novice nun begs for consolation from her mother superior after being seduced by her cousin; a young and naïve traveling actress named Altagracia reassures her mother that "los hombres, mamacita, son inofensivos" (men are harmless, mama).[69] The letters consistently adopt an intimate tone of conversation and confession among friends, sisters, or other women with similarly close relationships.

Most of Nervo's "Cartas de mujeres" are disconnected from the others in the series, and each must be read as a unique story. One character who breaks this convention of a single appearance is Estefanía, an actress who responds in three letters to the questions of an admiring reporter, in what seems to be a fictional public relations ploy to support her stage career. Andreas Kurz reads Estefanía as a veiled reference to Sybil Vane, an actress character in *The Picture of Dorian Gray*, by Oscar Wilde, whose highly publicized trial and conviction for "gross indecency" in 1895 made headlines around the world and sparked innumerable discussions of non-normative sexualities and Decadentism. Kurz concludes that Nervo used Estefanía as a coded announcement of his interest in Wilde's forbidden novel, a subtext that would be apparent to other writers but not to his broader readership, in this way protecting himself from a potentially severe public backlash during the conservative Porfiriato.[70] Both Decadentist aesthetics and the theme of acting are clearly of interest to Nervo, as the nested identity poses multiply: Nervo sneaks by as Prevostito, who poses as Estefanía, who is herself passing as a frivolous actress, when she is a veiled announcement of Nervo's admiration for the work of the pariah hero of Decadentism, Oscar Wilde.

Much of the allure of "Cartas" stems from the illusion that we are reading someone else's mail, that we have somehow, within the socially acceptable pages of a mainstream newspaper, stumbled into the illicit intimacy of a peeping Tom. Many critics note the intimate tone and orality of Nervo's work in general, which they associate with the famous "femininity" of his writing; of the book of poetry *En voz baja* (In a Quiet Voice), for example, José María Martínez writes that "lo feminizante del libro se puede vincular ... con el tono confidencial o *en voz baja* querido del poeta, es decir, con el tono propio del espacio social privado, que en las fechas de Nervo solía estar asociado a la presencia femenina" (what's feminizing about the book can be linked ... to the confidential or soft tone, beloved by this poet, that is, to the tone proper to private social spaces, which in the time of Nervo tended to be associated with women's presence).[71] Elsewhere, Nervo's performance of pathos includes discussions of his own sickness, weakness, and neurasthenia, contributing to a constructed sentimental bond with the reader.[72] In the "Cartas" under examination here, this confidential tone is unmistakable and exaggerated by Prevostito's pose as a sister, girlfriend, or daughter of the letter recipient.

I would suggest that the letters, when considered together, exhibit two opposite movements on the part of this writer. On the one hand, Nervo plays at his feminine pose and makes it an obvious game for the historical reader to share, in effect poking fun at the letter-writing characters and the feminine, frivolous world they represent. Sergio Márquez Acevedo proposes that the characters are "concebidos como estereotipos" (conceived as stereotypes), a dynamic that supports this joke shared between writer and reader at the characters' expense.[73] The masculine pseudonym of the byline supports this logic, and the diminutive suffix of "Prevostito" adds a ludic note that invites sardonic readings of the letters, such that the letters stop short of attempting to pass as truly written by women. In this light the letters must be considered a double-voiced discourse that both invites a female readership who might take them seriously, and forges a homosocial bond among men by identifying women as different, laughable, and inferior.

As this ongoing joke develops, however, Nervo presents us with a quite varied cast of female characters and subtly points out the challenges and paradoxes of their lives, which often result from a confrontation with modernity and the pressures it put on gender roles. Thus, the second possible reading of the *Cartas*, co-existent with the first, is as a critique of women's social position in Porfirian Mexico. In a letter titled "Desde el pueblo" (From The Town), for example, a provincial mother beseeches her son to take care of himself in an unfamiliar and threatening capital city; another, "El niño" (The child), exploded the myth of blissful motherhood as the letter-writer complains about her newborn son, describing what would today be identified as postpartum depression; a third, titled "Después del divorcio" (After the divorce), signed "Esther" and addressed to "Papacito," gives tragic voice to a young child who, along with her mother, has lost financial security, social position, and emotional stability following her parents' divorce and her father's complete abandonment. This letter from Esther appeared on January 31, 1899, approximately fifteen years before divorce gained legal protection in Mexico, and in a public sphere defined by the conservative Catholic mores of the first lady, Doña Carmen. The character of Esther is more emotionally resonant than a stereotype and raises fraught moral and legal issues in a public forum, with an ambiguous accusation of both the father's abandonment and of a society that limited the mother's options for economic independence. Esther's plaintive question—"¿Verdad que tú sí me quieres?" (Is it true that you do love me?)—demands that her father and society attend to the needs of the vulnerable.[74]

The "Cartas de mujeres" series delves into the most intimate confessions of devalued subjects of the new city, attending to the miniscule details of emotion and granting importance to even the frivolous. Nervo offers his own definition of Modernismo and the Modernista poet in a 1907 chronicle simply titled "El modernismo," which proposes that poets' heightened sensitivity has allowed them to focus on the miniscule or even invisible as a pathway to understanding the great truths of existence. A poet's senses, he writes, "se han ido afinando y hemos empezado a ver 'hacia dentro'. Hemos comprendido que . . . lo verdaderamente grande en el Universo, las fuerzas que lo rigen y la explicación de sus enormes destinos, está en lo infinitamente pequeño, en lo imperceptible, en lo invisible" (have been gradually refined and we have begun to "see within." We have understood that . . . what is truly great in the Universe, the forces that govern it and the explanation of its enormous destinies, is in the infinitely small, in the imperceptible, in the invisible).⁷⁵ Nervo points to something that goes beyond perfecting a traditional skill of observation, however. In his interpretation modern poets had to reinvent language in response to a new historical reality, what he calls "nervios modernos" (modern nerves), and which we can take to mean the disjointed, jangling experience of modernity: "para auscultar estos latidos íntimos del Universo, así como también las íntimas pulsaciones de los nervios modernos del alma de ahora, hemos necesitado nuevas palabras" (to sound out the intimate heartbeats of the Universe, as well as the intimate throbbing of the modern nerves of today's soul, we have needed new words).⁷⁶ Homosocial Modernismo emerges in response to this need: "a esta imperiosa necesidad de expresión, . . . ha respondido un grupo de hombres, a veces inconscientes, pero instintivos" (to this imperious need for expression, a group of men—sometimes unconscious but always instinctual—has responded).⁷⁷ Nervo's modernist aesthetic of the miniscule reorganizes hierarchies of value and makes possible a focus on the overlooked details and undervalued subjectivities of the modern city, in which orality and *lo popular* (the popular or working-class) emerge as critical signifiers in his broader aesthetic project.

If in Nervo's early work, a double-voiced discourse permits both a reading at the expense of women (i.e., by subtly mocking the female letter-writers and the feminine more broadly) and one sympathetic to their challenges, as we have seen with the "Cartas de mujeres," in his later work a tone of misogyny becomes unmistakable. His chronicle "El ser neutro" (The Neutral Being, 1921), for example, proposes that the world needs a sexless third category of person, a "neutral being" that, as neither a man nor a woman, would possess "todas las delicadezas, todas las ternuras femeninas, todo eso que vamos buscando en la mujer, sin lograr encontrarlo sino por excepción" (all the delicacies, all the feminine tenderness, everything that we are seeking in women, without managing to find it, with few exceptions).⁷⁸ The narrator imagines a *ser neutro* with a temperament even more feminine than what he finds in real women, who have proven less delicate and tender than he hoped. The implied identity of Nervo as the narrator, thanks to the use of the first-person singular, combined with the interlocutor of "mi amigo" (my friend), creates a homosocial scene for this fantastical critique of real women. Nervo goes on to describe the "neutral being" as "algo así como ciertas representaciones de ángeles, sin androginismo" (something like certain representations of angels, without androgyny), that is, lacking the confusing or threatening characteristics of the androgyne or hermaphrodite.⁷⁹ Despite a "feminine" temperament for the neutral being, Nervo uses masculine pronouns—Spanish grammar of the time required him to choose, after all—suggesting a fundamentally masculine identity. While delicate feminine temperaments become the territory of men in this chronicle, women's bodies are not absent; in this three-person system, she tends to housework and keeps out of the way of the narrator and his companion, the angelic *ser neutro*: "Mientras ella piensa en los trapos, comadrea, murmura, riñe con los criados, nosotros podríamos pasear al lado del 'Ángel'" (While she thinks of rags, gossips, mutters, quarrels with the help, we could walk alongside the "Angel").[80] The chronicle can be read as a fantasy of a world in which idealized femininity defines identity and social interaction, stepping in to meet the narrator's spiritual needs, while his real *compañera* (companion) tends to the material realities of daily life and has no discernable needs of her own.

A longer quote is helpful in characterizing the deep misogyny of this chronicle, "El ser neutro":

> La mujer es demasiado vulgar. En su juventud tiene la frescura excitante sin idealidad ninguna y se convierte pronto en ánfora de hastío, donde apenas sobrenada una gota de miel.
>
> En la madurez, llega a una fealdad a veces misteriosa, sin ganar, en cambio, *alma*.
>
> Cuando piensa un poco, resulta por lo general de una pedantería insoportable. Felizmente, casi no piensa nunca.
>
> Desear a un ser así, adorarlo, hacer de él la finalidad de nuestros años mozos y aun de nuestros años maduros, es, sin duda, una de las humillaciones más grandes que nos ha infligido el Genio de la Especie, brutal e imperioso.
>
> Woman is too vulgar. In her youth she has an exciting freshness without any ideality at all, and she soon becomes an amphora of weariness, where barely a drop of honey floats.
>
> In maturity, she arrives at a sometimes mysterious ugliness, without gaining *soul* in exchange.
>
> When she thinks a little, in general she ends up insufferably pedantic. Happily, she almost never thinks.
>
> To desire a being like this, to adore her, to make her the purpose of our youth and even of our years of maturity, is, without a doubt, one of the greatest humiliations that the Genius of the Species, brutal and imperious, has inflicted upon us.[81]

The narrator of "El ser neutro" considers women to be repugnant, charmless, and nearly incapable of thought, and treats their conventional role as man's mate as his great humiliation. He also fantasizes about excluding them even from a passive, supporting role in culture as muses, readers, or interlocutors with men. The chronicle closes by imagining a world in which the *ser neutro* provides men with a spiritual companion, while women are relegated to the role of breeding stock: "Entonces la mujer servirá solo para concebir y dar a luz, y ese ser maravilloso será el colaborador natural de todos los genios, de todos los santos" (Then woman will serve only for conceiving and giving birth, and that marvelous being will be the natural collaborator of all geniuses, of all saints).[82] Nervo relishes a fantasy of leaving women no role in culture whatsoever.

Our examination of Nervo's work has shown that, under the protection of a pseudonym, the "Cartas de mujeres" series allowed him to play with feminine voices and to raise questions about limited social options and fraught gender roles in Porfirian Mexico. The early chronicle series reveals his interest in *lo popular* and women's (fictional) discourse as an opportunity to explore notions of voice, style, and writerly authority, especially in relation to an intimate language of sensitivity, sentiment, and attention to the minutiae of social interactions. This series presents a Modernista sense of self founded on a posture that performatively calls attention to its own visibility, purporting to make public the most guarded secrets of a private, feminine realm. The additional texts discussed above suggest that Nervo generally humored and flattered his female readers, and was perhaps charmed by the intimate tone and attention to detail that they represent in his work, but he also came to disdain what he perceived as their frivolity and inability to understand or contribute to cultural, aesthetic, or spiritual endeavors. In "El ser neutro," his fantasy of women's non-subjectivity is unusually cruel among Modernista work, sharply excluding women from any thought, creativity, or community. Indeed, that very exclusion is what makes possible Nervo's fantasy of a spiritual-aesthetic communion between male artists, whom he saved from the distasteful experience of noticing their own gender—their own materiality, perhaps—with the removal of its opposite.[83]

This chapter has explored approaches to femininity in the work of Nervo, Gutiérrez Nájera, and Darío as examples of a discourse that permeated Modernismo more broadly. Particularly in the earlier years of the movement, these authors marshalled femininity to the cause of redefining writerly subjectivity, taking advantage of the opportunity it offered to explore new positionalities with voice and tone. Darío highlighted his poetic innovation and ambition with metaphors of sex and reproduction that set women firmly in the role of poetic object, as with "De invierno," the "Palabras liminares" of *Prosas profanas*, "Sonatina," and "Ite, Missa Est." Nájera played with the changes that modernity brought to urban space and literary style in "La Duquesa Job" and invited female readers to the "home" of the *Revista Azul* in "Al pie de la escalera," establishing a tone of mannered innovation for the new magazine. Nervo assumed a variety of feminine poses in his "Cartas de mujeres," suggesting that women's voices offered an attractive opportunity for writerly exploration and even ambiguous social critique, but he also fantasized about a complete exclusion of women from all cultural and interpersonal roles beyond reproduction. The feminine is clearly a rich category of Modernista thought that writers brought into aesthetic debate and innovation.

In the next chapter we will turn to the notions of femininity that emerge in Modernista representations of Paris, in a slightly later moment of the movement's innovations, to consider the shifts in Modernismo in that space of production of globally hegemonic modernity. We will see that the discourse of femininity supported Modernistas' renegotiation of their peripheral position and exclusion at the banquet of modernity; it helped them to articulate a particularly Latin American identity under the conditions of modernity; and it provided them with a vision for what possible future might be culturally appropriate for Latin America, among an array of possible modernities on offer.

CHAPTER 2

CRÓNICAS DE PARÍS

Darío and Gómez Carrillo
on the Feminine Modern

In early 1906, shortly after arriving in Paris from her native Peru, Zoila Aurora Cáceres recorded in her diary some of her initial interest in the Guatemalan Enrique Gómez Carrillo, who a few months later would become her husband. Although he was the most important writer of newspaper chronicles around the turn of the twentieth century in Latin America, it was not his fame or larger-than-life public persona that attracted her, but rather his innovative and distinctive writing style: "he leído una crónica de Gómez Carrillo; aunque no llevase su firma le habría reconocido por el estilo: es lo mejor que yo conozco en literatura castellana; siempre encuentra la novedad de la frase, siempre sorprende con lo imprevisto y envuelve el conjunto de elegancia, de sonoridad; más que una lectura parece que se hablase con él" (I've read a chronicle by Gómez Carrillo; even if it didn't have his signature, I would have recognized him by its style: it's the best that I know in Castilian literature; he always finds the novelty in phrasing, he always surprises with the unexpected, and he envelops the whole with elegance, with sonority; more than a reading, it seems like one talks with him).[1] The approachable sense of orality that Cáceres observed in Gómez Carrillo's prose, combined with elegance, sonority, and "novelty in phrasing" to create an innovative and recognizably individual style of writing, two of the goals most foundational to Modernista discourse.

Cáceres was not the only writer of the time to comment on the Guatemalan's distinctive style, although others phrased their opinions differently. What stood out for Amado Nervo, for example, was the frivolity of Gómez Carrillo's prose and, even more surprisingly, Carrillo's opinion that frivolity was a positive characteristic of literary style, rather than an insult. For Nervo, the Guatemalan's daily chronicles excelled at conveying "esa actualidad salpicada de un vago perfume y de un poquillo de oro . . . como el sutil polvillo que levantan las *victorias* de las duquesas, de las actrices y de las cocotas en las avenidas del *Bois*. ¡Ha sentido y comprendido tan bien a París!" (that timeliness, sprinkled with a vague perfume and a little bit of gold... like the subtle powder raised by the *victories* of the duchesses, the actresses, and the cocottes on the avenues of the *Bois*. He has felt and understood Paris so well!).[2] Frivolous, light, and reminiscent of the women of the Bois de Bologne, Nervo points to a feminine aesthetic in Carrillo's chronicles and the Paris they convey, while Cáceres avoids these associations; with Nervo, we see the Modernista obsession with gendered language in action. Understanding the relationship between the city of Paris and the Modernista discourse of femininity—the focus of this chapter—will allow us to see the fundamental similarity of these two assessments. It will also support a fuller understanding in later chapters of Cáceres and other women writers who rejected the Modernista approach, which considered literary style through metaphors of gender.

Not long after Cáceres's observations, Ventura García Calderón (1886–1959), another young writer from Perú who happened to be chancellor of the Peruvian Consulate in Paris, penned a profile of Gómez Carrillo, further characterizing his modern frivolity as focused on the visual pleasures and carefree enjoyment of urban space in that quintessentially modern city. García Calderón describes an afternoon the two spent together, observing the evening spectacle from a comfortable café terrace, sipping absinthe, and enjoying their view of sociability and consumerism on the busy boulevard. Among the many clichés associated with the City of Light, women's bodies draw their attention: "todas coquetas, todas adorables, todas deseadas, pasan encendiendo con su gracia un deseo tan grande, tan impersonal, tan imposible, que ya no es vulgar lujuria, sino el magnífico ritmo de la sangre en delirio" (all coquettish, all adorable, all desired, they pass by, sparking with their grace a desire so great, so impersonal, so impossible, that it is no longer vulgar lust, but rather the magnificent rhythm of blood in delirium).[3] These depersonalized and strangely uniform women inspire a universal, overwhelming desire in their observers, peripheral subjects whose dominating gaze establishes their belonging in the space of modernity that claimed global hegemony. The scene of homosocial bonding and voyeurism hinges on the particularly modern spectacle of women's casual access to city streets. In this profile, which served as prologue to Gómez Carrillo's 1909 book, *El libro de las mujeres* (The Book of Women), García Calderón is eager to demonstrate his own familiarity with a formula of the young Latin American man in Paris, in which Parisian women became a focal point for a generation of men who published newspaper chronicles throughout Latin America. Their work consolidated an enduring image of Paris as the privileged space for the spectacle of women's beauty.

García Calderón's prologue repeatedly links frivolity and Paris to Gómez Carrillo and his writing. When García Calderón insists that Carrillo's prose bears "la marca de París" (the brand of Paris), he means a modern Parisian style defined by lightness and an avoidance of pedantry: "Solo quiere ser simple, ser vivaz; él cree, como Anatole France, que se pueden decir graves cosas en leves prosas" (He wants only to be simple, to be lively; he believes, like Anatole France, that serious things can be said with light prose).[4] This vivid, nimble style is "prosa moderna, flexible á todas las complicaciones y las sinuosidades de un espíritu parisiense, prosa tornasolada, cambiante como ciertas sedas y ciertas alas" (modern prose, responsive to all the complications and the sinuisities of a Parisian spirit, irridescent prose, changeable like certain silks and certain wings).[5] García Calderón goes on to specify that Carrillo is an urban writer—"compone sus mejores prosas en el tumulto de un café, frente al tumulto del bulevar" (he composes his best prose in the tumult of a cafe, facing the tumult of the boulevard)—as well as something of a nomad, best defined by the "femenina inconstancia de su alma errante" (the feminine inconstansy of his wandering soul).[6] He agrees with Amado Nervo's proposal above that frivolity is the defining characteristic of Guatemalan's prose: "¿Frívolo? Cuando así lo llaman, sonríe sinceramente divertido. Es frívolo de buena gana. Diré más: orgullosamente" (Frivolous? When they call him that, he smiles, sincerely diverted. He's frivolous with enthusiasm. I take that one step further: with pride).[7] García Calderón even titles his prologue "La frivolidad de Gómez Carrillo" (The Frivolity of Gómez Carrillo).[8]

Some twenty years later, not long after Gómez Carrillo's 1927 death, the identification of his work with frivolity remained strong. The Venezuelan Rufino Blanco-Fombona (1874–1944) recalled Gómez Carrillo as a paragon of Modernismo's frivolous and "feminine" style:

> Las crónicas y los volúmenes de este escritor me parecen, en efecto, obritas maestras de frivolidad. No lo constato como reproche. Más bien lo haría

como elogio.... En nuestra lengua castellana,... solemne y campanuda, no conozco á nadie que haya escrito con más viveza alada, con más elegante suavidad femenil, con más gracia. La gracia de Carrillo no es chiste, sino ligereza, burbuja de espiritualidad, cosa de encanto.

The chronicles and volumes of this writer strike me as, in effect, little master works of frivolity. I do not establish this as a reproach. I would rather do it as praise.... In our Castilian language,... solemn and bombastic, I know of no one who has written with more winged vivacity, with softer feminine elegance, with more grace. Carrillo's grace is not a joke, but rather lightness, bubbles of spirituality, something of charm.[9]

Here Blanco-Fombona echoes García Calderón in reversing the usual connotations of frivolity: accusations become praise, and superficiality is considered charming. The link he traces between frivolity, artificiality, and femininity is an aesthetic one focusing on Gómez Carrillo's writing style. As we saw with García Calderón, he points out these characteristics in the Guatemalan's references as well:

No se preocupa sino de las piernas de las bailarinas, de las sonrisas ingenuas ó complicadas de las cocotas, de los trajes y gestos de las actrices.... Porque uno de los grandes servicios prestados por este fauno gentilísimo á nuestras pesadas y aburridas literaturas castellanas es la introducción de la mujer en las letras.... ¡Con qué *odor di femina* ha perfumado nuestras prosas!

He's worried only about the dancers' legs, the cocottes' naive or complicated smiles, the actresses' wardrobes and gestures.... Because one of the great services lent by this exceedingly pleasant fawn to our heavy and boring Castilian literature is the introduction of woman into literature.... With what *odor di femina* he has perfumed our prose![10]

In an obvious exaggeration, Blanco-Fombona credits Carrillo with introducing both women and a "feminine" aesthetic into trans-Hispanic literature. While he leaves that aesthetic undefined, its meaning here can be deduced from the other words that accompany it: "superficial," "frivolous," "soft elegance," "winged lightness," "smiles, mischievousness, flirtations," "grace." A frivolous or feminine style, then, is one that emphasizes elegance and carefree pleasure, as it avoids themes that might contradict this levity.

This chapter explores Gómez Carrillo's theory of a feminine Paris as a discourse on aesthetics that mediated postcolonial modernity for Latin

America, a discourse of significant importance, because the reprinting of his work in mass-circulating periodicals gave him unparalleled influence on Latin American perception of new styles of life in the French capital. Femininity as a carefree and celebratory representation of modern life is recurrent and even obsessive in his work, in tandem with his discourse of modern frivolity, which comes to function as a synonym. Hundreds of his chronicles appeared throughout the continent and in Spain in numerous mainstream newspapers, including *La Nación* and *La Razón* of Buenos Aires, Madrid's *El Liberal* and *El Imparcial,* and *El Cojo Ilustrado* of Venezuela, in addition to in his native Guatemala and elsewhere. His insertion in Modernista circles is clear in his extensive publication in specialized magazines as well.[11] Carrillo saw his work reprinted in a ripple effect throughout the trans-Hispanic journalistic space. He also fluidly split books into chronicles and repackaged chronicles into books, of which he published more than eighty in his lifetime. His voluminous body of work, which also included novels and plays, positioned him as the single most prevalent voice from Paris, the city that so defined one type of modernity for trans-Hispanic readerships in this period. His fame also stemmed from his flamboyant personality, which Andrew Reynolds has described as "deliberately excessive" and "performative," pointing out that it "helped to increase his prestige."[12] Carrillo's work largely fell into oblivion later in the twentieth century, although he has received some recent scholarly attention for his travel writing, his discourse of cosmopolitanism, his treatment of WWI, and his role knitting together a concept of trans-Hispanic literature.[13] His incredibly copious body of work supports a variety of readings.

Here we will analyze a topic all but untouched by scholars, the theory of a feminine modernity that Gómez Carrillo developed in relation to Paris, including a gendered style that shaped perceptions of modernity throughout Latin America. Consideration of Rubén Darío's own personifying approach to Paris will provide a comparison and an additional perspective on Carrillo's writing. Carrillo encouraged Latin Americans to imagine themselves choosing one style of modernity over another for their own futures, favoring a style directly related with core Modernista values of beauty and pleasure and a privileged social position for the male artist or writer, in opposition to the constructed alternative of a modernity exemplified by the United States and defined by industrialism and greater rights for women. The chapter will close by considering how Carrillo's proposal responded to period anxieties about Latin America's peripheral position in relation to the globally hegemonic modernity associated with the French capital.

A Francophilic tradition in Latin America predates Modernismo, as numerous scholars have demonstrated. In *Modernistas en París: El mito de París en la prosa hispanoamericana modernista* (Modernistas in Paris: The Myth of Paris in Modernista Spanish-American Prose), Cristóbal Pera explains that the city took on the status of myth in nineteenth-century Latin America, at first through readings of French writers including Victor Hugo, who created their own myth of the city. The myth later came to permeate Latin Americans' own writings, including Sarmiento's *Viajes por África, Europa y América* (Travels through Africa, Europe, and America) of 1849, and the city developed denser symbolic and metaphorical meanings. It eventually formed a rather consistent system that transcended any writer's single influence or even the influence of writers as a group, becoming what Walter Benjamin called the "capital of the nineteenth century."[14] Discussing *Viajes por África*, Marcy Schwartz characterizes Sarmiento's mode of describing Paris as traditional, to which the turn of the century writers would respond: "Sarmiento's writing creates a hierarchical relationship between Paris and Latin America. Paris is perfection and harmony, the artistic and organizational model that inspires Latin American progress. Foreigners are supposed to conform and adapt to Parisian behaviors."[15] What Jacinto Fombona calls the "necesario viaje a París" (necessary trip to Paris) was part of the education of young men of the peripheral oligarchy, just as Paris was the most important stop on the increasingly common *grand tour*, in which young Latin Americans (and especially men) acquired the cultural capital that would establish their position in adulthood. Indeed, statistical analysis by Jens Streckert indicates that "journeys to Paris virtually became an obligation for everyone interested in progress or in belonging to the elite."[16]

Around the turn of the twentieth century, this swelling flow of Latin Americans to Paris included a broader array of people beyond the elite, such as professionals and bohemians, although the group continued to be dominated by men. Beatriz Colombi describes them as a "colonia conformada por diplomáticos, cronistas, poetas, críticos, traductores, viajeros ocasionales, desplazados, exiliados, jóvenes promesas o novelistas establecidos" (colony made up of diplomats, chroniclers, poets, critics, translators, occasional travelers, displaced people, exiles, promising youths, or established novelists).[17] The lettered productivity of this generation, especially in journalism, is one reason that it consolidated an enduring image of Paris in the Latin American imaginary: "El grupo más numeroso está formado por los cronistas de los grandes periódicos continentales o españoles que constituyen la vanguardia de esta migración" (The most numerous group is made up of chroniclers from the great continental or European newspapers, who constitute the avant-garde of this migration).[18] Streckert uses French census records and witness testimony to demonstrate a significant increase of Latin Americans in Paris in 1901, which he attributes to the Paris World Fair of 1900.[19] Jason Weiss points out that "the *modernistas* were the first generation of professional writers, dedicated predominantly to their art.... Paris was the center of the world to them."[20]

By 1900, the city's earlier associations with aristocratic finery and popular revolt were fading and being replaced with notions of a modernity defined by cosmopolitanism, carefree hedonism, and artificiality. Several influential members of Spanish American Modernismo had taken jobs as diplomats or newspaper correspondents in Paris, which was increasingly seen as the central location of the movement. Colombi has examined this convergence of Latin Americans in Paris in the first decade of the twentieth century, particularly around the time of the World's Exhibition of 1900, dubbing the French capital a "Mecca" for intellectual networks from the global periphery.[21] Following a brief stay in 1893, Darío arrived in 1900 as a foreign correspondent, sent by *La Nación* of Buenos Aires to document the exhibition in Paris, much as Amado Nervo was sent by *El Imparcial* of Mexico. Other writers living there or staying for extended visits included Rufino Blanco-Fombona, Manuel Ugarte, Alcides Arguedas, and the García-Calderón brothers, Francisco and Ventura. The Paris they encountered inspired awe with both its real attributes and its mythological status, and the Modernistas and especially Gómez Carrillo were influential in extending the reach of the city's evolving mythology. By writing about a glamorous, frivolous Paris in mainstream newspapers, he popularized these new associations of the city, as he returned obsessively to notions of femininity in its representation.

DARÍO'S PARIS OF ENSUEÑO AND COMMERCIALIZATION

Among the many trans-Hispanic chroniclers working from Paris in this period, Rubén Darío has been the most examined by scholars. *La Nación* of Buenos Aires sent him there as a foreign correspondent in 1900, following more than ten years of his regular contributions to the newspaper and about five living in Buenos Aires.[22] The French capital had held a powerful symbolic value for Darío and many of his contemporaries, offering them a sort of ground zero of an aesthetic tradition associated with idealism and distanced from mundane concerns. Mariano Siskind has examined Darío's concept of the "French Universal," proposing that the French tradition "must be read as the horizon of *modernismo*'s worldly imagination."[23] At first Darío writes exultantly about a living, poetic tradition he encountered there, a tradition that carried over from his prior readings perhaps more than it responded to immediate observation. However, if Darío had long imagined from afar his full participation in world literature in the form of engagement with French and Parisian literary communities—and via his participation, the arrival of trans-Hispanic literature to a full plenitude of modernity on a global horizon—his real, lived experience of the French capital quickly took a different form. He began a long process of disappointment with his exclusion in that space of production of globally hegemonic modernity, and with a present that seemed to hurtle ever faster toward the dangerous unknown. The mythical Paris of plenitude lingered, in a productive opposition in the representation of Paris that recurs throughout Darío's career, frequently with the metaphor of a beautiful but duplicitous woman. While he initially represented Paris as a locus of aesthetic perfection, innovation, and unfailing good taste, it was also a hotbed of a fraught modernity that he considered dangerously commercialized.

When Darío arrived in Paris in 1900, he was optimistic and held high expectations of the city. He wrote in his memoirs about the French capital as a permanent fixture on his personal map of prestige:

> Yo soñaba con París desde niño, a punto que, cuando hacía mis oraciones, rogaba a Dios que no me dejase morir sin conocer París. París era para mí como un paraíso en donde se respirase la esencia de la felicidad sobre la tierra. Era la ciudad del Arte, de la Belleza y de la Gloria; y, sobre todo, era la capital del Amor, el reino del Ensueño. E iba yo a conocer París, a realizar la mayor ansia de mi vida. Y cuando en la estación de Saint-Lazare pisé tierra parisiense, creí hollar suelo sagrado.
>
> I dreamed about Paris since childhood, to the point that, when I said my prayers, I begged God not to let me die before seeing Paris. For me Paris was like a paradise where one would breathe the essence of happiness on Earth. It was the city of Art, of Beauty, and of Glory; and, above all, it was the capital of Love, the realm of Reverie. And I was going to see Paris, to realize the greatest desire of my life. And when in Saint-Lazare Station I stepped upon Parisian soil, I believed I trod upon sacred ground.[24]

Darío's Christian metaphors (paradise, Glory), alongside references to pagan tradition (Beauty, sacred ground), endow the French capital with an air of mystical reverie. The city is similarly overwhelming in "París y los escritores extranjeros" (Paris and the Foreign Writers), in which he compares it to a drug and to a bewitching woman:

Hay quienes hacen de París su vicio. Hablo del París que produce la parisina, del París en que la existencia es un arte y un placer. Tal París embriaga de lejos. . . . El paraíso, un verdadero paraíso artificial, se reconoce a la llegada. El hechizo está en el ambiente, en las costumbres, en las disposiciones monumentales, y sobre todo en la mujer. La parisiense sólo existe en París.

Some make Paris their vice. I speak of the Paris that produces the Parisian woman, the Paris in which existence is an art and a pleasure. That Paris intoxicates from afar. . . . Paradise, a true artificial paradise, is apparent upon arrival. The spell is in the air, in the customs, in the monumental layout, and above all in the women. The Parisian woman exists only in Paris.[25]

Darío associates the city with women, comparing their effects to a religion, a drug, or a great love affair: always attractive but dangerously unpredictable.

Darío's idealism and optimism remain strong in his first chronicle written from the Exposition, suggesting that the fabled City of Light was following through on its poetic promise. He idealizes the city with a tone of awestruck revelry, finding the long-sought *ensueño* (reverie) he identified with poetry, despite his unmistakably modern vantage point: "Visto el magnífico espectáculo como lo vería un águila, es decir, desde las alturas de la torre Eiffel, aparece la ciudad fabulosa de manera que cuesta convencerse de que no se asiste a la realización de un ensueño. La mirada se fatiga; pero aún más el espíritu ante la perspectiva abrumadora, monumental" (Seeing the magnificent spectacle as an eagle does, that is, from the heights of the Eiffel Tower, the fabulous city appears in a way that makes it hard to convince yourself that you are not experiencing a dream becoming real. The gaze becomes fatigued; but the spirit does so even more, facing the monumental, overwhelming view).[26] The fair condenses characteristics previously attributed to the surrounding city, in an experience that was only made possible by modern engineering. Darío's amazement is so intense that it leads to sensory fatigue ("the gaze becomes fatigued"). Our nomadic poet-chronicler continues to have faith in the fabled aesthetic experience of Paris and, for now at least, is able to link the poetic city to the modern city of industry and commerce.

Quickly, however, Darío's ability to reconcile urban modernity with his experience of poetic *ensueño* is tested, as Paris starts to reveal itself as commercialized and sordidly devoted to the bottom line. In "El viejo París" (Old Paris), his third chronicle on the Fair, dated 30 April 1900, he narrates his visit to a half-completed reconstruction of medieval Paris that has a sharp air of artificiality, illuminated anachronistically by modern electric lights.

The poet emphasizes the falsity of his surroundings, even as he relishes the essence of the historical city and its yearned-for aesthetic blessing:

> Asuntos de amor, actos de guerra, belleza de tiempos en que la existencia no estaba aún fatigada de prosa y de progreso prácticos cual hoy en día. Los layes y villanelas, los decires y rondeles y baladas[,] que los poetas componían a las bellas y honestas damas que tenían por el amor y la poesía otra idea que la actual, no eran apagados por el ruido de las industrias y de los tráficos modernos.

> Matters of love, acts of war, beauty from times when life was not yet fatigued with practical prose and progress like today. The lais and villanelles, the refrains and rondels and ballads, which the poets composed for the beautiful and honest ladies that had a different idea of love and poetry from the present one, were not drowned out by the noise of modern industry and traffic.[27]

Here, a recreation of old Paris conjures nostalgia for a mythical city that Darío knows only from literature, a mythical city where poets' social roles were secure and where women valued the poets' work. In spite of the artificial facades, the construction underway and the untimely (or perhaps *too timely*, too modern) details, this simulacrum of medieval Paris still communicates the Parisian essence that Darío seeks, allowing him to believe in an old-fashioned version of love and of poetry, and substituting the drudgery of practical, modern prose with cloak-and-sword chivalry. And yet, industry and modern traffic threaten to invade from the margins of the simulacrum, calling attention to the artificiality of the scene.

These early hints of disillusionment with Paris and its aesthetic promise would become more frequent and consistent. Darío comments in particular on the commercialization of art in the French capital, even sharing his belief that his own writing seemed drained of spiritual value in that environment.[28] He warned also against the dangers of industrial progress, as with a Parisian subway accident that killed ninety commuters in 1903: "Si el progreso ha de venir así, mejor que no venga" (If this is how progress must come, better that it not come at all.)[29]

The prostitute has a privileged place in Darío's representation of the French capital. He especially associates the city with courtesans, who reflect a commercialized form of what he considers the city's feminine nature: "En París no sólo hay grupas y sonrisas de venta, y cafés alegres. Mas, entre todos los que vienen, nadie prefiere Madame Curie a Mademoiselle Liane de Pougy. Y París, sobre todo, es mujer. Es la hembra" (In Paris there are not just rumps and smiles for sale, and happy cafés. Yet, among all who come, no one prefers Madame Curie over Mademoiselle Liane de Pougy. And Paris is, above all, women. It is female).[30] While both were famous, Curie and de Pougy marked extreme points on Darío's spectrum of modern types of Parisiennes: the first was a physicist, chemist, and the first female professor at the University of Paris; the other, a beautiful and storied courtesan. Darío acknowledges this diversity but makes clear that only one contributes to the draw of Paris for young men from Latin America. He clarifies that the courtesan is a false promise and always deceptive, truly a man-eater: "A París viene todo el oro de nuestras minas, en monedas y en pensamientos; y a los que llegan fuertes, jóvenes, sanos, con la primavera en el alma, París los devuelve enfermos, viejos, rotos" (All the gold of our mines, in coins and in thought, comes to Paris; and those who arrive strong, young, healthy, with springtime in their souls, Paris returns them sick, old, broken).[31] The image communicates not only the vulnerability these travelers felt in Paris; it also reminds us that this coming-of-age experience was strictly gendered and available to men only. Here, the fear of being consumed in the French capital stems from an anxiety specific to the peripheral man who finds himself lacking his accustomed social capital in a new milieu.

The male writer's precarity in Paris is thus directly tied to questions of identity and national origin. Parisians' ignorance of Latin America inspired in them a pervading sense of rejection, rather than the belonging that Darío had long imagined. In the formulation of his contemporary, the Argentine Manuel Ugarte writes, "esta sensación de inferioridad aparente, por encima de las equivalencias reales, la tuvo Darío hasta el fin. No pudo desprenderse de ella durante su larga permanencia en París" (Darío had this feeling of apparent inferiority, beyond all the real equivalencies, up to the end. He could not free himself of it during his long stay in Paris).[32] Colombi notes that many Latin Americans in Paris at this time shared Darío's sense of isolation and perceived inferiority: "en los testimonios, las cartas y las memorias abundan los lamentos de extranjería y el sentimiento de saberse intrusos en París" (in the testimonies, letters, and memoires appear abundant laments of foreignness, of the feeling of being intruders in Paris).[33] Darío credited this sense of rejection to Paris's status as the center of global hegemonic culture, which allowed its residents to imagine that they had no need to learn about other places and their cultural production:

> Para el parisiense no existe otro lugar habitable más que París, y nada tiene razón de ser fuera de París. Se explica así la antigua y tradicional ignorancia de todo lo extranjero y el asombro curioso ante cualquier manifestación de

superioridad extranjera. Ante un artista, ante un sabio, ante un talento extranjero, parecen preguntar: ¿Cómo este hombre es extranjero y sin embargo, tiene talento?

For the Parisian, no other place than Paris is inhabitable, and nothing has any reason to exist outside Paris. This is the reason for their old and traditional ignorance of everything foreign, and the curious astonishment in response to any sign of foreign superiority. Before a foreign artist, sage, or talent, they seem to ask: How can this man be a foreigner and nonetheless have talent?[34]

Marked as an outsider by his language, the very element in which he realized his own vision of modernity, Darío felt that his origins and national identity barred him from participating fully in his adopted home.[35] Colombi describes Darío in Paris as eventually "un sujeto diaspórico, resistente a cualquier conciliación con su nuevo aquí-ahora" (a diasporic subject, resistant to any reconciliation with his new time and place).[36] Within this context of pervasive disappointment and rejection, perhaps what most surprises is that Darío continued to use "Parisian" as a descriptor for literary style: "Yo he sido más apasionado y he escrito cosas más 'parisienses' antes de venir a París que durante el tiempo que he permanecido en París. Y jamás pude encontrarme sino extranjero entre esas gentes" (I have been more impassioned and I've written more "Parisian" things before coming to Paris than during the time I have lived in Paris. And never could I consider myself anything but a foreigner among those people).[37]

In December of 1904, Darío describes Parisians as "un público de política, bolsa y automovilismo" (a audience interested in politics, stock markets and car-racing), generally unable to appreciate poetry or anything else that required slowing down from their busyness and distraction.[38] His tone shades into cynicism one month later when, in "El año nuevo de París" (New Year in Paris), he uses formerly honeyed tags with new irony, giving them a disparaging ring: "Lo cierto es que se vive una atmósfera folletinesca desde hace tiempo . . . . Tal es la existencia presente en la dulce Francia" (The truth is that we have lived a melodramatic atmosphere for a while. . . . Such is current life in sweet France).[39] Imagining what a foreigner might think upon arriving for the first time in the legendary city, he wonders, "Aquí pasa algo. . . . ¿Es una enfermedad colectiva? ¿Por qué se siente aquí en el ambiente la presencia de un mal flotante?" (Something is happening here. . . . Is it a collective illness? Why does one feel everywhere the presence of a floating evil?).[40] Finally, dubbing Paris "el atrayente paraíso de mi juventud" (the attractive paradise of my youth),

Darío draws a clear line between that imagined paradise and the real city in which he lives. No longer can he see the city as his muse:

> ¡Cómo no voy a sentirme extranjero aquí, donde he perdido todas mis ilusiones que he traído de un París de arte sincero, de noble entusiasmo, de generosidad intelectual! Aquí no puede sentirse a sus anchas sino el que se ha saturado del elemento ambiente, el que se ha parisienizado. Yo no he podido echarme el alma al hombro, cambiarme de piel y lanzarme a la corriente.

> How could I not feel like a foreigner here, where I have lost all the illusions I brought of a Paris of sincere art, noble enthusiasm, intellectual generosity! Here no one can feel at home except someone who has saturated himself with the environment, who has Parisianized himself. I have not been able to throw my soul on my back, change my skin, and jump into the current.[41]

For Darío, Paris has come to represent vulgar commercialism rather than the aesthetic idyll of *ensueño*. Forced to choose, he does not hesitate: he remains a poet and gives up on becoming Parisian.[42]

Darío considers Gómez Carrillo to have an unusual place among Latin Americans in Paris. The Guatemalan arrived before others of his generation, and he spoke French much better than most. He also managed to gain some recognition with a French readership, which for other Latin Americans was generally out of reach. Interestingly, Darío considers Carrillo's residence in Paris to be a direct and immediate contributor to his writing style. He commented in 1892 that "con el tiempo que ha pasado en París ha cambiado del todo: su criterio estético es ya otro; sus artículos tienen una factura brillante aunque descuidada, alocada" (with the time that he's spent in Paris he's changed completely: his aesthetic criteria is different now; his articles have a brilliant craftmanship, although careless, crazy).[43] In "París y los escritores extranjeros" (Paris and foreign writers), Darío writes that Carrillo's recognizable writing style resulted from his contact with the French capital, again personifying the city as a prostitute: "París le dió su gracia verbal, su versatilidad femenina, su sonrisa y el gusto por el refinamiento de sus placeres. . . . No creo que pudiera nunca separarse de París, aunque haya llegado a reconocer más de una de las falsías y engaños de la adorable cortesana que lo hechizó" (Paris gave him his verbal grace, his feminine versatility, his smile and his taste for the refinement of Paris's pleasures. . . . I don't think that he could ever separate from Paris, even if he might come to recognize more than one of the deceits and tricks of the adorable courtesan who bewitched him).[44] Here Carrillo's "feminine versatility"—perhaps a veiled reference to Carrillo's famous unpredictability—is a gift from Paris-as-courtesan, who inspires his refinement, taste for pleasure, and even the flexibility and liveliness of his prose.[45] In this case, "feminine" as a descriptor of Paris and of writing can be understood to communicate that it is attractive and enjoyable but unstable.

Darío's admiration for Carrillo's style was not constant, however, and in a letter to the Spaniard Miguel de Unamuno he criticized the Guatemalan's prose as "tonterías" (nonsense) that "no harán sino que se distinga entre lo que París tiene de sólido y verdaderamente luminoso, y el article de París, que fascina a nuestros snobs y bobos de la moda" (will do nothing but distinguish between what of Paris is solid and truly luminous, and the Parisian article, which fascinates our snobs and fools for fashion).[46] Here Darío positions Carrillo's signature "article de París" (Parisian article) as fashionable but silly and counter to a more authentic Parisian tradition of artistic leadership. Darío thus associates the French capital with two literary styles: one is laudable (solid and luminous), while the other is a mere fad, lacking in depth, and best avoided. Darío even laments his own role in popularizing the latter style of chronicle: "no sabe usted lo que he combatido el parisianismo de importación, que he tenido la mala suerte de causar en buena parte de la juventud de América" (you don't know how much I have combatted the Parisianism for import, which I've had the bad luck of causing in a good part of the youth of America).[47] Although he regrets his role in a widespread adoption of the "article de París," he nonetheless remains faithful to his inspiration in French literature, reminding Unamuno that Spain has failed in this regard: "La innegable indigencia mental de nuestra madre patria nos ha hecho apartar los ojos de ella; no es culpa nuestra" (The undeniable mental indigence of our motherland has caused us to look elsewhere; it is not our fault).[48] It is noteworthy that Darío's disappointment with Paris extends even to his own literary innovations in relation to that city.[49]

GÓMEZ CARRILLO'S CRÓNICA DE PARÍS

Both Darío and Gómez Carrillo enjoyed unusual renown as chroniclers of Paris, but Darío's work has been more examined by scholars, despite the fact that Carrillo likely had even greater circulation in newspapers of the time. His writing was also more closely identified with an ostensibly Parisian style, and in it we most clearly see the consolidation of a feminine modernity as integral to Modernista thought. He arrived in Paris in 1891 as a teenager, possibly following the advice of Darío, who claimed to have pointed him toward "el camino de París" (the road to Paris).[50] As a result, when other writers in Spanish converged on the French capital in 1900, he was prepared to serve as guide to the spaces and intellectual networks associated with bohemian (or post-bohemian) Paris, a service that he continued for years. Carrillo pursued a career in journalism and, eventually, diplomacy, living primarily in France until his death in 1927. Among Modernistas, he was exceptional because he was not a poet, and instead dedicated his considerable energies entirely to prose and especially the newspaper chronicle. These he collected in books including *Almas y cerebros* (Souls and Brains), *La vida parisiense* (Parisian life), *El modernismo* (Modernismo), *El libro de las mujeres* (The Book of Women), *Vistas de Europa* (Views of Europe), *Entre encajes* (Among lace), and *Sensaciones de París y de Madrid* (Sensations of Paris and Madrid), etc. His travel writing included *El alma japonesa* (The Japanese Soul), *La Grecia eterna* (Eternal Greece), *De Marsella a Tokio* (From Marseille to Tokyo), among other books. For Colombi, Gómez Carrillo "fue el cronista del éxito, el que alcanzó la gran época de las veladas *La Plume* y se hizo notorio por su frecuentación con los famosos" (was the successful chronicler, the one who reached the great era of the *La Plume* soirées and became notorious for his contact with famous people).[51] His early work from France introduced a concept of world literature to trans-Hispanic readers, as Siskind has explored.[52] Around 1900 he consolidated his concept of a feminine modernity as an approach to urban experience and as an aesthetic that he encountered in Paris, and which he offered to the modernizing republics of Latin America as a model for their own future.

Antonio Cortón, in his prologue to Carrillo's *El alma encantadora de París* (The Charming Soul of Paris), describes the Guatemalan as, simply, "un parisiense" (a Parisian).[53] Darío similarly extols Carrillo's familiarity with the city in "París y los escritores extranjeros":

> Gómez Carrillo es un caso único. Nunca ha habido un extranjero compenetrado del espíritu de París como Gómez Carrillo. . . . Él es quien dijo que el secreto de París no lo comprendían sino los parisienses. Los parisienses ¡y él! Si no ha llegado a escribir en francés es porque no se dedicó a ello con tesón. Mas en su estilo, en su psicología, en sus matices, en su ironía, en todo, ¿quién es más parisiense que él? Muerto Jean Lorrain, no hay entre los mismos franceses un escritor más impregnado de París que Gómez Carrillo.

> Gómez Carrillo is a unique case. Never has a foreigner understood the spirit of Paris as well as Gómez Carrillo. . . . He's the one who said that the secret of Paris is only understood by Parisians. By Parisians, and by him! If he hasn't begun writing in French, it's because he hasn't dedicated himself with

determination. Yet in his style, in his psychology, in his subtleties, in his irony, in everything, who is more Parisian than him? With Jean Lorrain dead, even among the French themselves there is no writer more impregnated with Paris than Gómez Carrillo.[54]

Darío's observations again point to the experience of Paris as consequential for a writer's literary style. He sets Gómez Carrillo as the standard of a "Parisian" aesthetic, which we can understand here as related to the Guatemalan's famous frivolity. Aníbal González has noted this association and extended it to include modernity also, proposing that eventually Gómez Carrillo "se convirtió en un oráculo de la modernidad (entendida, rudimentariamente, como todo lo que pasaba en París)" (became an oracle of modernity [understood, rudimentarily, as everything that happened in Paris]).[55] The trademark levity of Gómez Carrillo's writing contributed significantly to his success, as María Luisa Bastos proposes in her analysis of triviality in his subject matter and style. Referring to a Carrillo chronicle on the American dancer Löie Fuller, Bastos points out that "el texto juega predominantemente en el nivel sensorial, en el nivel de los significantes, a expensas del significado" (the text plays predominantly on the sensorial level, on the level of signifiers, at the expense of the signified); what she calls his "técnica trivializadora" (trivializing technique), achieved with heavy recourse to anaphora and repetitious syntax, "da al texto lo que hoy percibimos como su marcada entonación kitsch" (gives the text what we perceive today as its marked kitsch intonation).[56] For Óscar Rodríguez Ortiz, "esta evidente sucesión de 'frivolidades' dibuja la tipología de una estética coherente: la bohemia, el decadentismo, lo simbólico, los sentidos insaciables como 'moral de las formas', el moderno sentimiento de lo rápido" (this evident series of "frivolities" sketches the typology of a cohesive aesthetic: bohemianism, decadentism, the symbolic, the insatiable senses as a "moral of form," the modern sentiment of the fast).[57]

As we have seen previously, a representation of the French capital as the epitome of beauty and of an aesthetic modernity is not unusual among Modernistas. Something that differentiates Carrillo, however, is his sustained attention to a discourse of femininity, in which Parisian modernity is made visible by Parisian women's urban activity, and that modernity is understood to be itself gendered as feminine, characterized by grace, lightness, and an impeccable sense of taste; in his own words, it is "ligero, voluptuoso, frou-froutante" (light, voluptuous, frou-frouing).[58] For example, in his memoire *En plena bohemia* (In Full Bohemia), he declares that Paris is "la ciudad santa del mundo moderno" (the sacred city of the modern world), and his own body of work is "un himno aparentemente frívolo, mas en el fondo muy lleno de fe grave, a la gloria, a la belleza y a las virtudes parisienses" (an apparently frivolous hymn, yet in truth very full of serious faith in the glory, beauty, and virtures of Paris).[59] The chronicle "El alma sublime de París" (The Sublime Soul of Paris), collected in *Vistas de Europa* (1919), continues to exhibit a deep investment in this mythology of Paris, which for him represents all the spiritual-aesthetic experience sought by Modernistas: "Es la gracia bendita entre las gracias," he says, "la sonrisa que florece cual una rosa, el encanto que todo lo embellece" (It is the blessed grace among graces, the smile that blooms like a rose, the charm that beautifies everything).[60] More than the center of French tradition, the city represented to him a collage of the world's best and most current aesthetic practices. He was an active traveler and writer of travel literature, but in his view Paris condensed a world of beauty: "Y es que París es un mundo, es que en París hay cien ciudades y cien aldeas, es que París tiene todos los cielos, todos los climas, todas las bellezas, todos los contrastes" (It's that Paris is a world, and it's that in Paris there are one hundred cities and one hundred villages, it's that Paris has all the skies, all the climates, all the beauties, all the contrasts).[61] His concept of femininity as a particularly modern style applies equally to his view of the city, to the women he describes there, and to his own, distinctive writing style. Paris as the quintessentially modern city was a privileged space from which to educate Latin American newspaper audiences on modern life and the modern styles that he considered appropriate to their culture and future.

The new prose styles associated with femininity and with Paris gained mainstream recognition as a genre, the *crónica de París* or the *crónica parisiense* (or what Darío above calls the *article parisiense*, Parisian article), in large measure thanks to the broad, mainstream circulation of Carrillo's work. The genre was often considered superficial; according to Ugarte, depth was all but impossible given the genre's subject matter of the vast and rapidly changing culture and current events in Paris, particularly when considered alongside the delayed temporalities of trans-Atlantic publication, which meant that "news" appeared three weeks late.[62] As a result, correspondents had to depend on a new and exciting writing style to sustain reader interest. For Ugarte, a frivolous style is the core of the chronicle's value: "en la hermosa frivolidad de esas crónicas que resbalan sobre la ciudad, sometiéndolos [los problemas más arduos] a la *blague*, hay un perfume tan penetrante de alma de artista que nadie se atreve a formular un reproche" (in the beautiful frivolity of these chronicles that slide over the city, subjecting them [the most arduous problems] to joking banter, there is a penetrating perfume of the soul of an artist, and no one dares to formulate a reproach).[63] Colombi refers to "la superficialidad de la elegante crónica parisina—con su previsible ironía, comentario pasajero, necesaria afectación" (the superficiality of the elegant Parisian chronicle—with its predictable irony, its passing commentary, its necessary affectation).[64] For Molloy, the style remained popular throughout Latin America long after it had been discarded elsewhere, thanks to the prestige and large readership of Darío and especially Gómez Carrillo; she credits their "crónica de boulevard" (boulevard chronicle) for the long life of Modernista rhetoric.[65] Frivolity, beauty, a concern with fashion, avoidance of "serious" topics, what Cáceres above called Carrillo's "novelty in phrasing": these are the elements that define the *crónica parisiense* and relate it to a discourse on femininity.

Gómez Carrillo's concept of a modern, feminine style functioned in his thought as a sort of protection against the dangers of the modern city. Much as we have seen already for Darío, he identified a vein of industrialism and work ethic in Paris that he considered undesirable, and he marshalled the representation of women and the idea of femininity to the cause of countering these dangers of the twentieth century. In this formulation, femininity is a desirable style that modern urban subjects should cultivate, in order to balance the city's increasing industrialism. Carrillo exalts in his role as observer of women in a chronicle titled "El bulevar día a día" (The Boulevard Day by Day): "¡Oh, estos ojos, estos labios, estas gargantas! ¡Cómo no ser pagano á la manera moderna, adorador de la *chair ideale*, fanático de la gracia, del encanto de la esbeltez de nuestras contemporáneas! En la uniformidad gris del siglo naciente, entre el humo de las fábricas, entre el rumor de los negocios, en medio de los trajes negros de los hombres, ellas son la alegría" (Oh, these eyes, these lips, these throats! How could we not be pagans in the modern way, adorers of the *ideal flesh*, fanatics of grace, of the charm of the slenderness of our ladies of today! In the gray uniformity of the new century, amidst the smoke of factories, amidst the hum of business, among the men's black suits, they are joy).[66] Here, the beautiful women of Paris provide a joyful remedy to the "gray uniformity" of modern industry and commerce, a variation on earlier models of the eternal feminine as passive, contemplative, or domestic, with a balancing effect on its opposite of ostensibly masculine industrial activity.[67]

Carrillo goes on to limit the women's expression to silent primping, revealing frivolity to have deeper meanings that elude language. He separates them both from voice and from the social category of the artist, which he occupies fully himself:

> Ellas no dicen nada. Y en silencio, con un poquito de desdén y otro poquito de lástima hacia nosotros, se consagran á cultivar sus propias bellezas, y se

> pulen como joyas, y se dan brillo y facetas como piedras preciosas, y se perfuman como flores y se adornan como altares. Y en lo que el filósofo sólo ve frivolidad, ponen algo más y algo mejor: ponen amor, ponen ternura, ponen fe . . . y el artista sincero se siente, como en los museos de obras maestras, acongojado de tanta belleza.
>
> The ladies say nothing. And in silence, with a little bit of contempt and another little bit of pity toward us men, they dedicate themselves to cultivating their own beauty, and they polish themselves like jewels, and they give themselves shine and facets like precious stones, and they perfume themselves like flowers, and they adorn themselves like altars. And where the philosopher sees only frivolity, they put something more and something better: they put love, they put tenderness, they put faith . . . and the sincere artist feels, as in museums of master works, anguished before so much beauty.[68]

Significantly, the sentiment of a "sincere artist" is necessary here to properly understand the women's performance of frivolity; while it is the women who cultivate beauty, Carrillo clearly does not include them in the category of artists. "El bulevar" presents a theory of modernist art as the product of sincere male artists viewing beautiful, vain, and silent women, two mutually exclusive groups whose combined efforts are necessary to combat the "gray uniformity" of modernity.

Carrillo's proposal that women and their beauty constituted a positive, necessary force to counteract the excesses of modern life has drawn little attention from scholars. These images circulated alongside threatening images of women that were also plentiful around the turn of the twentieth century—the femmes fatales, viragos, and deceptive prostitutes, often racialized or associated with immigration, illness, or class mobility—and these have received more scholarly analysis, particularly in the visual arts. The representation of beautiful women as a dangerous temptation is frequent. In *Las hijas de Lilith* (Lilith's Daughters), Erika Bornay interprets images such as these as reactions against new opportunities available to women in society, particularly in England and France, tracing the development of "aquel miedo finisecular hacia la mujer y, como consecuencia, aquella agresividad que se desencadenó contra ella" (that turn-of-the-century fear of woman and, as a consequence, that aggresivity that was unleashed against her).[69] Similarly, in *Idols of Perversity*, Bram Dijkstra analyzes these and related images in literature, painting, and other media, as a particularly pervasive misogyny resulting from evolutionary theory.[70] Literary scholars have also studied period anxieties related to many variations of disruptive gender expression, non-normative masculinities, and the negative and threatening connotations of women's sexuality.[71] Carrillo's representation of *Parisiennes* intervenes in this panorama with a markedly different tone, directing our attention to the frivolous with a flood of lighter imagery. At the same time, however, it is clear that he participated in the exclusion of women from creative agency and emphasized instead their potential as passive muses for creative men, including himself. They functioned as a sort of screen upon which he projected his own theory of modernity.

Gómez Carrillo's *Psicología de la moda femenina* (Psychology of Feminine Fashion, 1907) includes material that probably first appeared in newspapers as chronicles of Paris the previous year, or around the time of his marriage to Aurora Cáceres, whose observations appear at the beginning of this chapter.[72] Collected as a long essay, it is a "miscellaneous" work with a patchwork or collage-like style that offers plenty of opportunity for digression.[73] *Psicología* examines Parisian women's obsession with fashion, which Carrillo calls "Nuestra Señora del Capricho" (Our Lady of Caprice), with a breezy tone that shades ambiguously into a joke.[74] Susan Kirkpatrick has called the book "un ligero y chismoso popurrí de anécdotas sobre la moda, el diseño y las artes parisinas" (a light and gossipy potpourri of anecdotes about fashion, design, and Parisian arts).[75] As if winking at his audience, the author discusses "frivolous" topics with a serious tone and proposes the need to formally educate the public in "la profundidad de las frivolidades. . . . La cátedra se impone, la cátedra de las elegancias femeninas" (the deepness of frivolities. . . . The course of study is required, the course on feminine elegance).[76] He lectures on the importance of elegance, which he understands as an art of fashion and adornment expressed through personal taste and consumerism. In this piece, Carrillo represents Parisian women as epitomizing taste and especially currency in a rapidly-changing consumer culture, while men, in sharp contrast, have no such freedom of expression with their own clothing: "Nada, en efecto, debe brillar en el tocado nuestro [de los hombres]; nada debe llamar la atención" (Nothing, in effect, must shine in our wardrobes [of men]; nothing should call the attention).[77]

As Carrillo celebrates new styles that allow him to foreground aesthetic debate, he strictly condemns any defeminizing of women's gender expression. At one point, for example, he rejects innovative fashions that lessen the visual differences between men and women, and forcefully condemns feminists and *yanqui* influence. Carrillo seeks methods to "hacer el milagro urgente de conservar á la arcilla femenina, á pesar del *sport* y de la hygiene, de la democracia y de la igualdad inteletual [sic] de los sexos, su gracia, su prestigio y su esplendor" (achieve the urgent miracle of conserving feminine clay—her grace, her prestige, and her splendor—in spite of sport and hygiene, of democracy, and of intellectual equality of the sexes).[78] Indeed, *arcilla* is an important metaphor: women are the clay with which Carrillo molds his philosophies and his literary performances of style, while the "psychology" of the book's title belongs to him and to others like him, that is, to male observers and philosophers. In a similar example, Carrillo considers Paul Adam's idea of a Palacio de la Mujer (Palace of Women) that, like a perverse World Exposition pavilion, would display living examples of the most elegant women from all the countries of the world. The fantasy recalls Darío's 1894 poem, "Divagación" (Divagation), a parade of women representing various nationalities or ethnicities, all inviting and sexually available to the male observer. Carrillo quotes Adam, agreeing with him, as we imagine Darío might, too: "'Nuestro siglo tiene el deber de crear ese panteón de la Belleza y de poblarlo de ídolos vivos. La acción sería útil y singular, pues así como el hombre fecunda el cuerpo de la mujer en el amor, la mujer fecunda el espíritu del hombre en la voluptuosidad'" (Our century has the obligation to create that pantheon of Beauty and populate it with living idols. The effort would be useful and singular, for just as man fertilizes woman's body in love, woman fertilizes man's spirit in voluptuosity).[79] Indeed, this vision of the Women's Palace reveals the deep misogyny of Carrillo's ideology, and reminds us that within Modernismo creative agency is a gendered privilege accorded strictly to men. The most modern of subject in this framework is the man who observes women and translates their performance of modern consumer culture into a modernist literary product.

Carrillo is clear that his idealized *Parisienne* is inspiring for her elegance and her talent combining old styles with new, the fad of the moment with the all-important individual touch. Andrew Reynolds is right to note that "the concept of chic as described by Gómez Carrillo rejects passivity and values personal creative agency."[80] At the same time, however, it is important to note that Carrillo drew a line separating women, including Parisian women, from creativity or agency as writers. He disdained women who crossed this line as *la mujer moderna* (the modern woman), whose literary or intellectual endeavors he considers banal: modern woman "no logra, en cuanto se hace artista ó pensadora, salir de la estela que deja la nave masculina" (doesn't manage, if she becomes an artist or a thinker, to go beyond the wake left by the ship of men).[81] His framework leaves no space for women writers' innovations or success, as their work is always interpreted as a drab and imperfect imitation of men's writing.

Although Gómez Carrillo's prose seemed to emulate his object, with his writing style taking on characteristics of beauty, lightness, and frivolity, his traditionalism is also noteworthy regarding gender expression, with strict and different expectations for women and men. For this reason it would be incorrect to interpret his discourse of a feminine writing style as an adoption of a womanly pose. He deploys this fascination with feminine style, rather, to situate himself, his reader, and more broadly Latin America in relation to the hegemonic modernity considered to emanate from Paris. In the final analysis, Carrillo's *crónicas parisienses* (Parisian chronicles) are more about his attitude toward a particular modernity than they are about news in the French capital. As Ugarte suggests, their value was in their style, and their attraction for Carrillo's avid readership likely stemmed from the chronicles' flair, confident attitude, and blithe fluency in the cultural codes that eluded the periphery and defined Paris as up to date. His chronicles gave his trans-Hispanic readership a sense of belonging in the rapidly changing cultural landscape, a position from which to understand and even pass judgement on the latest fads in Paris. In this process he contributed to a broad association of the period between modern style, femininity, and the French capital.

One of the ways the chronicle of Paris positioned Latin Americans within the space of production of globally hegemonic modernity was by situating Latin American culture as a branch of the French tradition. Here too the language is heavy on metaphors of gender. Ugarte explains the national associations of prose styles and links them to gender norms: he discusses the "crónica latina" (Latin chronicle, referring to both writing in both French and Spanish) as "bella" (beautiful) and "agradable" (pleasant), in contrast with the "sajona" (Saxon) chronicle of New York, which he describes as "sólida" (solid) and "útil" (useful).[82] This contrast delineates two styles of modernity as they are expressed in literary aesthetics, suggesting one style of modernity as preferable over another for Latin America's own future. Ugarte insists on this point of collective "Latin" identity: "Nuestro espíritu es inquieto, inconstante y apasionado. La raza latina es una raza de poetas. Y la 'crónica' es el género que sintetiza sus cualidades y sus defectos" (Our spirit is restless, fickle, and passionate. The Latin race is a race of poets. And the 'chronicle' is the genre that synthesizes its qualities and defects).[83] Paradoxically, it would seem that the most apt genre for a "race" of poets is not poetry at all, but the chronicle. As Vera Helena Jacovkis observes, "así como la crónica se reivindica precisamente por sus defectos (es superficial, frívola), son estos mismos defectos los que la relacionan con el 'espiritu' latino (que es 'inconstante', 'inquieto', 'apasionado')" (just as the chronicle is revindicated precisely for its defects [it is superficial, frivolous], these same defects are what relate it to the Latin "spirit" [which is "restless," "fickle," and "passionate"]).[84] Frivolity thus functions in Gómez Carrillo's prose as literary style that communicates his proximity to French culture, his ability to relate that expertise to Latin American culture, and his concept of a feminine, modern style as the prerogative of a masculinist approach to the production of literature.

BUENOS AIRES, OR PARIS IN AMERICA

Gómez Carrillo's interest in the feminine modern extended to other cities as well, as if measuring other locations against the Parisian standard. This is particularly noteworthy in *El encanto de Buenos Aires* (The Charm of Buenos Aires, 1914), in which he describes the Argentine capital as partially modern, partially feminine, and on the right track in emulating Paris, although a latent primitivism continued to threaten disruption. *El encanto* is a collection of chronicles following Carrillo's trip to the Argentine capital between May and July of 1914, and which operate in a mode of constant comparison between that city and Paris.[85] Upon awaking in his hotel room the first day in Argentina, what he hears and sees convinces him that he must be in the capital of France. The two cities are so similar that he claims to lose track of his whereabouts. "Y en la modorra del lecho, decíame: 'Es una ilusión, puesto que no estoy en París, sino en Buenos Aires.' Pero hé aquí que al abrir la ventana me convenzo de mi error. Es en París en donde estoy, no en Buenos Aires" (And in the drowsiness of bed, I said to myself: "It's an illusion, given that I am not in Paris, but rather in Buenos Aires." But lo and behold that upon opening the window, I convince myself of my error. This is Paris around me, not Buenos Aires).[86] Throughout the rest of the book, Carrillo praises Buenos Aires for its similarity to Paris, pointing out a desirable culture of frivolity and artificiality in the American city's recently remodeled streets.[87] He considers the two cities to be so similar that he feels he knows everything about Buenos Aires, although he has never visited the city before: "Nada en sus detalles me parece desconocido. Nada me choca. Nada me sorprende" (Nothing in its details seems unknown to me. Nothing shocks me. Nothing surprises me).[88] At times, Buenos Aires is even more Parisian than Paris, and he praises the Argentine capital as "un París más rico, más sonriente, más feliz de aspecto que el de Europa" (a Paris richer, smilier, and happier-looking than the one in Europe).[89] Here, the signifier "Paris," rather than referring to a city in France, becomes a neat package of all that the city represented to the writer: beauty, style, artificiality, a carefree attitude toward life.

Gómez Carrillo bases his comparison of Buenos Aires and Paris on specific, concrete aspects of the two cities. The Avenida de Mayo (May Avenue), on which his hotel is located and the place that he turns to first in describing

Buenos Aires, is like the great Parisian boulevards; Palermo emulates the Bois de Bologne (Bologne Wood).[90] Carrillo's description of Calle Florida (Florida Street), which he considers a unique combination of the traits of various European cities, amounts to an original summary of the beauty that he considers possible in a specifically American modernity:

> Todo lo que pueda soñarse de lujo, de alegría, de encantadora frivolidad, de buen gusto suntuoso, se halla reunido en esta calle. . . . Y su belleza, su carácter, su estilo, si puedo expresarme así, está justamente en no ser una copia de ninguna arteria europea. . . . No, no es un reflejo. Es tal vez una síntesis, hecha con arte exquisito, de todo lo que hay en Europa de más distinguido, de más animado, de más brillante, de más moderno.

> Everything that could be dreamed in terms of luxury, happiness, charming frivolity, sumptuous good taste, is brought together in this street. . . . And its beauty, its character, its style, if I can put it that way, is precisely in not being a copy of any European streets. . . . No, it is not a reflection. It is perhaps a synthesis, made with exquisite art, of all that Europe offers of more distinguished, of more animated, of more brilliant, of more modern.[91]

In *El encanto de Buenos Aires*, the Argentine capital comes to represent modern urban life alongside Paris, thanks to its brilliance, animation, and "charming frivolity." Once again, we see an implicit definition of a preferred modernity as based on aesthetic perfection, artifice, and luxury, rather than industrial productivity.

Only one feature of Buenos Aires distances it from the modern perfection that Paris represents for Carrillo: the regular street grid, which he considers undeniably and irremediably ugly.[92] In the chronicle "Las calles de la City" (The Streets of the *City*), he writes that "en Buenos Aires, tan limpio y tan alegre, la belleza resultaría enteramente parisiense de no ser por las malditas líneas rectas, que hacen imposible las perspectivas y que imponen la monotonía" (The beauty of Buenos Aires, so clean and so joyful, would be entirely Parisian, save for the damned straight lines, which make perspectives impossible and impose monotony).[93] The utilitarianism and efficiency of the colonial Spaniards created a dull grid design, and the long boulevards of recent reforms were similarly uninspiring. In all periods, Carrillo favors urban space shaped by what he calls the "wise caprice of centuries":

> Cada vez que nos encontramos entre bulevares recién construídos experimentamos una sensación penosa de uniformidad y de monotonía. La gracia

pintoresca de los laberintos antiguos, creados por el sabio capricho de los siglos, no ha seducido nunca á los fundadores de ciudades. Para que una población sea artística, casi puede asegurarse que es preciso que haya nacido del azar. En cuanto los hombres, conquistadores ó reformadores, se proponen hacer algo, no llegan sino á la belleza higiénica y cómoda, que es la peor de las bellezas.

Every time we find ourselves in newly built boulevards, we feel an awful sensation of uniformity and monotony. The picturesque grace of ancient labyrinths, created by the wise caprice of centuries, has never seduced founders of cities. For a population to be artistic, we can be almost certain that it is necessary for it have been born randomly. As soon as men, conquistadors or reformers, propose to do something, all they manage is a hygienic and comfortable beauty, which is the worst of the beauties.[94]

Here Carrillo considers an inherent ugliness to be characteristic of all American cities since the time of their founding, but also the result of recent attempts at urban reform. These cities are an enduring, material marker of the Americas' colonial history and peripheral status.[95]

The street grid functions in Carrillo's discourse, then, as a problem from which spectators must be distracted, if a city is to be apprehended as beautiful. He considers Buenos Aires exceptional in that it has partially surmounted its monotonous street grid and, thus, the visual reminder of its colonial history. He writes that what saves Buenos Aires from its ugly American foundations is Porteños' unfailing good taste, which led them to create an artificial appearance of age when remodeling their city. Despite the city's newness—a friend tells him, "Todo lo he visto yo salir del suelo" (I have seen all this rise up from the soil)—Carrillo praises the simulacrum of age he sees in the Argentine capital, where "una delicada pátina que parece obra de siglos da al conjunto un tono gris suave, agradable, de muy buen gusto" (a delicate patina that appears to be the work of centuries gives the whole a soft gray tone, agreeable and of very good taste).[96] In this manner, Americans' cultivation of good taste can overcome their cities' humble, humiliating origins. The artificiality of the Buenos Aires facade does not trouble him. Indeed, Carrillo posits artificiality in general as a positive aspect of modernity and one that links it to a concept of feminine style: "Todo lo grande, todo lo fuerte, todo lo recio, diríase que aquí se afina y se engalana con galas casi femeninas" (Everything great, everything strong, everything robust, we could say that here it is refined and adorned with almost feminine elegance).[97]

A chronicle titled "Entre flores y sonrisas" (Among Flowers and Smiles) describes the upscale neighborhood of Palermo. Carrillo praises "la divina frivolidad criolla" (the divine Creole frivolity) and sees in the neighborhood the self-conscious display that he has identified as modern when discussing Paris: "Todo es alado, todo es vaporoso, todo tiene un sutil aire de artificio y de teatro en el magnífico paseo" (Everything is winged, everything is vaporous, everything has the subtle air of artifice and of theater in the magnificent promenade).[98] When residents of Buenos Aires enact a ritualized display of their artifice and beauty in the Palermo promenades, Carrillo is enthusiastic upon viewing the parade of young Porteñas. Once again, his praise of the Argentine capital is phrased as a comparison with Paris:

> ni pueden tener mayor belleza ni pueden tener más distinción [las señoritas de Palermo]. Aunque sea algo pesado compararlo todo con París, en las parisienses hay que pensar viendo á las porteñas distinguidas que animan las magníficas alamedas de Palermo.... En todo caso, si no superiores, tampoco son inferiores plásticamente, rítmicamente, suntuariamente.

> they [the young ladies of Palermo] could not have more distinction. Although it might be dull to compare everything to Paris, it is of the Parisian ladies that we must think, when viewing the distinguished Porteñas that animate the alamedas of Palermo.... In any case, if they are not superior, neither are they inferior plastically, rhythmically, luxuriously.[99]

This narrator's voyeuristic eye metonymically transfers the girls' beauty to the city surrounding them. Carrillo's objectifying gaze inspects the girls' physiques, rhythms, and wardrobes as he might examine merchandise in a department store. Moreover, the señoritas' "distinction" corresponds to their knowledgeable interaction with their surroundings, that is, their posture, and performance of a particularly modern femininity. Here, taste is the metric for judging Argentina's success at the task of overcoming colonial history, for not seeming behind the times or uneducated. Carrillo uses this metric to evaluate the country's entry as an equal into the imagined universality of Parisian-styled modernity.

El encanto de Buenos Aires turns readers' attention to Porteña women on numerous occasions, and most references underline the similarities Carrillo sees between Buenos Aires and Paris. He accords young women responsibility for a city's visual effect, lauding them for their successes but censuring their shortcomings. He even calls them to a "patriotic" project of urban beautification downtown:

Ah, niñas de Palermo, deliciosas niñas morenas, que andáis como maniquíes de la rue de la Paix: cuán triste es que no os decidáis, renunciando á vuestros hábitos, algo recelosos y también algo orgullosos, á pasearos igualmente por las calles céntricas de Buenos Aires! Ya sabéis que esas calles tienen fama de ser feas. Si vosotras las animárais, serían deliciosas. . . . Porque venir hasta aquí [a Palermo] sólo para admirar vuestro encanto, casi es considerarlos cual un espectáculo de lujo, cual un espectáculo raro. ¿Cómo no comprendéis, ya que sois patriotas, que el mejor medio de dar prestigio á vuestra ciudad es engalanarla con el constante don de vuestras gracias? Las parisienses lo hacen en su París.

Ah, young girls of Palermo, delicious brunette girls, who walk like mannequins on the Rue de la Paix: how sad it is that you do not decide, renouncing your somewhat suspicious and also somewhat proud habits, to promenade as much through the central streets of Buenos Aires! You already know that those streets are famously ugly. If you animated them, they would be delicious. . . . Because to come all the way here [to Palermo] only to admire your charm, one must almost consider you a luxury spectacle, or a rare spectacle. How do you not understand, since you are patriots, that the best way to give prestige to your city is by adorning it with the constant gift of your graces? The Parisian ladies do it in their Paris.[100]

As he continues to leverage his knowledge of Paris and that city's prestige in his comparison with Buenos Aires, Carrillo drives home the girls' responsibility as guardians of their city's (and even their nation's) aesthetic status. In spite of his playful and initially positive tone, his estimation of these "mannequins" from a fashionable Parisian street falls short of expectations, and he criticizes them for not displaying themselves in a more convenient location. By better living up to their task of display, they would contribute to their country overcoming its American ugliness, the mark of its colonial origins.

GÓMEZ CARRILLO'S PARIS AND PERIPHERAL SUBJECTIVITY

This chapter has taken up the *crónica de París* or *crónica parisiense* of the influential Modernista Enrique Gómez Carrillo, considering his treatment of the genre alongside Rubén Darío's similar approaches and Carrillo's chronicles of Buenos Aires. We have seen that Carrillo's chronicles of Paris gave his trans-Hispanic readership a sense of belonging in Paris and in modernity by aligning Latin America with French culture, as something like cousins on the "Latin" branch of a global family tree. We have also seen that he emphasized the role of taste and distinction in communicating a city's modernity—which he defined as its similarity to Paris—and the role that he assigned women, to perform that taste in city streets. For Carrillo, a great deal was a stake in women's use of public space, as well as in the strict gendering of roles in relation to creative agency. Indeed, a nation could even aspire to overcome its colonial history and assume dignified parity with the most admired countries abroad by remodeling public space appropriately and educating its young ladies about their performance requirements within that space.

Certain elements of Carrillo's theory resonate with other authors of his time, among them the belief that Latin American culture was a branch of the French or Roman tradition (i.e., Mediterranean but not Spanish). Other writers made similar proposals, José Martí and José Enrique Rodó among them, but what distinguishes Carrillo in this discourse of a pan-Latin identity is his gendered rhetoric of modern style, which he marshaled to the cause of imagining Latin America's own possible modernity based on a cultural affinity with Paris.[101] Significantly, his logic hinged on a strict division of creative labor, in which women performed their knowledge of modern pastimes and taste in public spaces, and men interpreted their performance and parlayed the inspiration they experienced into a reinvigoration of literary style as light, flexible, and innovative. This process, moreover, gave men from the periphery an imaginary position (and perhaps an imaginary position of importance) in that central space for the production of globally hegemonic modernity, a relatively stable social position from which to envision their own role in Paris and their region's possible future.

Both here and in Chapter 1, I have proposed that Modernismo imagined French modernity and an implicit, future Latin American modernity, as feminine, in opposition to an ostensibly masculine modernity represented by the industrialism of the United States. Another frequent comparison was Spain and its discussion of "virile" literature for authors that would come to be called the Generación del 98, as we have considered in Chapter 1, such that by rejecting ostensibly masculine models of culture, Carrillo also signaled his interest in moving beyond the traditionalism of his Spanish contemporaries. Modernistas' identification of a stylistic femininity in their own work and that of other Latin Americans thus contributed to this perception of a cultural affinity with France and of an imminent Latin American modernity that would be culturally appropriate because it followed a French model. In this way, appropriating femininity as a positive descriptor related to modernity allowed them to renegotiate their own inferior status in a global hierarchy of cultural prestige. Although it is true that many Latin Americans favored a modernity represented by United States and New York—earlier, Sarmiento saw an example worth emulating in the North American urban design and educational systems, for example, and Gómez Carrillo's contemporary Clorinda Matto de Turner sought a model for women's rights there, as we will see in Chapter 3—the focus here has been on an obsession with modern femininity in the Latin American imaginary around the turn of the twentieth century.

As the Modernista journalists with broadest circulation, Darío's and Gómez Carrillo's proposals resonated throughout a trans-Hispanic cultural space for decades, shaping perceptions of modernity and of Latin American identity in a period of rapid historical change. By the time of Darío's death in 1916, they were perhaps equally renowned and identified with Modernismo, a point that is easy to forget today, given that Gómez Carrillo's vast body of work has been relatively little examined by scholars.[102] Darío's monumental contribution to Spanish-language poetry was an important difference between the two, but this alone does not explain his continuing recognition, in contrast with Carrillo's fall to the wayside. It is plausible that at least some measure of Carrillo's oblivion results from his discourse of femininity and the frivolous, which contributed to a perception of his work's triviality and limited relevance over time. María Luisa Bastos interprets frivolity in Gómez Carrillo's work as an example of his responding to reader demands, particularly those of a non-specialist readership that might not have recognized or cared about the difference between more high-brow art and what she calls Gómez Carrillo's irritating superficiality and "cursilería irredimible" (irredeemable tackiness), an extreme version of frivolity.[103] She argues that aspects of Carrillo's work that we might find tiresome today are in fact critically and historically significant, and stem from his interest in communicating novelty. His role, then, as something of a tour guide to the latest fashions of Paris, which required that he always appear to be up-to-date, shaped his style as a market-driven writer who was able to answer a demand from his readership: the demand for modernity, for Paris, and for frivolity.

This chapter has developed a fuller understanding of what was at stake in that desire for the frivolous, for lightness. In the historical context of Carrillo's newspaper circulation, this discourse represented for his readers an expression of their own belonging in modernity, supporting their imagining of a particularly Latin American or trans-Hispanic place at the table of a modernity perceived to be universal. At the same time, his discourse of feminine, modern style presented a less drastic shift in gender roles than those sought by advocates for women's rights, and one that curtailed women's potentially radical interventions, limiting their threat to tradition. His discourse as it was expressed in literary style was, moreover, pleasurable and accessible to the casual reader, a point that should not be underestimated when considering his success. His work from Paris contributed significantly to the broad circulation of the Modernista ideology of modern, feminine style. The next three chapters will consider women writers' responses to Modernista ideas of a feminine aesthetic, alongside their very different opportunities in relation to that movement's intellectual networks.

CHAPTER 3

ALTERNATIVE MODERNITIES

Exile and the Re-invention
of Clorinda Matto de Turner

On December 14, 1895, the Peruvian novelist and journalist Clorinda Matto de Turner (1852–1909) became the first woman nominated to membership in the Ateneo de Buenos Aires, a prestigious writer's club in her new home of Argentina. She was a well-known novelist, but she was also an exile struggling to reinvent her professional life in a new and largely unfamiliar country, and for this reason she had little social capital to spare when facing her audience. An address on *indigenismo* (Indigenism), the topic that had brought her fame some five years before for her novel *Aves sin nido* (Birds without a Nest), would have been both interesting and unthreatening to her male listeners, for whom racial issues in the Andes would have seemed exotic and unconnected to their own daily lives. She decided instead, as the first woman to speak from the podium of the Ateneo, to leave *indigenismo* aside and focus on a pressing issue that presented a challenge to almost any organization of trans-Hispanic writers like the Ateneo: the exclusion of women writers from their ranks. In her speech, Matto discussed women's education as the great, peaceful effort of modernity, perfectly suited to "el terreno fértil de nuestra América" (the fertile terrain of our America).[1] She insisted that "trabajan millares de mujeres productoras que, no solo dan hijos á la patria, sinó, prosperidad y Gloria! Éstas son LAS OBRERAS DEL PENSAMIENTO de quienes voy á ocuparme en seguida" (thousands of productive women work, not only giving children to the homeland, but also prosperity and Glory! These are the WOMEN THOUGHT-WORKERS, whom I will discuss in what follows).[2]

In her address, Matto went on to name and describe more than ninety women writing throughout the Spanish Americas, from Mexico and the Caribbean to Chile and Argentina, showcasing her extensive knowledge of and contact with a sprawling network of women writers. In closing, she reminded her audience of the particular challenges that these "heroines" faced:

> [Que] la enumeración, aunque incompleta, que he hecho, sirva de recuerdo agradecido para las obreras del pensamiento en América del Sur; verdaderas heroinas, repito, que no solo tienen que luchar contra la calumnia, la rivalidad, el indiferentismo y toda clase de dificultades para obtener elementos de instrucción, sinó hasta correr el peligro de quedarse para tías, por que [sic], si algunos hombres de talento procuran acercarse á la mujer ilustrada, los tontos le tienen miedo.

> May this enumeration I have made, albeit incomplete, serve as a grateful reminder for the women thought-workers in South America; true heroines, I repeat, who not only have to fight against slander, rivalry, indifference, and all sorts of difficulties to access elements of education; they even have to run the risk of becoming old maids, because, while a few talented men try to get to know the educated woman, the silly ones are afraid of her.[3]

Matto de Turner here asks her audience to choose between supporting women's education and professional opportunities, or counting themselves among the "tontos" (silly ones) who fear them. The rhetorical strategy was perfectly designed for a group of self-important men in a public setting. In this way she initiated her membership in the Ateneo, launching a frontal attack on the exclusion of women as active literary participants and members, and decisively refuting the assumption that women writers were rare and isolated. She took up space for women writers, and, in a gesture that continues to bear political power today, she insisted on saying their names.[4]

This chapter examines Matto de Turner's professional reinvention during her exile in Buenos Aires, where she lived until her death in 1909. We will attend to her strategic engagement with writerly networks that helped her to advance her career despite the setback of a sudden exile. These multiple, interconnected networks include trans-Hispanic writers around the world; women writers from a similarly sprawling geography; largely homosocial writers' groups in Buenos Aires (be them male, as with the Ateneo, or female as with the Sociedad Proteccionista Intelectual [Intellectual Protectionist Society]); and the Peruvians exiled with her from Piérola's Peru. We will especially attend to her engagement with performance traditions to cultivate a community of women writers using rituals legitimized by traditional social roles, such as mother and godmother. These staged events provide a space for women's mutual support, memory work, and political organization, a niche within a broader literary field that excluded them. Matto's staged events particularly highlight the intergenerational character of her work, with a series of women mentors and protegées reaching back into the nineteenth century and forward into the twentieth, as part of her insistence on ushering a new tradition into existence. Her persistent interweaving of speeches and periodical publication allowed her to build the supportive community that she needed in this moment of personal reinvention.

Clorinda Matto de Turner was born in Cuzco and grew up there and on her family's nearby estate, then lived for about ten years in Tinta after marrying an English businessman. Upon his death in 1881, she moved to Arequipa to pursue her budding career as a writer and stave off bankruptcy. There and later in Lima she became renowned as a writer of *tradiciones* (traditions) in the style of her friend Ricardo Palma; as a journalist and newspaper founder and director, particularly after she became director of *El Perú Ilustrado* (Illustrated Peru) in 1887; and as an *indigenista* novelist, especially following her international hit *Aves sin nido* in 1889. Matto's public support for President Andrés Avelino Cáceres caught her in the violence of his ousting by Nicolás de Piérola. Following the destruction of her home and her feminist press, La Equitativa (The Equitable), and the burning of her effigy in the plazas of Lima and Cuzco, she was forced to abandon the Peruvian cultural field in which she had built a name.[5] Matto de Turner fled first to Chile, where she felt out of place in a culture still celebrating its victory over Peru in the War of the Pacific, and in May of 1895 she crossed the Andes and the pampas, headed to Buenos Aires. She arrived full of optimism about her future and the new opportunities that Argentina would offer, with a capital city that buzzed with excitement, modernization projects, and literary debate. It was significantly larger and more cosmopolitan than Lima, with immigration creating such rapid growth that half of Buenos Aires residents were immigrants in the year of her arrival.[6] Its closer connection to Europe meant that the winds of modernity blew stronger. Another contrast with Lima proved challenging, however: the Argentine capital had a less cohesive tradition of women writers and was little accustomed to women's professional activity. Matto was a middle-aged widow, alone, with savings to last only six months. As a professional forced to rebuild her career in a new environment, she faced a daunting task.

Matto de Turner did not respond to this moment of personal upheaval by installing her personal brand in a new urban space where it made little sense. Although her novels had been well-received in Argentina prior to her arrival, especially *Aves sin nido*, novels were not the primary mechanism of achieving literary prestige in her new environment, where a combination of poetry and journalism were a stronger currency.[7] Similarly, her signature theme of *indigenismo* was less pressing far from the Andes, in a city preoccupied with another underclass, that of a flood of poor immigrants from Europe. As a result, she set aside her prior commitment to *indigenismo* and the novel, maintaining instead her efforts in journalism and redoubling her attention to both the women's cause and the building of a trans-Hispanic literary community. Her primary space of activity for these efforts was a new magazine, *Búcaro Americano: Periódico de las Familias* (American Vase: Periodical of Families), which she launched in February 1896, about eight months after her arrival. One of the magazine's stated goals reflected her continuing commitment to women's educational and professional opportunities, but another, that of organizing and showcasing the best new trans-Hispanic literature, was newer to Matto and responded directly to the need to create a socio-professional space for herself in the Argentine capital.[8] Although directing the magazine did little to ease her economic hardship, particularly during the first years of her exile, Matto did eventually recover from the brink of poverty thanks to her work as a teacher in the Escuela Comercial de Mujeres (Women's Commercial School) and the Escuela Normal de Profesoras (Normal School of Women Professors).[9] *Búcaro*'s unusual success—it continued publication irregularly until 1908—reconfigured the map of trans-Hispanic literary production, tracing a network across great distances and spotlighting the social, literary, and educational interventions of women at every turn.

Buenos Aires in the 1890s was the time and place of Modernismo's first cohesion in physical spaces on a continental level, that is, the first time that aesthetic advancements (for which Rubén Darío's *Los raros* and *Prosas profanas* of 1896 have been taken as an example) coincided with a sizable international community of young writers in the same city, making possible a new group consciousness facilitated by Darío's role as spokesperson for the movement. What I wish to study here is the role of Buenos Aires Modernismo as a foil for Matto de Turner's self-reinvention. The literary movement was a constant presence that she strategically engaged, kept at a distance, and ultimately critiqued. This chapter examines *Búcaro Americano* alongside Matto's correspondence and speech performances, with reference also to historical records of the city's modernization, to sketch an emplaced view of her reinvention in the urban space and social field of the Argentine capital. We will see that, despite sharing with many Modernistas the circumstance of an immigrant and a journalist, Matto never really considered an active engagement with Modernismo to be an option for her. She included the work in her magazine as part of her commitment to offer an overview of new literature in Spanish, but she critiqued the movement's treatment of women and proposed instead a different approach to modernity based on education and professional opportunities for women.

BOHEMIANS AND TRADITIONALISTS IN THE ATENEO DE BUENOS AIRES

Lettered sociability in Buenos Aires was already active when Matto arrived, due to both its home-grown tradition and a burgeoning immigrant community. The Nicaraguan Rubén Darío arrived in Buenos Aires on August 13, 1893, renowned for his 1888 publication of *Azul . . .* in Chile and for his *crónicas* in *La Nación* of Buenos Aires, perhaps the most influential modern daily of South America.[10] He immediately started working in the newspaper's press room and participating in other spaces of lettered sociability. His arrival inaugurated a new era of Porteño bohemianism, in which journalism went hand in hand with poetry and nightlife. As Darío recalls in his *Autobiografía* (Autobiography), "casi todas las composiciones de *Prosas profanas* fueron escritas rápidamente, ya en la redacción de *La Nación*, ya en las mesas de los cafés, en el [bar] Aue's Keller, en la antigua casa de Lucio, en la de Monti. 'El coloquio de los centauros' lo concluí en *La Nación*, en la misma mesa en que Roberto Payró escribía uno de sus artículos" (almost all the compositions of *Profane Proses* were written quickly, some in the pressroom of *La Nación*, some at café tables, in Aue's Keller bar, at Lucio's old house, at Monti's. I finished "The Centaurs' Conversation" in *La Nación*, at the same table where Roberto Payró was writing one of his articles).[11] The flexible environment and the writers' layered sociability allowed them to seize inspiration wherever it struck and to develop ideas together at any time. The friendships and euphoric productivity of a new literary community are clear in Darío's memoir: "De ese vibrante grupo del Ateneo brotaron muchos versos, muchas prosas; nacieron revistas de poca vida, y en nuestras modestas comidas a escote creábamos alegría, salud y vitalidad para nuestras almas de luchadores y de *rêveurs*" (From that vibrant Ateneo group sprouted many verses, many pieces of prose; short-lived magazines were born, and in our modest, family-style meals we created joy, health, and vitality for our souls of fighters and dreamers).[12] While the Nicaraguan's influence clearly energized and coalesced the young *letrados* in Buenos Aires at this time, it had an opposite effect on the traditionalists: Roberto Payró's memoir indicates that "el mundo literario estaba exasperado, y en todos los centros intelectuales se rugía en pro o en contra de Rubén Darío. . . . En nuestro mundo literario no se ha visto jamás, sin duda no volverá a verse agitación semejante" (the literary world was exasperated, and in all the intellectual centers everyone bellowed for or against Rubén Darío. . . . In our literary world such agitation has never been seen before, and surely will never be seen again).[13]

Perhaps the most important organizing space for the city's artistic-literary field—what Payró called the "mundo literario" (literary world)—was the Ateneo de Buenos Aires, which began meeting in mid 1892 in the home of Rafael Obligado, in an extension of traditional *veladas*. The coterie chose as its first president Carlos Guido y Spano, an Argentine poet at the height of his prestige and seniority, but he resigned in October, and Calixto Oyuela, characterized by a "casticismo intransigente" (intransigent traditionalism), was narrowly elected as his successor.[14] In the same period the Ateneo took possession of its first headquarters on the newly opened Avenida de Mayo at the corner of Piedras, where the Café Tortoni was and still is located. Sections were established for history, natural sciences, and social sciences, and the Ateneo's formal inauguration followed on April 25, 1893. Later that year Carlos Vega Belgrano, patron of Modernismo, became Ateneo president. The Ateneo enjoyed multi-generational interest and cosmopolitan participation from its earliest moments. Darío's arrival energized and brought cohesion to the younger, more international faction that previously had lacked a sense of group identity, and as a result the Ateneo as a whole began a shift toward the modern and the new.[15] Early debates revolved around authors' rights and payment, which the younger generation advocated, to the chagrin or outrage of the older participants. In late 1894, the organization settled into its more permanent location at the new Bon Marché building at Florida and Córdoba, known today as the Galerías Pacífico.[16] This is the space depicted in photographs in a *Búcaro Americano* article titled "La mujer en el Ateneo argentino" (Woman in the Argentine Ateneo) in March of 1896, the same issue that offers a profile of Vega Belgrano and his portrait on its cover. The Ateneo's locations were all central, stylish, and part of the renovated Buenos Aires that was just then being unveiled.[17]

Laura Malosetti Costa underscores the variety of activities associated with the Ateneo: its headquarters hosted concerts, exhibits, and speeches.

In addition, its younger members associated with Darío and Modernismo created a climate of "bohemia y alcohol y discusiones que se prolongaban hasta la madrugada. . . . Así, entre las conferencias, las libaciones nocturnas y la redacción de los diarios, fue gestándose en torno al Ateneo una nueva manera de ser escritor, más profesional y menos patriarcal que la que todavía cultivaban Guido, Oyuela, Mansilla y Obligado" (bohemianism and alcohol and discussions that lasted into the early morning. . . . Thus, amid the conferences, the noctural libations, and the newspaper writing, a new way to be a writer took shape around the Ateneo, more professional and less patriarchal than the way cultivated by Guido, Oyuela, Mansilla, and Obligado).[18] Malosetti Costa's characterization of the young *letrados* as more "professional" than the traditionalists reflects their middle-class background and their economic dependence on work, while the traditional, "patriarchal" alternative reflected older systems of patronage that largely limited the lettered city to the wealthy.[19] Like the younger Athenians, Matto was also dependent on the economic fruits of her labors; however, Malosetti Costa's point about the bohemian nature of this "new way to be a writer" suggests women's lack of access to the spaces of literary networking.[20] This bohemianism was markedly homosocial, in an exacerbation of a characteristic common to literary life of the time, and Modernista sociability seems to have included no women who participated as writers. Indeed, it is possible to read Darío's *Autobiografía* and conclude that Buenos Aires had no women writers during his five years residing in the city.[21]

Although literary practice in the Ateneo varied, its early members were all men, and the organization initially barred women's membership. For Néstor Tomás Auza this fact "más que una exclusión parece una afrenta" (more than an exclusion, seems to be an affront).[22] Numerous women were present at Ateneo events in the audience; for example, so many women attended the inauguration that they filled the main room, relegating men to the reading room where the speeches could not be heard.[23] In his detailed, seventy-page description of the Ateneo, however, Giusti mentions no literary women as active participants. He also does not mention their absence, indicating the perceived normalcy of women's exclusion at the time. Precedent for women's membership nonetheless existed with the Ateneo of Lima, which had admitted women since the 1870s. During his presidency Vega Belgrano successfully advocated to modify the association's statues to allow the membership of women, and that status was offered first to the famous novelist, Matto de Turner, recently arrived from Peru. The active participation of women writers in the Buenos Aires Ateneo was null before her membership in early 1896, and afterward it continued to be very rare.[24]

Indeed, a professional woman like Matto de Turner would not participate in the nighttime sociability of Modernistas: it likely would not have interested her, and the real and symbolic risk of public spaces at night were significant for a woman in this period. She could nonetheless participate in Ateneo *conferencias* (conferences), and for this reason her absence after her speech is surprising. A few months after her own speech there, Matto writes to her friend Ricardo Palma that two other Peruvians had given addresses after her, but "no fui ni a una ni a otra. Sé estos pormenores por Vega Belgrano" (I did not go to either. I know the details from Vega Belgrano).[25] The laconic tone gives no hint of her reasons, which might have included boredom or simple busyness, but in fact her disappointment with the Porteña literary community was not limited to the Ateneo, nor to her fellow Peruvians. "Literariamente," she commented to Palma two months later, "aquí, el movimiento es malo. Todos se preocupan del comercio y de los negocios" (in literary terms, here the movement is bad. Everyone is worried about commerce and business).[26] The euphoric sociability and synergy of the literary scene was simply not accessible to her, despite what her membership in the Ateneo might suggest. Her strategic engagement with the Ateneo included acceptance of formal opportunities, and she took advantage of connections of all sorts. At the same time, however, that engagement was severely limited by both a broad culture of women's exclusion, as well as by her overwork related to teaching and the directing of *Búcaro*.

In addition to legitimizing her participation in lettered Buenos Aires sociability, Matto's membership in the Ateneo provided her with a connection to most of the important writers in that city, and she clearly took advantage of that access to gather contributions for *Búcaro*. She included poems and chronicles from its members, as well as publishing their writing and visual portraits regularly, but the frequency of these gestures is higher for the traditionalists than for the "Bohemians." Guido y Spano, for example, appears often in the pages of *Búcaro*. In one note, Matto narrated a visit to his sickbed in January of 1899 to greet him on his birthday, describing him as "el león engrillado, como el águila enjaulada" (the shackled lion, like a caged eagle).[27] She goes on to lavish praise on his personality and writing: "todo en él es dulzura, alegria, vibraciones del arpa ëolia que canta junto á su lecho con tonos enseñados por él mismo á los sauces que inclinan la copa y á los musgos que alfombran la pradera" (everything about him is sweetness, joy, vibrations of the Aeolian harp singing at his bedside, with tones that he himself taught to the willows bowing their fronds, and to the mosses that carpet the meadow).[28] In September of that year, she reproduced Guido y Spano's portrait on the magazine's cover and profiled him in "Nuestras miniaturas" (Our miniatures).[29] Several of his poems appear also, in addition to notes about him or dedications in other issues.[30] Her comfort level with the older traditionalists is apparent in her commentary on a letter he had received, which she reprinted in *Búcaro*. The piece was not exactly a willing contribution, as she had swiped it from his desk while visiting: "Yo en mi anhelo de traer algo de aquella fiesta para este Búcaro querido, extendí la mano en un descuido de [su esposa] Micaela y cometí el hurto de un papel que resulta ser de los más expresivos, cuya copia va enseguida para restituir el original en descargo de mi conciencia" (In my desire to bring something of that party to this beloved Búcaro, I extended my hand when [his wife] Micaela was not looking, and I committed the theft of a paper that ended up being very expressive, a copy of which you will find below, so I can return the original in defense of my conscience).[31] The purloined letter, from Julio Migoya García, wished Guido y Spano a happy birthday, waxed poetic on his "virtudes cívicas y preclaro talento" (civic virtues and illustrious talent), and associated his poetry with the history of Southern Cone independence.[32]

Among the Athenians affiliated with Darío's younger group, Carlos Vega Belgrano—another mediator and promotor, like Matto de Turner herself—was treated many times in *Búcaro*, but Darío himself, very little. Matto even used iconic tags like "el príncipe azul" (the azure prince) to refer to the Nicaraguan obliquely.[33] Seen from this perspective, her insertion in the Porteño lettered field can be understood as strategic contact with both Athenian currents, but a privileging of the traditionalists. Without affiliating fully with either faction, perhaps because neither had a tradition of including women writers, she initiated professional friendships with the main literary actors in turn-of-the-century Buenos Aires, excepting only the most radical figures, be that for their political proposals (as with the socialists or anarchists) or for their decadentist aesthetics and the bohemian character of their sociability. Her only mention of Darío in her correspondence with Palma comments dryly that he was "algo dejado para el trabajo" (rather careless about work).[34]

The fourth number of *Búcaro* includes "La mujer en el Ateneo argentino," a note in which Matto remembers her own legitimation as a lecturer and an Ateneo member. She links the organization's inclusion of women to an Americanist argument in favor of women's progress in Latin American society, describing it as a "centro intelectual llamado á ser el foco desde donde se reparta calor y vida á las personalidades artísticas y literarias en este lado del mundo de Colón" (intellectual center called to be the point from which warmth and life will be shared with artistic and literary personalities on this side of Columbus's world).[35] Matto criticized the treatment of Emilia Pardo Bazán by the Real Academia Española (Royal Spanish Academy)—thus participating in a trans-Hispanic moment of women's shared protest that can be traced in historical periodicals today—and insisted that the Americas were the most promising space for women's literary and professional activity.[36] She also reminded her readers that, in terms of women's professional opportunities, neither Spain nor Argentina was the most advanced or modern of countries: "América es, ciertamente, la que imprimirá el verdadero carácter á las escritoras del porvenir. . . . Entre las sociedades que con igual propósito han nacido en la América latina, corresponde al Ateneo de Lima la primacía de no haber restringido, desde su creación, el ingreso á la mujer" (America is, certainly, what will imprint true character upon women writers of the future. . . . Among the societies with the same purpose born in Latin America, the first not to restrict women's entry, from the time of its creation, was the Athenaeum of Lima).[37] The broad growth that Matto identified in the Americas, as opposed to the greater traditionalism in Spain, undoubtedly contributed to her successful installation as a *letrada* in Argentina: although a cohesive tradition of women's professionalism was lacking there, the sheer scope and speed of change in the literary field allowed her enough flexibility to find a foothold.

Matto's engagement with the Ateneo de Buenos Aires is an example of her strategic positioning in relation to the mainstream literary field of her new city. Matto did not fit within any pre-established roles in the Argentine capital, and she was forced to carve her own path among different factions surrounding her. Early in her exile, when she was pressed with the need to refashion her career in Buenos Aires, we see an adept but careful relationship to the city's lettered sociability. On this point I agree with Vicens, who considers the Peruvian's varied socio-professional interventions in the lettered scene of Buenos Aires to be "estrategias de supervivencia de Matto de Turner en el exilio; son diferentes maneras de ocupar espacios en la escena literaria del momento: hacer circular sus textos, su nombre y, a través de estos hechos, visibilizar y legitimar su propia impronta autoral" (Matto de Turner's survival strategies in exile; they are different ways of occupying spaces in the literary scene of the moment: she circulates her texts, her name, and, through these efforts, makes visible and legitimizes her own authorial mark).[38] In contrast with mainstream creative communities, which were largely homosocial and male, networks of professional women generally welcomed men's involvement; with fewer resources at their disposal, both social and economic, they turned to alternative mechanisms of community formation.

PERFORMANCE AND TRANSMEDIAL INTERVENTIONS

"Las obreras del pensamiento" is somewhat well known among scholars today, but another of Matto's speeches, presented about six weeks later, has gone unremarked. It would seem at first glance quite different from "Obreras": Matto presented it outdoors, in the Cementerio del Norte (Northern Cemetery, also known as Recoleta), before a primarily female audience. Instead of focusing on a synchronous network of dozens of writers as she had with "Obreras"—or what Ana Peluffo calls "una visión sororal de la cultura que es más horizontal (y rizomática) que vertical" (a sororal vision of culture that is more horizontal [and rhizomatic] than vertical)—here Matto emphasizes one writer's difficult life and tragic death, and the diachronous lessons to be drawn for a community.[39] Rather than map a spatial network, that is, she traced a genealogy of women writers through time and across generations. This performance is a eulogy that Matto presented before a crowd gathered around the fresh grave of the Uruguayan novelist Lola Larrosa de Ansaldo, one of the more than ninety women writers that Matto had named in "Obreras del pensamiento."[40]

Larrosa had been felled by tuberculosis in her late thirties, following a life of economic hardship marked by her husband's disability.[41] In her speech, Matto emphasizes Larrosa's tenacity when forced to leave the domestic sphere to support her family:

> ella, tuvo que buscar por sus propias manos el sustento de ese esposo enfermo y de ese tierno niño. La abnegada mujer se lanzó al torbellino de la Sociedad, llevando la pluma en la mano; con las ideas en el cerebro, y, con el dolor en el corazón! Sus libros, sus revistas; acaso, le dieron pan escasísimo, pero, cuando ella también comenzó a enfermar y su frente se inclinó como el endeble lirio sin aire y sin sol, las más desesperantes exigencias sitiaron ese hogar infortunado.

> with her own hands she had to seek support for her ill husband and for her tender child. The selfless woman threw herself into the whirlwind of Society, with her pen in hand; with ideas in her brain, and pain in her heart! Her books, her magazines; they provided but scarce bread, but when she also began to fall ill and her brow bent, like the weak lily lacking air and lacking sun, the most desperate demands besieged her unfortunate home.[42]

The economic necessity and moral imperative of a writer's fair remuneration for her work are apparent in Matto's address, echoing discussions elsewhere in Buenos Aires about writers' professionalization, as we have seen occurring in the Ateneo and among Modernistas employed in journalism. Although other writers seemed unaware of women writers' economic demands, the latter had in fact a prior history; for example, Juana Manso discussed women's paid "carrera literaria" (literary career) as early as 1854.[43] The occasion for Matto's performative lament is not Larrosa's funeral, but rather the dedication of a plaque at her graveside by the Sociedad Proteccionista Intelectual. Matto impresses upon her audience that the nearly eight hundred women members of this society, founded two years earlier, wished to honor Larrosa as their beloved "socia consejera" (counselor member).[44]

Like a tree drawing stability from its deep roots to reach higher, Matto draws on a history of women's mutual support and professional-affective sociability, projecting their collective advancement into the future. In her cemetery speech she refers to the nearby resting place of her friend and mentor, the Argentine writer Juana Manuela Gorriti, wishing that she could erect a mausoleum to honor Gorriti with a plaque "que diga á las hijas y á las nietas de las escritoras: AQUI REPOSA LA MAS ILUSTRE ENTRE AQUELLAS" (that would say to the daughters and granddaughters of the women writers: HERE LIES THE MOST ILLUSTRIOUS AMONG THEM).[45] With these "daughters and granddaughters," Matto articulates a matriarchal, exclusively female genealogy of writers that reaches back into the nineteenth century and forward into the twentieth, strengthened by its historical consciousness and its marks upon public space, as with the plaque and the longed-for mausoleum. Indeed, she proposed that the memory object, the plaque in the shape of an open book, would serve as "noble estímulo á las que emprendan el camino alumbrado por la antorcha de la inteligencia cultivada, allanado en sus escabrosidades por la fé en los mejores destinos de la mujer, en las generaciones que nos sucedan" (noble stimulus to the women who would take the path illuminated by the torch of cultivated intelligence, the path's roughness smoothed by the faith in woman's better destinies, in the generations to come).[46] This gesture resonates with Vicens's proposal that Matto's intergenerational efforts are intentional and foment a social space amenable to her contributions: Matto identified two generations of women writers and set her sights on a role mediating between them, imagining "el lugar que pretende diseñar la novelista para sí misma: Clorinda ha compartido espacios y periódicos con todas ellas (ya fallecidas) y es *quien es capaz de articular ese grupo de pioneras con el que está dando sus primeros pasos literarios en ese momento*" (the place that the novelist would design for herself: Clorinda has shared spaces and periodicals with all the women writers (at this point dead) and *it is she who can articulate that group of pioneers with the group that is taking its first literary steps in that moment*).⁴⁷ In her speech, Matto endeavors to preserve a memory of pioneering women writers and their challenges. She goes on to envision the book-shaped memory object as a concrete invitation for future generations to write: it was "la plancha donde, mas tarde se inscribirá la verdadera glorificación de las mujeres que sobresalgan por el talento, la virtud y el trabajo, trinidad de nuestros ideales progresistas" (the plaque where later will be written the true glorification of women who stand out for their talent, virtue, and work, that trinity of our progressive ideals).⁴⁸

Matto's remarks on this occasion were part of a longer program, and when giving a later speech, María Emilia Passicot was "tremblorosa por la emoción" (trembling with emotion).⁴⁹ The emotional speaker, with her hand shaking as it holds notes, reminds us of the emplacement of the scene, the physical proximity of its players to each other, their warmth shared amid the surrounding tombs. The togetherness of this "sentimental community"—I borrow the phrase from Ana Peluffo, who analyzes "performative aspects of public sisterhood"—flowed into shared tears and renewed commitments that *took up space* for women writers, reinterpreting that place in terms that supported their needs.⁵⁰ Vicens has analyzed "escenas sororales" (sororal scenes) of women writers meeting a new, professional friend, a description of intimate sisterhood that allows us to account for these encounters' sentimental language.⁵¹ These concepts undergird Matto's performative eulogy at the graveside of Larrosa: the public performances and narrativized sororal scenes are two ways of taking up space, of promoting physical togetherness to offer mutually legitimizing support.⁵²

This affective sociability bound together a developing community that we can access today only partially, through the printed remnants found in archives: considering the performance itself, beyond the printed speech moldering in dusty boxes, demands a creative engagement to reconstruct the imaginaries that have otherwise been lost. Matto's eulogy interweaves the writing of professionals with their friendships, the rituals of social obligations, and the shared circumstances of women's more limited access to public space and the written word. It illustrates both the power of affective performance and the strategies of personal and collective growth, suggesting a largely invisible substrate to women's writing in this period. Indeed, similar scenes of togetherness must have been frequent, ranging from calling on a friend at her home, to the performance of devotion represented by inscribing her album with a personal note, to attending and commenting on social or cultural events, such as theatrical productions. Although their ability to publish their writing was severely limited by patriarchal tradition, it could be shared more intimately in *veladas* (evening events) and other literary performance. Latin American women's writing of the nineteenth century appears due for a broad re-imagining of what the archive has struggled to preserve.

Today we have access to Matto's eulogy because she printed it less than a week later in the first issue of *Búcaro Americano*, much like her earlier speech, "Las obreras del pensamiento en América del Sur," considered in this chapter's opening. That is, her campaign for women's professional networks started with the performance of speeches before live audiences—in both the Ateneo de Buenos Aires and in the cemetery at Larrosa's graveside—and then converted those texts into magazine articles that would expand her audience and give her proposals more permanence. Matto's speeches built on an earlier practice of gathering to validate women's cultural contributions, one example of which is the Lima *veladas* hosted by Juana Manuela Gorriti in the 1870s and by Matto in the 1880s.[53] In this way, these writers participated in what Francesca Denegri has identified as the "primera generación de mujeres ilustradas en el Perú" (first generation of Peruvian women writers).[54] Particularly associated with Gorriti—who according to Isabel Tauzin Castellanos was "la mujer que más inspiró a las peruanas" (the woman who most inspired Peruvian women)—these gatherings brought recent literary production into a performance format and in the space of a home, amid music, presentations of visual art, patriotic song, and similar cultural production.[55]

The Lima *veladas* were presided over by a woman, featured the work of both women and men, and were occasion for the rituals of community formation. In one famous example, a young Clorinda Matto de Turner visited from the highlands and was ceremoniously received in Gorriti's *velada*, where the hostess—more than thirty years her senior and serving as "sacerdotiza del arte, como heraldo de la fama" (priestess of the art, as herald of fame)—crowned her with laurel.[56] Rocío del Águila writes that "esta ceremonia que se difundió en una serie de periódicos funcionó como una suerte de *bautizo literario* para Matto de Turner y selló su aceptación dentro de los círculos letrados capitalinos" (this ceremony became known in a series of periodicals and functioned as a sort of *literary baptism* for Matto de Turner, sealing her acceptance within the lettered circles of the capital).[57] Moreover, Peluffo has pointed out "el elemento performático de esta coronación ya que las mismas escritoras se ocupaban de invitar a periodistas o cronistas a las soirées para que publicitaran en la prensa lo que ocurría en ellas" (the performative element of this coronation, given that the same women writers took it upon themselves to invite journalists or chroniclers to the soirées, so they would publicize their activities in the press).[58] Alongside their activation of performance to create space for women writers, the *veladas* utilized a language of sentiment that metaphorically frames women's professional interventions as the natural result of loving relationships: the baptism formalizes the protection of a godmother for her goddaughter.

Matto's graveside eulogy reveals her awareness of the deeply and unavoidably political nature of the personal. She attributes the particular melancholy produced by Larrosa's death to the conflict between the deceased's poverty and her social responsibilities as a woman. Larrosa's economic reality demanded that she support her family, but fair compensation for her work was out of reach (much like affordable childcare, one imagines). The irreconcilable nature of that conflict creates the suffering that for Matto defines Larrosa's unhappy life, and the emotion runs deep precisely because the eulogist herself identified with this predicament. Indeed, at the time of this speech, Matto was herself struggling economically due to the sudden and violent circumstances of her exile, and not for the first time. Most importantly, Matto and Larrosa were not exceptional in their vulnerability, and every woman hearing her speech could be subject to the same precarity.

It is significant that Matto's approach in this eulogy differs markedly from her male contemporaries' treatment of dead women, particularly those of Rubén Darío and other Modernistas, for whom the dead women of Decadentist and Romantic tradition represented ciphers of aesthetic mystery and a platform from which to project the poet's own voice. In this regard they are illuminated by the framework of Elisabeth Bronfen in *Over Her Dead Body: Death, Femininity, and the Aesthetic* (1992), which examines representations of the "dead feminine body clearly marked as being other, as being not mine."[59] Bronfen explains that for many fin de siècle writers, "femininity and death cause a disorder to stability [and] mark moments of ambivalence, disruption or duplicity."[60] For Matto, in contrast, the deceased evoked identification and a sense of vulnerability, not otherness. The world in her view was already disordered, and her discourse sought to provide stability with the clarity of its critique. The approach of Timothy Secret in *The Politics and Pedagogy of Mourning* would seem more applicable to Matto's eulogy, particularly in its intimate linking of the political with mourning. Secret builds on the work of Derrida, noting: "No justice . . . seems possible or thinkable without the principle of some responsibility, beyond all living present, within that which disjoins the living present, before the ghosts of those who are not yet born or who are already dead."[61] True justice, in Secret's framing, reaches beyond those it might immediately affect, those presently alive, to include past and future lives in its embrace. For Matto, historical consciousness of both injustice for women and their mutual support practices provides a foundation for building a different future.

LOOKING FORWARD, LOOKING BACK

Women writers drew on traditions of gathering, of performance, and of trans-medial movement from performance to periodical text for the purpose of legitimizing their work and building a network of support; they also had a tradition of professional mentorship across generations that functioned according to its own codes, distinct from those of men, who had other tools at their disposal including formal education or publication via patronage. One movement (from performance to text) makes possible another (of rising recognition for a woman writer). Similarly, the rhetoric of rituals for building family relationships serves metaphorically to foster professional relationships, as with Gorriti's "baptism" of Matto. In these cases, women built professional legitimacy, using their zones of traditional expertise (family, private, performance) to make incursions into zones coded as masculine (professional, public, print).[62]

Matto returns emphatically to the trans-medial, pro-sororal tradition of the *veladas* in the inaugural number of *Búcaro Americano*. The issue's very first article, titled "Bautismo" (Baptism), introduces the new magazine by replicating Gorriti's baptismal ritual in written form, explicitly tying the new magazine project to that tradition and representing it as part of a broader sentimental community. The "birth" of *Búcaro* has not been easy, Matto writes. In contrast with earlier projects, which she calls "hijos de mi pensamiento" (children of my thought), this new magazine is "hijo de mis dolores, nacido en el ostracismo al que me condena el duelo del hogar con la muerte de un hermano idolatrado y el infortunio en la política provocado por las convicciones difíciles de quebrantar" (a child of my pains, born in the ostracism to which my grieving home condemns me, with the death of a beloved brother and the political misfortune provoked by the convictions difficult to break).[63] Despite this difficulty, Matto nonetheless professes admiration for her beautiful child and takes pride in providing it with the traditional functions of a baptism, that is, announcing a name and charging community members with fomenting its growth. Indeed, the naming of the "child" resonates with the naming of women writers in Matto's then-recent speech, "Las obreras del pensamiento": she reminds us that "en el derecho de ser y de existir está el derecho de llamarse" (in the right to be and to exist, is the right to a name).[64] In this naming ceremony of a different sort,

Búcaro will receive the protection of three "godmothers," who are profiled in a future issue.[65] This sort of editors' note was of course requisite upon the debut of a new magazine, but the rhetoric of intergenerational family ties and a supportive sisterhood is significant in that it frames Matto's reformist, sometimes challenging intervention into public discourse as legitimate and necessary.[66]

Thus far we have considered three texts in the first issue of *Búcaro Americano* that drew on traditions of performance: the magazine's introductory announcement, "Bautismo"; Matto's Ateneo speech, "Obreras del pensamiento," repurposed as an article; and her graveside eulogy for Larrosa. Matto found another opportunity to emulate women's spaces of sociability at the end of each number of *Búcaro*, where she printed a "Social" column, usually signed by Azul del Monte, a pseudonym of unknown authorship. This type of column permitted a collage-like fragmentation, in which the author quoted letters or reviews penned by others, to highlight parties, theater productions, betrothals, and society comings and goings. Taking advantage of the traditional flexibility in this section, del Monte gathered letters from others—such as the Baronesa de Blanc, who promises to report regularly on the latest fashions in Paris—and even included veiled advertisements. Del Monte's advice on sleeve styles, skirt shapes, and whether this season's hats should have feathers or flowers surely helped to expand the magazine's readership. Rather more surprisingly, it is in this "Social" section that we find Matto's speech from Larrosa's graveside, adding a lugubrious and straight-forwardly political note where readers expected a light tone. She denies the note its own title or graphic integrity, camouflaging it in the magazine's section most clearly coded as for women only. What she gains with the text's location in the "Social" section, however, is its emplacement in a social scene and a concrete location, with Del Monte's framing observations about the scene of the event. She preserves the sense of a performance. That this trans-medial movement, from performance to print, would occur in the most "feminine" of journalistic spaces, suggests that in this case femininity is license for flexibility and experimentation, for escape from the more disciplined practices of the rest of the magazine's organization.

Matto clearly cultivated the literary talent of younger women. The "Social" section that Matto disrupted with her eulogy noted that one young woman at the cemetery event was "la bella señorita Zoila Cáceres" (the pretty young lady Zoila Cáceres) also known as Aurora Cáceres, who is also considered in Chapters 2 and 5. Then twenty-four years old and on the brink of starting her own literary career, Cáceres would eventually carry forward the values of intergenerational support, as the closing of this chapter will explore;

however, on her arrival in Buenos Aires she was not yet fully schooled in or committed to that process, and showed all the exploration of a young person searching for her path.[67] Cáceres had arrived in the Argentine capital with her family, including her father the former Peruvian president, General Andrés Avelino Cáceres, following the Piérola coup d'état that removed him violently from office. Matto also formed part of this wave of Peruvian exiles descending on the Argentine capital in 1895, and Cáceres's involvement in *Búcaro* suggests that Matto took her young compatriot under her wing.[68] The first *Búcaro* publication signed by Eva Angelina, Cáceres's lifelong pseudonym, is titled "La emancipación de la mujer" (The Emancipation of Woman) and appears in issues six and seven (15 May and 1 June, 1896); it is relatively well-known among scholars today as a strident argument in favor of women's education.

What scholars have not remarked, however, is that Cáceres appears to have first written for *Búcaro* in the previous issue, number five, signing rather coyly with her initials of ZAC. This note also fits within the "Social" section and focuses entirely on fashion, as would some later contributions.[69] ZAC was also the byline for stand-alone articles in issues eight through eleven, with a travel narrative about northern Argentina.[70] In these, the author describes visiting northern Argentina to escape the Buenos Aires autumn, which, she writes, "me iba matando el espíritu" (was killing my spirit).[71] She further masks her identity by referring to Andrés Avelino Cáceres, who was honored in a procession she witnessed in Salta, not as her own father, but as "un compatriota de Vd., el general Cáceres" (a compatriot of yours, the General Cáceres), addressing the letter to Matto de Turner as the magazine's editor.[72] Although the authorship of these narratives is inconclusive, the rarity of the signed initials and the narrative's similarity with Cáceres's future writing, in terms of subject matter and style, suggests that it is in fact hers.

This travel narrative is relevant to our discussion of professional women's intergenerational support for two reasons. First, the author's reluctance to sign her name can be interpreted as a sign of her youthful uncertainty or perhaps her decorum as she experimented with her developing role in the lettered city. Particularly alongside the more strident tone of "Emancipación de la mujer," a sense of exploration is clear: Cáceres is trying on different writerly hats with her earliest publications. Secondly, the travel series marks one limit to the feminist genealogy under examination. My phrasing here is similar to Peluffo's when she discusses "sororophobic" emotions of envy and rivalry among women writers, but this situation is better described as an occasion of simple ignorance or a missed opportunity.[73] The first destination on the itinerary of ZAC is Rosario de la Frontera, followed by Salta, both locations treated more extensively than later stops, which included Tucumán, Córdoba, and Rosario de Santa Fe. She describes Rosario de la Frontera and Salta as locations of a spa and a religious procession, but does not mention their history as the birthplace and family home of her own "grandmother" in our feminist genealogy, Juana Manuela Gorriti. Cáceres misses this opportunity for another eulogy that Matto would have deeply valued, neglecting to inscribe herself into a family tree extensively developed by other writers, and in which she clearly participated. Either her commitment to that genealogy was not yet cemented, or she simply had no idea of the hallowed ground she walked.

Nearly thirty years later, Cáceres's greater experience would lead her to respond very differently in a similar situation. Matto died in 1909 in Argentina, and in 1924 the Peruvian congress called her remains home. By this time, Cáceres was an activist in her own right, experienced with organizing women's and writers' associations in France and Peru. In the same year, in fact, she contributed significantly to an association called Feminismo Peruano (Peruvian Feminism), which she would serve as president for life.[74] For the occasion of receiving Matto's mortal remains in Lima, Cáceres organized a convoy representing twelve different women's societies to accompany her from the railway station to the cemetery, where a series of speeches paid homage to the deceased, in effect reprising Matto's own performance of graveside memory work for Larrosa de Ansaldo.[75] Although many details of this event are unknown—we lack photographs or complete speeches, for example—it is clear that Cáceres placed great importance on honoring the remains of her mentor. The togetherness and staging of the event were important, the memory work and the *taking up of space*. Cáceres remembered Matto's lessons, and she carried them forward into the fast-changing social landscape of the mid-twentieth century. Indeed, in her *Álbum personal*, which we read in detail in Chapter 5, Cáceres included a clipping from an *América Latina* profile of Matto, which calls her "sin disputa, una de las primeras figuras literarias de América Latina . . . y obrera infatigable" (without a doubt, one of the primary literary figures of Latin America . . . and an indefatigable working woman).[76]

Cáceres's turn of phrase cites Matto's speech and essay, "Obreras del pensamiento," echoing some thirty years later and across the Andes, when, in a final continental displacement, the exile returned after death. We can read Cáceres's event as an explicit continuation of Matto's efforts to build a community of women writers using performance and togetherness, demanding public space for women writers. The eulogistic note of both events highlights the importance of memory work in building that community. Indeed, Matto fought at every turn to identify, support, and promote a new tradition of women writers that bridged geographies both vast and local. She may be the most consequential such figure in the history of Latin American women writers.

PROFESSIONALISM AND FRIVOLITY

Matto de Turner's approach to navigating the intellectual networks of her new home corresponds to her image as a practical and hardworking professional, unencumbered by idealism of the aestheticizing sort. She developed a skepticism of Modernismo over time. By 1906 her rejection of the movement had strengthened: "No comulgamos en la religión de la escuela modernista ni decadente, respetamos, sí, toda escuela con tal que los adeptos sean verdaderos, y por eso preferimos al poeta en sus encantos de hogar, sencillos como besos de niño, cristalinos cual gota de rocío, tierno como arrullo de paloma" (we do not partake of the religion of the Modernista or Decadent schools; yes, we respect all schools as long as their followers are true, and that is why we prefer the poet within the charms of the home, simple like children's kisses, crystalline like a drop of dew, tender like the cooing of a dove).[77] In this formulation, she rejects Modernistas because she considers them artificial or inauthentic (i.e., they are not "verdaderos"), where authenticity is associated with the home and with simplicity, clarity, and affection. Despite maintaining a "Bibliografía" (Bibliography) column on new publications in *Búcaro*, Matto was reticent regarding important Modernista publications, such as Darío's *Los raros* and *Prosas profanas* of 1896, and Leopoldo Lugones's *Las montañas del oro* (The Mountains of Gold) of 1897.[78]

Susana Zanetti observes that Matto nonetheless included many Modernistas in the magazine:

> la mayoría de los poetas masculinos considerados—por inclusión de sus poesías o en notas—son modernistas, aunque la elección de los textos o los rasgos poéticos comentados *silencian aquello que por excelencia define al movimiento*, como son el enriquecimiento de la percepción, la exaltación del placer sensual en los afectos, en el cuerpo o en la poesía, o los postulados de la autonomía del arte. Los poemas modernistas reproducidos son los presuntamente más decorosos, menos transgresores respecto de las concepciones morales y estéticas que los textos femeninos incluidos en la revista evidencian.

the majority of male poets considered—by the inclusion of their poems or in notes—are Modernistas, although the choice of texts or the poetic characteristics commented upon *silence that which par excellance defines the movement*, such as the enrichment of perception; the exhaltation of sensual pleasure in emotions, in the body, or in poetry; or postulates of art's autonomy. The Modernista poems reproduced are the presumably most decorous, least transgressive regarding moral and aesthetic conceptions, than evinced in the women's texts included in the magazine.[79]

Although Matto avoided the more innovative or radical themes favored by Modernismo, as Zanetti describes, it is important to note that she participated in the same debates on modernity and its liberating progress: for the Modernistas, that liberation would be aesthetic, releasing them from the habits of tradition and provincialism, while for Matto the liberation would be for women, in educational and professional terms. Significantly, these differing approaches to the promise of modernity coincided in their efforts to build a trans-Hispanic literary community through correspondence, travel, and the circulation of periodicals, as well as to foment that community's professionalization.[80]

Previous chapters of this book have examined the predominant image of women in Darío's work of this period and in Modernismo more broadly as passive, ornamental, and representative of beautiful frivolity. This image of the feminine is perhaps where Matto came into irreconcilable conflict with Modernismo, and she constantly criticized frivolity for its incompatibility with a social purpose for women.[81] According to Zanetti, Matto "destaca la función social de la mujer en el hogar, la beneficencia y la religión, al tiempo que rebate los estereotipos de pasividad, de inferioridad o de una personalidad absorbida sólo por frivolidades" (highlights the social function of woman in the home, charity, and religion, as she refutes the stereotypes of passivity, inferiority, or of a personality absorbed solely by frivolities).[82] Matto instead frames frivolous women as anachronistic, for example by commenting, in a note on the Mexican writer Laura Méndez de Cuenca, that "la mujer frívola está llamada á escuchar sólo el eco de su propia voz en el derruído caserón de las añejas prácticas" (the frivolous woman is called to hear only the echo of her own voice in the fallen mansion of former practices).[83] Although Matto did not favor more radical feminist proposals like women's suffrage, her condemnation of superficiality and idleness was consistent. This critique drew on preexisting debates in both Argentina and Peru—as reflected for example by *Blanca Sol*, an 1889 novel by the Peruvian Mercedes Cabello de Carbonera—but it sharpened during her years in Buenos Aires.

Elia M. Martínez, a Normalist professor and member of the editorial staff of *Búcaro Americano*, joined the attack on frivolity with her article "Las mujeres frívolas" (Frivolous women), marking a contrast between the preferred models for women in the River Plate region and in Peru. Matto selected this piece for publication on June 1, 1896, about one year after her arrival in Argentina:

> La evolución rápida y favorable que se nota en pró del desenvolvimiento femenino... resplandece en las yankées [sic] de la América del Norte y trasciende con vuelos gigantescos en las naciones del habla latina y en las demás del Continente Sud-Americano, para destacarse en las mujeres del Perú, [pero] brillando por su ausencia las mujeres del Plata; el alma se oprime por inmensa mole, ante *la indiferencia de la nacionalidad argentina*, que debiera por su origen y tradiciones llevar en alto el buril de la gloria que cincela el talento de la mujer de alma y corazón.

> The rapid and favorable evolution we can see in favor of women's development... shines among Yankee women of North America and transcends with gigantic leaps in the nations of Romance languages and in the rest of the South American Continent, standing out with the women of Peru, [but] conspicuous in its absence with the women of the River Plate; the soul is oppressed as if by a great weight before the *indifference of the Argentine nation*, which should, due to its origin and traditions, lift high the chisel of glory that carves the talent of women of soul and heart.[84]

Martínez accuses Argentina of indifference toward women's advancement, despite the enthusiasm she sees elsewhere for this endeavor; as we have seen in Chapter 2, the problem and fascination of frivolity was circulating as a discourse mediating encounters with globally hegemonic modernity, thanks in part to the work of Enrique Gómez Carrillo and other Modernista chroniclers. Ten years later and still living in Buenos Aires, Matto continues to argue against the frivolous or ornamental woman, defining her in "La mujer moderna" (Modern Woman) as a non-productive consumer and therefore useless. A woman who works is preferable because she is less vulnerable: "La sociedad acepta con preferencia á la mujer trabajadora sobre la mujer adorno," she insists. "Como bien ha observado un notable sociólogo; una mujer que no trabaja, sobre todo si pertenece á una familia pobre, está continuamente expuesta á inminentes peligros propios del estado de miseria en que se agita, debido sencillamente á que siempre consume algo y no produce nada" (Society accepts with preference the working woman over the decorative woman. As a notable sociologist has observed, a woman who does not work, especially if she belongs to a poor family, is continually exposed to imminent dangers resulting from her impoverished state, because she always consumes something, and she produces nothing).[85] Although the shades of her argument shift over the years, her critique of women's perceived lack of involvement in work and other serious matters, was constant.

However consistent her personal campaign against frivolity was, however, Matto softened her critique enough to find promotional space in *Búcaro* for "La Ciudad de Londres" (The City of London), perhaps in exchange for financial support of the magazine. This large, modern department store in Buenos Aires, in the style of a French *grand magasin*, had an elegant location at the corner of the Avenida de Mayo and Peru. The recommendation of the business tends to appear in the "Social" page, near the end of each issue, for example in this note signed by "Josefina":

> La mujer elegante es, indudablemente, la que más aguza el ingenio humano. Cada nueva estación parece que trajese la última palabra al respecto, y sin embargo, vemos que lo pasado fue nada en relación al presente. *La Ciudad de Londres* es la gran colmena donde se elabora lo grandioso, lo deslumbrante, lo *chic*, pero, declaramos que las novedades para Semana Santa y Páscuas, que ha recibido de Europa, sobrepasan lo regio del asunto. Vayan las hermosas lectoras á la gran *Ciudad* . . . y juzgarán por sí mismas de la recomendación que les hago.
>
> The elegant woman is, undoubtedly, the one who most sharpens human ingenuity. Each new season would seem to bring the last word on this issue, and yet, we see that previous seasons were nothing in relation to the present. *The City of London* is the great beehive where the grandiose, the dazzling, the *chic* is produced, but, we declare that the latest designs for Holy Week and Easter, received from Europe, go above and beyond the magnificent. Go, beautiful readers, to the great *City* . . . and you will judge my recommendation for yourselves.[86]

This discussion of fashion fits nicely within the traditional topics of the "Social" section discussed earlier, reminding us of the multiple discourses, registers, and needs that Matto juggled as she assembled each issue.

Despite the emphasis of the "Ciudad de Londres" promotions on elegance and consumerism, Matto finds a way to relate them to her support for women's work and education, and she uses them to pivot the discussion of fashion and shopping toward women's professional opportunities. In the following issue, in a director's note titled "La mujer trabajadora" (The Working Woman)—that is, fore-fronted as the first article in the issue, rather than buried in the fragmented "Social" section, at the end—Matto praises the department store for employing more than 300 women: "¡Cuántas señoras, qué de señoritas, infinidad de niñas adolescentes salvadas del hambre y del dolor, en aquella colmena humana que les brinda la sabrosa miel del trabajo debidamente remunerado!" (How many ladies and young ladies, an infinity of teenaged girls, saved from hunger and pain, in that human beehive that affords them the tasty honey of duly remunerated work!)[87] She draws sweeping conclusions, offering the store's employment of women as proof that "el esfuerzo oficial y la voluntad individual, se estrechan para dar unidad á la acción impulsora del progreso de la mujer" (official effort and individual come together to give unity to the action propelling women's progress).[88] Indeed, Matto's own employment as a professor at the Escuela Comercial de Mujeres likely explains the relationship between her magazine and the department store, as the Ciudad de Londres became a workplace for many of her graduates. She closes the note expressing hope that "las primeras señoritas que de aquella [Escuela Comercial de Mujeres] salgan, con su carrera comercial terminada, encontrarán en la Ciudad de Londres el campo en donde utilizar sus conocimientos" (the first young ladies to leave [that school] with their commercial studies complete, will find in the City of London the field in which to utilize their knowledge).[89] In addition to the possibility that she received financial compensation from La Ciudad de Londres, Matto gains from her relationship with the business in that it serves her as a platform for advancing women's education and employment opportunities.

After the last issue of *Búcaro* was published on May 15, 1908, Matto's rejection of female frivolity continued its prominent position in her writing, shaping her reactions to Spain and France during a 1908 trip, when she studied women's education systems on behalf of the Argentine government.[90] The resulting book, published posthumously as *Viaje de recreo* (Recreational Trip, 1910), compared French and Spanish approaches to modernity, with an opposite preference as compared to Modernista Francophilia. Vanesa Miseres explains that "Francia se le presenta como una nación negativamente moderna. En su camino al progreso, esta última nación ha resignado a la familia a un rol ínfimo, aspecto que la aleja significativamente del ideal modernizador de Matto basado en la solidez del núcleo familiar" (France seems to her a negatively modern nation. In its path toward progress, that nation has relegated the family to a negligible role, an aspect that distances it significantly from Matto's modernizing ideal based on the solidity of the nuclear family).[91] Although Matto perceived the French emphasis on women's education as positive, she insisted that the purpose of that education should be to better support the traditional family unit, rather than women's autonomy.[92] In contrast with her critique of France, she identified strongly with Spanish culture and reaffirmed a "family" closeness with the former colonial power.[93]

In "Despedida" (Farewell) published in the last issue of *Búcaro Americano*, Matto explains that she is leaving for "playas europeas" (European shores) to address health concerns, but she will continue collecting material for future issues of the magazine, "cuya vida está tan íntimamente vinculada con mi vida y en cuyas páginas luce el pensamiento de los escritores de la América del Sur" (whose life is so intimately tied to my own, and in whose pages the thought of South American writers shines).[94] She takes continuing pride in her project to connect the trans-Hispanic literary community, and it seems that Matto planned to continue production of *Búcaro* after returning from her trip, but, when that time came, she only managed to complete the memoire *Viaje de recreo* before her death on October 25, 1909. This final issue also contains pieces by Leopoldo Lugones, Amado Nervo, and Rubén Darío (tagged incorrectly as Guatemalan), showing that her publication rate for important Modernistas had not slackened.[95] Darío contributed a short prose piece, "Pálida como un lirio" (Pale as a Lily), that evokes the *princesa* of "Sonatina" and continues the themes of feminine passivity and the muse as a platform for the writer's own voice.[96] Matto, in contrast, maintained her commitment over years to a platform that promoted her own work amid the magazine's dense network of others' voices, in which women were especially represented. She had no choice but to build the social role of the woman writer in the Buenos Aires of her exile, both by promoting her own work and public persona, and by promoting a broader network of women writers, within which her own public figure was legitimized and became legible.

CLAIMING SPACE FOR WOMEN WRITERS

Trans-Andean travel and an expanding socio-professional network were important tools to build career prospects for women writers, who created new opportunity by reaching beyond their national literary fields. A challenge for scholars today is that this transnational movement dispersed their work, and when their writings were not valued by the next generation, particularly by a generation of scholars seeking to define a national canon, many items were lost.[97] In addition, these women writers often had no descendants attending to their papers, exposing them to even deeper oblivion throughout the twentieth century, until varied scholars including feminists began scratching in the archives. What this chapter demonstrates is that nineteenth-century women writers were no less foundational than their male counterparts, and that they—particularly Clorinda Matto de Turner—worked tirelessly to build a space for women's writing, education, and professionalism.

If exile disconnected Matto from Peruvian institutions at the end of her life, contributing to the disappearance of her late work in both Peruvian and Argentine literary history, it is in part due to the sexism of her environment and of the mechanisms of canonization that rendered her less legible by the demands of national literary history. A transnational approach allows scholars to consider both her influence as a novelist in Peru and her reinvention in Argentina, which inspired her to pursue new directions as she recommitted herself all the more tenaciously to women's advancement. She also drew on her unparalleled transnational network to build a vision of trans-Hispanic letters that granted significant space to women's contributions, responding at every turn to the need for their professional advancement. The success of *Búcaro* as a complex and long-lasting project is evidence of Matto's hard work and steadfastness. It also points to her significant social and cultural capital, which, when we remove the national lens so common to twentieth-century literary history, comes into focus as on par with that of the period's most successful men of letters.

This chapter has examined the Buenos Aires reinvention of Clorinda Matto de Turner, particularly focusing on her engagement with spaces of networking and sociability—such as the Ateneo de Buenos Aires and the pages of her new magazine, *Búcaro Americano*—and on the role of performance to build a name for herself in her new environment. We have seen that speeches gave Matto a platform to legitimize her professional interventions into the Buenos Aires literary field, and she took those opportunities to insist on the deep and broad community of women writers that faced persistent exclusion. This is to say that in creating a space for herself, she did the same for innumerable others: she built the community and the tradition that she needed. When speaking for audiences of primarily women, her language of sentiment and shared struggles affirmed that community's mutual support and took up space for women writers; before predominantly male audiences, her skills of logic and persistence left no doubt as to the importance of women writers on a transnational scale. Her historical consciousness and cultivation of younger women writers, moreover, built an intergenerational network that endeavored to preserve a memory of writers past: the ritual of her own welcome in Gorriti's Lima *veladas* of the 1870s resonates some twenty years later in her remembrance of Gorriti after the older woman's death, just as it echoes in the reception shown to her own mortal remains in 1924 by her protegée, Aurora Cáceres, following their travel from Buenos Aires to Lima. Matto's speeches enjoyed a transmedial afterlife as printed text that expanded their audience and further legitimized her proposals for a modernity based on improving women's educational and professional opportunities, a proposal sharpened by its contrast with Modernismo's approach to modern femininity as decorative, frivolous, and passive. The Buenos Aires obsession with modernity shaped both these proposals and brought them into productive juxtaposition between 1895 and 1909.

In the next chapter, we will consider the different manifestations of writerly sociability across the River Plate in Montevideo, and the efforts of another woman writer, María Eugenia Vaz Ferreira, to reconcile her roles, which she considered incompatible, as a woman and a poet.

CHAPTER 4

RAREZA

María Eugenia Vaz Ferreira and Montevideo's "Generation of 1900"

Following Rubén Darío's consolidation of Decadentist thought in Latin America with his 1896 collection *Los raros*, the cultural category of *rareza* found fertile ground around the continent. This is nowhere truer than in Uruguay, where the "Generation of 1900" (usually called the Generation of 900 in that country) made a lasting imprint on national literary production. Ángel Rama situated many of these eccentric writers within a national tradition in his anthology of Uruguayan prose, *Cien años de raros* (One Hundred Years of Eccentrics, 1966).[1] The country has more recently been called a "tierra privilegiada de raros y precursores de venas originales" (privileged land of eccentrics and precursors of original pathways), as the *rareza* defining this particularly Uruguayan genealogy has become broadly recognized.[2] Valentina Litvan and Javier Uriarte, in their preface to *Raros uruguayos: Nuevas miradas* (Uruguayan Eccentrics: New Views), deconstruct "una cierta rareza uruguaya" (a certain Uruguayan strangeness) as a literary current, proposing that by the twenty-first century "'raro' se ha convertido en un calificativo habitual y donde lo marginal ha transitado al centro" (*raro* has become a habitual descriptor, the place where marginality has moved to the center).[3] Today, the marginal has become canonical in the Uruguayan literary tradition. Paradoxically, strangeness defines the norm.

Histories of Uruguayan *rareza* go back to a foundational moment with Montevideo's "Generation of 1900," in which the Decadentist fascinations of Spanish-American Modernismo reached a fever pitch. If one vein of Modernismo shied away from locating the body at the center of aesthetic production, rejecting the sexualization of European Decadentism (as Molloy proposes with the "body phobias" of Martí and Rodó), it is in Montevideo that we see the opposite, the fullest embrace of the excessive body.[4] Cultural innovation flourished there in the intense sociability of irreverent *cenáculos*, or coteries, within the context of liberal Batllismo, a political period defined by the two presidencies of José Batlle y Ordóñez between 1903 and 1915. Poets' clubbishness contributed to their bohemian excesses and aesthetic innovations. Women writers of the period, however, were not included in the creative synergy of the groupings, of which Consistorio del Gay Saber (Consistory of Gay Wisdom) and the Torre de los Panoramas (Tower of Panoramas) were the most influential.[5] Indeed, for Carina Blixen, between 1800 and 1920 "los roles masculinos y femeninos se hicieron cada vez más fijos y se acentuaron para la mujer los moldes de la pasividad" (masculine and feminine roles became increasingly fixed and accentuated the mold of passivity for women).[6]

This chapter will examine the social field of Montevideo's poets within the political and cultural context of Batllismo, delving especially into the work and life of María Eugenia Vaz Ferreira (1875–1924), who has been nearly forgotten today outside her country. We will see that despite Montevideo's effervescent sociability for writers and its relative openness to challenging aesthetics, even in the field of gender representation, innovative women poets struggled to find or create a space for their work. The forceful brilliance of Delmira Agustini found unusual recognition during her lifetime, in part due to her family's intense support of her writing; at the same time, however, her poet contemporaries infantilized and sexualized her, and their interest in her work often seemed to result from her own self-representation within those hierarchical modes of sociability. Vaz Ferreira's rejection of these modes of interaction helps us to understand her sense of never having a social space that allowed her to be both a woman and a poet. Throughout her career she pondered the mutual exclusivity of these social roles.

Raised in the leafy Montevideo neighborhood of El Prado, where her influential family hosted regular salons, María Eugenia Vaz Ferreira was educated at home, according to the standards for girls' education at the time.[7] Although her older brother Carlos, who would become an important pedagogue and philosopher, attended university, this was unheard of for women at the time. Indeed, it was rare even for men, as Emir Rodríguez Monegal reminds us that "los escritores del 900 fueron en realidad autodidactos" (the writers of the Generation of 1900 were actually autodidacts).[8] She was tutored by accomplished relatives, developing her skill in painting with her cousin Julio Freire, and in music, particularly piano of the Romantic composers, with her uncle, the well-known musician León Ribeiro. Vaz Ferreira excelled as a musician and even became a composer for piano, an absolute rarity for women of her time and place.[9] As a teenager she began declaiming her verse in social gatherings and publishing in the local press, including such poems as "Monólogo" (Monologue) in *La Razón* in August of 1894, and "La eterna canción" (The Eternal Song), "La sirena" (The Mermaid), and "A una golondrina" (To A Swallow) in *El Día* between February and May of 1895. She preferred presenting her poetry in person over publication, but also became uncomfortable as the center of attention: when her friend Alberto Nin Frías was preparing an essay on her work, she shared her poems but requested that he not circulate them or feel pressured to comment, asking, "No sería mejor el silencio absoluto?" (Would not absolute silence be best?).[10] By 1905 her recognition had grown enough that Raúl Montero Bustamante included eleven of her poems in his anthology *El parnaso oriental: Antología de poetas uruguayos* (The Eastern Parnassus: Anthology of Uruguay Poets), in which he describes her as "sin duda la primer [sic] poetisa de América y la más grande que ha tenido el país" (without a doubt, the first poetess of the Americas and the greatest that the country has had).[11] This recognition marks perhaps the highest point of her prestige, before Delmira Agustini began to overshadow her with her first book publication in 1907. Vaz Ferreira's original, one-act plays in verse— *La piedra filosofal* (The Philosophical Stone, 1908), *Los Peregrinos* (The Pilgrims, 1909), and *Resurrexit: Idilio Medioeval* (Resurrexit: Medieval Idyll, 1913)—premiered in the Teatro Solís of Montevideo and marked important social events in the local calendar.[12] Hugo Achugar rightly emphasizes that she should be remembered not only as a poet, but as a multifaceted artist, due to the varied modes of her creative production.[13]

The images that most shape collective memory of Vaz Ferreira today are the spinster, the possibly mad eccentric, and the university professor wrapped in a purple cloak who declaimed her poetry before an audience of rapt students. Language of peculiarity threads through critical response to her work. Although the loneliness and melancholy of her later life are clear, in her youth the poet was sociable, iconoclastic, and fascinating to her friends, the *mimada* (pet) of the effervescent arts scene around turn of the century Montevideo. In Crispo Acosta's recollection, "ella fue siempre la mujer que no se aviene con la rigidez inútil. . . . Pareció rara" (she was always the woman who would not go along with useless rigidity. . . . She seemed strange).[14] Similarly, around 1903 a very young Agustini considered Vaz Ferreira's "extravagances" to be an integral part of the older woman's brilliance:

> Todo en ella es encantador, desde su vigoroso talento poético hasta sus deliciosas extravagancias de niña ligeramente voluntariosa; y ¡pensar que tal vez hay personas lo bastante malignas para reprobárselas! ¡Ignorantes! Quitad el fulgor a un astro y dejará de serlo; quitad el perfume a una rosa, y será algo así como un cadáver embalsamado . . .; quitad a *María Eugenia* sus caprichos, y dejará de ser María Eugenia.

> Everything about her is charming, from her vigorous poetic talent, to her delicious extravagances of a slightly headstrong girl; and to think that there might be people evil enough to condemn her for them! Ignorants! Take the brilliance from a star, and it will stop being a star; take the perfume from a rose, and it will be something like an embalmed cadaver . . .; take from *María Eugenia* her caprices, and she will stop being María Eugenia.[15]

Vaz Ferreira also consistently expressed this perception of her own eccentricity in her poetry, exploring an incompatibility between women's social roles of the period and her own vocation as an artist. Tania Pleitez Vela has written that the poet perceived "una fatal incongruencia entre su *yo* y el mundo exterior que la intentaba determinar" (a fatal incongruence between her sense of self and the outside world that tried to determine her); in her youth, Vaz Ferreira's "frivolidad exterior" (external frivolity) was a "coraza" (shield) that later fell away.[16]

Indeed, Vaz Ferreira's poetry reveals that through the years this shield came to be replaced by an isolated melancholy that dominates collective memory of the poet. It is noteworthy, however, that both youthful frivolity and the illness of her mature years allowed her to evade convention, to dodge expectations for female respectability and protect her own exceptionality as well as her social identity as a poet and artist. In this regard Blixen reminds us of a similarity between Vaz Ferreira and Agustini, noting that "es posible pensar que la idea de 'excepcionalidad' en la que tanto abundan las crónicas sobre la poesía y la persona de Delmira y María Eugenia fuera un refugio que les proporcionaba una manera de no someterse ni romper el sistema de reglas opresivo" (it is possible to consider the idea of 'exceptionality,' so abundant in the chronicles about the poetry and the person of Delmira and María Eugenia, as a refuge that provided them with a way neither to submit, nor to break the oppressive system of rules).[17] In these women poets' historical context, difference was deviance, and *una poetisa* (a poetess) was strange and inherently dangerous due to her contrast with social norms.[18] Her exceptionality as an artist and a poet excluded her from full participation in bourgeois society, even as it provided new, limited freedoms and space for limited self-determination.

ILLNESS AND IDIOSYNCRASY

In Uruguay around the turn of the twentieth century, the woman poet was made legible by her public persona of illness, and in the case of Vaz Ferreira, artistic talent and poor health form the foundation of her *rareza*.[19] Her illnesses included sciatica and renal dysfunction, which may have contributed to mental health difficulties. She also suffered from hyperacusis—a painful oversensitivity to sound, which would seem particularly unbearable, given her vocation as an artist of poetry and of voice—and from claustrophobia, perhaps related to conflicts with her difficult mother.[20] Blixen reads the numerous references to nervous illnesses in the papers of Vaz Ferreira and Agustini as "una manera de ser mujer en un medio agobiante" (a way to be a woman in a stifling environment), as well as indication that writing was not sufficient to "romper moldes y crear otros" (break molds and create new ones).[21] Indeed, Vaz Ferreira's body of work points to a profound dissatisfaction with the social roles available to her, even as her relative privilege afforded her greater access to cultural circles and education than most women of her time and place enjoyed. Her epistolary and poetry repeatedly reference her perception that the social roles of poet and woman were mutually exclusive. Where the social role of the woman writer was lacking, other recognizable "types" could step in. In this regard Vaz Ferreira was a pioneer in the tradition of the *rara avis* female poet, significantly shaping the conditions under which her later counterparts would find greater renown, including Agustini and Juana de Ibarbourou in Uruguay, as well as Alfonsina Storni in Argentina and the Nobel laureate Gabriela Mistral of Chile.[22]

Vaz Ferreira's unconventionality gave rise to many anecdotes that are difficult to separate from myth. The young artist rejected social convention, once declaring to a friend that her highest aspiration was to become a garbage man.[23] She sat down to chat with vagabonds, even as she avoided some required gatherings of high society.[24] She attended a party while wearing one black shoe and one white because, as she explained to a friend, "no era un pajarito que debía mover sus dos pies al mismo tiempo" (she was not a little bird who had to move her two feet at the same time).[25] Crispo Acosta recalls her in terms that evoke an "Eulalia," the *marquesita* (little marchioness) from Darío's poem "Era un aire suave" (There Was a Soft Air): "Ella era inquieta y caprichosa; revolvía los salones del gran mundo con la tempestad de sus risas; contestaba a carcajadas las tonterías del buen tono" (she was restless and capricious; she stirred up the salons of the social world with the tempest of her laughter; she answered the silliness of social mores with cackles).[26] Vaz Ferreira was also adventuresome, modern: in February of 1914, she soared over the Montevideo Hippodrome as the first Uruguayan woman to fly in an airplane, her bravery all the clearer when another flight at the same event ended in a crash landing.[27] The poet never married, although eventually she established a residence independent of her family home.[28] In 1912 Vaz Ferreira became a secretary at the new Women's University, where she also accepted a second position as professor of letters in 1915, thus participating in the first generation of Uruguayan women to be active professionally in the public sphere.

From a young age, Vaz Ferreira was the primary caretaker for her controlling mother, Belén Ribeiro Freire, with whom she had a difficult relationship.[29] Vaz Ferreira's writing recounts their disagreements over her vocation as a poet. At the age of eighteen she first publicly recited her poetry, presenting "Monólogo" at the Club Católico while accompanied by her older brother. The poem relates her mother's discouragement of María Eugenia's poetic vocation:

> . . . mamá no quiere,
> pues me está reprimiendo todito el día
> que, por Dios, no haga versos, que eso es muy malo
> que me quedo soltera seguramente, si hago poesía.
> Y pese á mis protestas y a mis razones
> aunque ya no la escuche cuando diserta,
> me trae á la memoria, como recurso,
> unas tías muy viejas, cuyo recuerdo me desconcierta . . .
> ¡Tendrá razón acaso! Temo que ustedes
> para sí estén diciéndose: "¡Ay! Si no trata
> de cambiar, le auguramos triste futuro . . .
> ¡Qué mal está esa niña con esos aires de literata!"

> . . . Mama doesn't want it,
> she's restraining me all day long,
> That for God's sake I must not write verses, that it's really bad
> And that I'll surely be left an old maid if I write poetry.
> And despite my protests and my reasons,

Although I don't listen to her anymore when she lectures,
It makes me recall, like an appeal,
Some very old aunties, whose memory disconcerts me . . .
¡Maybe she's right! I fear that you
Must be saying to yourself: "Ah! If she doesn't try
To change, we predict a sad future . . .
How bad off that girl is, with those airs of a literary lady!"[30]

In this poem the external conflict with her mother created an internal struggle for the poet: her mother's nagging creates doubts about her own future, doubts that take the form of imaginary gossip permeating her social environment, such that even her audience ("ustedes") is assumed to disapprove of her. Although Vaz Ferreira's social pressure to abandon poetry—and perhaps by extension her other artistic endeavors—created anxiety and difficulties for her, it is also apparent that she felt her vocation to be powerful and undeniable, and thus all the more challenging in an unsympathetic environment. "Monólogo" goes on to lament sardonically:

Se aprecia más hoy día que á una poetisa,
una niña hacendosa, seria, que sabe
recortar bien los puños deshilachados de una camisa.

What's appreciated today more than a lady poet,
is an industrious girl, serious, who knows
how to properly trim the threadbare sleeves of a shirt.[31]

At this young age, Vaz Ferreira has a clear understanding of both her vocation as poet and the incompatibility of that vocation with the social role of a young woman.

A letter from Vaz Ferreira to her close friend Alberto Nin Frías describes her mother's apparent mental illness, which contributed to the poet's suffering. Although undated, the letter is likely from 1902 to 1904, when Nin Frías was preparing a study of her work.[32] She writes: "Mamá, a quien adoro, y que me adora (creo) y que es lo único que tengo en el mundo, es conmigo de una crueldad increíble. No se si Vd. habrá oído hablar de una grave enfermedad nerviosa que hace que se mortifique y contrarie constantemente á la persona que mas se quiere—esto le pasa á ella conmigo. Ahora tiene Vd. la clave de mi tristeza" (Mama, whom I adore, and who adores me [I think], and who is all I have in the world, is incredibly cruel to me. I don't know if you might have heard of a serious nervous illness that makes a person torment and contradict constantly whomever the person loves most—this is how she treats me. Now you have the key to my sadness.)[33]

The letter goes on to describe a quarrel about a marriage engagement, adding to the suggestion of the poem "Monólogo" that Vaz Ferreira's freedom of movement and marriage prospects were a principle focus of family disagreement. The letter, moreover, sheds light on how the poet's desire to avoid provoking her mother caused her to retreat from public interaction, which she characterizes as a sort of banishment ("destierro"):

> Anoche cuando Vd. vino, yo me asomé por uno de los cuartos interiores adonde acostumbro á desterrarme por horas y aun por días enteros; lo ví a Vd. y oí como mama me negó. Se imaginará cuanto habré sentido. . . . Hace como dos meses fue aceptado como pretendiente un amigo del fraterno, que segun se opine, era un novio brillante—mama estaba contenta—pero al cabo de este tiempo noté que no sentia por él lo que era necesario y hace 5 ó 6 dias resolví terminar el asunto—esto le tiene enojadísima.
>
> Last night when you stopped by, I peeked through one of the interior rooms, where I usually banish myself for hours or even for whole days; I saw you and I heard how mother denied me. You can imagine how I must have felt. . . . About two months ago a friend of the *fraterno* [brother] was accepted as fiancé, who is thought to be a brilliant groom—mother was happy—but after some time I noted that I did not feel for him what was necessary and about 5 or 6 days ago I decided to end the matter—this is has her exceedingly mad.[34]

In this instance, Vaz Ferreira retreats from desired social interaction to avoid and protect herself from her mother. The scene is all the more painful when we consider the poet's claustrophobia, and allows us a glimpse of how her reclusiveness, famous later in her life, developed in her youth, alongside her mother's overbearing, controlling character. Vaz Ferreira's use of the passive voice (he "was accepted as fiancé") reflects her precarious decision-making power regarding her own engagement.

Illness came to define both Vaz Ferreira's social isolation and the public image of the woman poet. Her chronic health difficulties worsened later in life, when renal insufficiency contributed to her melancholy nature.[35] Toward the end of her life Vaz Ferreira longed for a "casa del silencio" (a house of silence), an underground home with two doors to facilitate escape in case of unexpected visits.[36] For Marita Fornaro Bordolli, "la María Eugenia transgresora fue transformándose, durante su vida, en 'la rara', si no en 'la loca'" (María Eugenia as transgressor eventually transformed herself into 'the eccentric,' if not into 'the crazy lady').[37] Particularly in her last few years, when illness led her to retire from teaching and to suffer increasing mental health challenges, she was known to wander nocturnal Montevideo, riding in streetcars or slowly walking the Prado park, where she stopped to touch her forehead to the earth three times at the stroke of midnight.[38] Eccentricities from this period dominate the anecdotes that friends recalled after the poet's death, and for some they become the main thread of her biography. Following her retirement in 1922, Vaz Ferreira died in 1924, probably after undergoing surgery related to renal failure.[39]

Although Vaz Ferreira chose not to publish her poetry in book form during her lifetime, in 1903 she organized a volume titled *Fuego y mármol*, and late in life she prepared her work for a posthumous collection, *La isla de los cánticos* (The Island of Chants), which her brother Carlos completed after her death. *La otra isla de los cánticos* (The Other Island of Chants) would follow in 1959, after Carlos's death, and María Eugenia's *Poesías completas* (Complete Poems) were finally published in 1986, edited by Hugo J. Verani, who considers her "la primera mujer uruguaya con voz lírica inconfundible" (the first Uruguayan woman with an unmistakable lyrical voice).[40] Scholars have proposed that Vaz Ferreira's poetry evolved from the Romantic meditations of her youth, to Modernista preciosity, to the more distilled, polished melancholy of her later years.[41] Although many poems treat outdoor spaces, particularly in her early work, her poetry can also be suffocating, alternately of the poetic voice who suffers the restrictions of her bourgeois milieu, or of a love interest only called "tú" (you), whom the poetic voice desires to control and enclose. The spaces of her poetry are primarily interior and hermetic; gazes turn inward toward the poet's own character, or to a tight social dynamic between two people. Particularly in her later years—which many critics have considered her most mature and developed poetic period, defined by a post-Modernista purification or boiling down to barer elements—Vaz Ferreira's poetry communicates frustration with blocked desires and stifled potential.

THE IMPOSSIBLE WOMAN POET

One of Vaz Ferreira's best-known poems, "La berceuse," foregrounds the poet's body as a space of artistic production in conflict with her social environment.[42] Here she employs a conversational tone, similar to that of the earlier-discussed "Monólogo":

> Era de noche, yo tocaba
> una berceuse de Chopin, y aún sin mirarlo bien sentía
> fijos en mí los ojos de él.
>
> It was night, I was playing
> a berceuse by Chopin, and without looking at him I still felt
> fixed upon me his eyes.[43]

The gaze-play of observer and observed highlights the female form as a locus of musical production, and the song becomes a proxy for what the two leave unsaid, until the pianist momentarily forgets their connection and concentrates all her attention on the art. The pianist-poet has felt rather than seen the man's gaze, and when she finishes the piece she is met with a disappointing surprise:

> Cuando después que hube concluido
> volví los ojos hacia él
> hallé los suyos ya cerrados.
> Nada me dijo, yo callé.
>
> When I had finished,
> I turned my eyes to him
> and I found that his were closed already.
> He said nothing, and I kept quiet.[44]

In this moment of silence, the piano stilled and the poet hushed, her bewilderment grows. If we read the listening man as a potential beau, the erotic anticipation prolonged by and reflected in the music leads to an image of the gentleman reclining next to the pianist, as if on a shared bed. Ironically, however, the would-be lover has fallen asleep. A *berceuse* is, after all, a lullaby:

> No sé qué extraño sentimiento
> hizo a mis labios sonreír
> al verlo tan serenamente
> adormecido junto a mí . . .
>
> I don't know what strange feeling
> made my lips smile
> upon seeing him so serenely
> dozing next to me . . .[45]

The "strange sentiment" and Vaz Ferreira's smile at the center of the poem point to her ambivalence about a defining paradox of her life. The poem depicts a dawning awareness of both her own effectiveness as an artist and her incompatibility with social norms: the man's slumber shows that her art has been too successful, as a lullaby that puts the listener to sleep. At the same time, the passion of her social relationships—what we could call her social performance—has been gravely misread.

The poem's final stanza jumps ahead in time, to an older poetic voice who has given up trying to understand her listener's slumber:

> ¿Fue real su sueño? ¿Fue un elogio?
> Aún hoy lo ignoro.
> Sólo sé que yo me dije sin despecho:
> "Fui más artista que mujer."
>
> Was his sleep real? Was it a compliment?
> Still today I don't know.
> I only know that I said to myself without spite:
> "I was more an artist than a woman."[46]

Here Vaz Ferreira reframes the poem as focusing on her own, changing feelings about the experience, rather than on the social interaction (or lack thereof) between two potential beaux. She articulates explicitly the theme of mutual exclusion between the social roles of artist and woman, and she clearly marks the space of the former as her more comfortable position. The phrase "sin despecho" is rich with meaning; *despecho* can mean anger or offense, suggesting the poet's *lack* of anger—i.e., her acceptance and forgiveness—in relation to both her own self as an artist and her lack of place in the world. At the same time, however, "sin despecho" carries the resonance of *pecho* (the breast) and *despechar* (to wean), returning us to the artist's female body and the social expectations it carried. With "sin despecho" the poem recalls the body as space of the poetry's origin, to the *pecho* (breast) as home to the rhythm of the beating heart and to the breath that supports voice, even as it projects in this case the curve of a feminine form. The poetic voice rejects a fragmentation of focus that would have her look away from her music, as she prioritizes her art over her social connections. In "La berceuse" Vaz Ferreira lays bare her own experience of continuity between the female body and artistic production, as she condemns broader society's perception of these social roles' mutually exclusion.

The concept of *destierro* (banishment or exile) as metaphor for Vaz Ferreira's social isolation appears at various moments in her writing. She describes an episode of debilitating sciatica as an inconvenience "que me tiene desterrada de casi todo" (that has me exiled from almost everything).[47] In one of her letters to Nin Frías, she laments that "todos somos desterrados de algo. Todos hemos escuchado el aullar en un rincón de nuestras vidas" (we are all exiled from something. We've all heard the howling in a corner of our lives).[48] In this light, exile from social interaction resulted from both her illness and her *rareza* as a woman artist. Indeed, Vaz Ferreira considers health and strength to be preconditions of sexual expression and social integration, while illness is a defining factor of her own experience and of the artist more generally, reflecting an image of the artist made popular by Decadentism in the period.

Another poem among her best known, "Los desterrados" (The Banished), joins the theme of unrealized erotic attraction, discussed above in "La Berceuse," to a reflection on metaphorical banishment. Like much of her work, this poem is difficult to date. It was included in *La isla de los cánticos* but is not known to have appeared in periodicals, perhaps due to its erotic theme.[49] The poem describes a sad and cold afternoon's walk, interrupted when the poet sees a metalworker and becomes a voyeur/voyeuse:

> yo lo vi gallardamente
> curvado sobre las fraguas.
> El cabello sudoroso
> en ondas le negreaba
> chorreando salud y fuerza
> sobre la desnuda espalda.
> Le relucían los ojos
> y la boca le brillaba
> henchida de sangre roja
> bajo la ceniza parda.
> Y era el acre olor del hierro,
> luz de chispas incendiarias,
> rudo golpe del martillo,
> vaho ardiente de las ascuas,
> que las mal justas rendijas
> hasta mí fluir dejaban
> con ecos de cosa fuerte
> y efluvios de cosa sana.
>
> I saw him gracefully
> curved over the forge.

> The sweaty hair
> darkening in waves
> gushing health and strength
> over the naked back.
> His eyes gleamed
> And his mouth shone,
> swollen with red blood
> under the brown ash.
> And the iron's acrid smell,
> light of incendiary sparks,
> rough strike of the hammer,
> burning exhalation of the coals,
> which the poorly joined bars
> let flow to me
> with echoes of something strong
> and floods of something healthy.[50]

The poet as a Peeping Tom (or Thomasina) is transfixed by the metalworker's display of physical strength and exertion. The hot interior space illuminated by flame contrasts sharply with the gloomy weather outdoors. The vivid sensual descriptions have an unmistakable erotic charge.

The poet laments to God her own sensate condition, wishing she did not suffer this unsettling spectacle in her loneliness—the metaphor of a solitary journey here has Biblical overtones—and she turns away from the metalworker to continue her tedious march.[51] At the same time, the fire she leaves behind reaches out as if attempting to embrace her:

> seguí la tediosa marcha,
> arropada entre las brumas
> pluviosas, y me obsediaban
> como brazos extendidos
> los penachos de las llamas
> y unos ojos relucientes
> adonde se reflejaba
> el dorado y luminoso
> serpenteo de las fraguas.
>
> I continued the tedious march,
> bundled up in the drizzly
> fog, obssessed by

> the feathers of the flames
> like reaching arms
> and some gleaming eyes
> that reflected
> the golden and luminous
> weaving of the forges.⁵²

The poetic voice returns to her lonely, gloomy normalcy, but carries with her the searing image of the metalworker's snakelike strength and sinuosity, and his comfortable control of the fiery space. Readers are denied any response from the metalworker: his eyes shine, reflecting the golden, dancing light of the forge, but we do not know if he sees her. The visually stunning combination of strength and sinuosity (*serpenteo*) is for the poet a glimpse of a world denied. Indeed, she can barely make out the sight through clouded window glass and cracked shutters, and she returns to the cold of her predestined journey of solitude.

Achugar interprets the verse "gushing health and strength" as a moment of seduction, proposing that this outpouring of health and strength separates the metalworker from the observer/poet, who is herself banished: "Es el derroche de salud y de fuerza lo que establece la frontera que separa lo 'visto' del 'yo lírico' identificado como parte de 'los desterrados'" (the profusion of health and strength is what establishes the border separating what is "seen" from the "lyrical voice" identified as part of "the banished").⁵³ Rather than separate the two figures with her banishment, however, "nosotros" (we) in my reading is reference to a group identity formed by the observer and the observed; the poetic voice so desperately longs for attachment that she fantasizes their "nosotros" into existence. In this interpretation the poet's title, "Los desterrados," conjures a shared banishment from what should be togetherness, and what for the poet was an exile from a social world that would allow a female poet to fully realize her sexual identity. She imagines that they are both exiled by circumstance from a desired connection: across class divides and without ever having met, what they share is this alienation from each other, as well as the isolated fervor of their life's work. On some level, then, the metalworker is an image of herself as a poet, alone with her talent and pouring her brilliance and passions into her craft.

Several of Vaz Ferreira's best-known poems revolve around a battle of domination between would-be lovers. "Holocausto" (Holocaust) fantasizes about the controlling characteristics and power of the poet's idealized love interest, whom she builds up as a sort of Neitzschian superman, a "vencedor de toda cosa" (conqueror of everything) on a cosmic scale.⁵⁴

The first half of the poem strings together a series of conditions describing how she will complement him and even sacrifice herself for him, should he prove himself worthy. Verses seven and eight refigure both the "tú" and the first-person voice as poets—"y si sabes el ritmo de un canto sobrehumano / silenciarán mis harpas una eterna melodía" (and if you know the rhythm of a superhuman song / my harps will silence an eternal melody)—thus shifting the erotic theme to one of a challenge between two writers.[55] The end of the poem brings a twist, however, when the game of conditions for him, and promises from her, shifts to an insistence on the poet's own creative power. The images associated with her are in some cases arrestingly original, in contrast with the more clichéd metaphors of the powerful "tú":

> Me volveré paloma si tu soberbia siente
> La garra vencedora del águila potente:
> Si sabes ser fecundo seré tu floración,
> Y brotaré una selva de cósmicas entrañas,
> Cuyas salvajes frondas románticas y hurañas
> Conquistará tu imperio si sabes ser león.
>
> I will become a dove if your pride feels
> The conquering claw of the powerful eagle:
> If you know to be fecund I will be your flowering,
> And I will sprout a jungle of cosmic entrails,
> Whose savage fronds, romantic and shy,
> Your empire will conquer if you know to be a lion.

"Holocausto" thus presents a poetic voice confident in her own creative powers, searching for a powerful and idealized poet-lover, but not confident about the chance of ever finding that person. Her own poetic prowess, moreover, might present a fatal flaw to their potential partnership. The poem's title suggests a sort of funeral pyre for her own hopes for a lover, as if she knows that the superman capable of balancing her own relentless and voracious creativity does not exist. This poem is an alexandrine sonnet, the metric most associated with Modernista verse, and with this form Vaz Ferreira positions herself in relation to Modernista tradition. An allegorical reading would suggest that the poet considered herself to be more powerfully creative than those around her, finding clear resonance with many poems by Agustini.[56]

Around 1902 through 1904, Vaz Ferreira mentioned a similarity between her poetry and Darío's for their combination of melancholy, neurosis, and coquettishness, showing her awareness of Modernista activity across the River Plate.[57] "Holocausto" is not the only Vaz Ferreira poem that can be read as a commentary on Modernismo, and she often employs a frustrated tone when referencing favored tropes of that movement. "Los torrentes" (The Torrents), for example, communicates annoyance with the stereotyping, fragmentation, and objectification of female bodies so common in the work of her period. First published in her posthumous *Poesías completas*, the poem opens with a passionate condemnation of this clichéd description of women, including shining golden hair and the "fruit of red mouths," recalling the *boca de fresa* (strawberry mouth) of Darío's princess in "Sonatina," another reference to the image as cliché. Here, anaphora emphasizes the dominant emotion of "odio" (hate):

> ...Odio la fruta de las bocas rojas
> que incitan a probar su miel hiblea,
> y la gracia armoniosa de las curvas
> raudas como las ánforas de Grecia...
> Odio la magna luz de las pupilas
> donde llamean fúlgidas hogueras,
> el mármol inviolado de las carnes
> y el ritmo turbador de las cadencias...
> Odio el alba solar de las sonrisas,
> odio la tibia suavidad morena:
> ¡Malditos sean los volubles ojos
> por quien en tantos odios me encendiera!

> ...I hate the fruit of the red mouths
> that incite tasting of their golden honey
> and the harmonious grace of the swift
> curves like the amphoras of Greece...
> I hate the supreme light of the pupils
> where glowing bonfires blaze,
> the inviolate marble of the flesh
> and the disturbing beat of the rhythm...
> I hate the sun's dawn of smiles,
> I hate the warm, dark-haired softness:
> Damn the fickle eyes
> for whom in such hatred I would burn![58]

Obvious Modernista tropes here include references to ancient Greece (*amphoras*), the Parnassian image linking women's beauty to polished sculpture (*the inviolate marble of the flesh*), an interest in color and visual contrasts (as with gold, brilliance, shine, light, burning, etc.), and the obsession with rhythm (*the disturbing beat of the rhythm*), particularly as all these tropes are marshalled to the task of portraying women in poetry. The repetition of "odio" leaves no doubt regarding the poet's impatience with fragmented women and other clichés of feminine beauty.

The closing verses of "Los torrentes" present a new ambiguity about Vaz Ferreira's position: for whom exactly, or in response to whom, does she burn with hatred? The object of her curse (*Damn the fickle eyes*) can be read as the eyes of another fragmented body like those she has described in the poem, suggesting that she is frustrated with the female beauty surrounding her; it can also be read as the objectifying gaze focused on stereotyped female bodies. Although dating this poem is difficult, the theme of the gaze on female bodies echoes our earlier discussion of "La berceuse" and again points to Vaz Ferreira's concern with the treatment of women artists and of female bodies in poetry. A second ambiguity, that of the poem's title "Los torrentes," can be read as reference to the saturation of the poet's cultural milieu with images of the sort she critiques, that is, images of clichéd female bodies objectified and fragmented in art; perhaps she felt the onslaught of images to be analogous to a river current that left her no footing. In an alternative interpretation, the title could refer to a flood of anger and hatred she experienced when observing these images.

Another of Vaz Ferreira's reflections on verse can be found in the brief poem "La rima vacua" (The Hollow Rhyme) which meditates on song in a nocturnal landscape.[59] The poet finds companionship in her natural environment not from the poetic cliché of the stars, who turn their backs to her, but from an ugly screamer of the pond's blurry nighttime depths. In this way, sound predominates over vision, and darkness over light:

> Grito de sapo
> llega hasta mí de las nocturnas charcas . . .
> la tierra está borrosa y las estrellas
> me han vuelto las espaldas.
>
> Grito de sapo, mueca
> de la armonía, sin tono, sin eco,
> llega hasta mí de las nocturnas charcas . . .
> La vaciedad de mi profundo hastío
> rima con él el dúo de la nada.

> The toad's cry
> reaches me from the nocturnal ponds...
> the earth is blurred and the stars
> have turned their backs on me.
>
> The toad's cry, grimace
> of harmony, with no tone, no echo,
> reaches me from the nocturnal ponds...
> The emptiness of my profound tedium
> rhymes with him, a duet of nothing.[60]

The toad's "grimace of harmony" is a grotesque mockery of traditional beauty. The gesture parallels the deadened, animal cry across the dark pond, which lacks both tone and resonance. The horrible song nonetheless speaks to the poet, who finds herself "rhyming" with the toad in a meaningless duet that is all animal sound, no human language. The poem's last word of "nada" underscores the preceding images of emptiness ("the emptiness of my profound tedium" and the title, Hollow Rhyme). Her weariness is frustrating but somehow comfortable, given the companionship of the toad and its consonance with the environment. Far from the perfectionistic harmonies of Darío's early work, as with *Azul . . .* and *Prosas profanas*, the power of this poetry is instead dissonant, interiorizing rather than performative, perhaps suggesting an approach closer to that of Lugones and Herrera y Reissig.[61] "La rima vacua" indicates a complex, mature poet concentrating her skills into a condensed individuality, a demonstration of poetic strength.

VAZ FERREIRA'S ARCHIVE

Today, new access to archival materials allows examination of complex friendships and unknown flirtations, bringing nuance and new questions to Vaz Ferreira's image as a solitary spinster. In the years following her death, friends and scholars speculated about her romantic entanglements and aspirations, with the names of Álvaro Armando Vasseur and Arturo Santa Ana appearing most often, but these theories are not supported by her archive.[62] Maintained in the Quinta Vaz Ferreira, the former family home of Carlos Vaz Ferreira, this archive has recently made materials available, including remnants of epistolary networks, drafts and notebooks, music compositions, paintings, and programs from the varied modalities of turn-of-the-century intellectual sociability, such as *tertulias* (gatherings), concerts, and theatrical productions.[63] María Eugenia's correspondence shows that she was in contact with Delmira Agustini, José Enrique Rodó, Pedro Miguel Obligado of Argentina, and the Brazilian poet Luís Guimarães (in 1902, regarding her translation of his work from the Portuguese).[64] Her received correspondence includes suggestive visiting cards, anguished letters related to a personal crisis, and metaphysical ruminations squirreled away alongside playful postcards. Traces of her flirtations with several men suggest that her social life was more active than her biographers have realized; their relationships appear to have been kept largely secret. The María Eugenia that emerges in this archive contradicts her solitary and unfriendly image maintained by Uruguayan collective memory.

Codes and secret languages run throughout the archive of María Eugenia Vaz Ferreira. In her family home, Carlos was known as Quele and María Eugenia was Pel; she also called him "Fraterno," while she was "Soror," or even "Sororísima nostra."[65] In this neo-Latinate game, their mother was "Mater" and their friend Vasseur joined in by referring to himself as "Super." Vaz Ferreira's received correspondence includes a letter from Vasseur that appears to be from around the same time as her letter to Nin Frías. Dated October 26, but lacking notation of a year, the letter relays that Vasseur has just had dinner with Carlos and "*A.C.M.*," a suitor of María Eugenia. It appears she had recently rejected his marriage proposal, possibly the same one discussed in relation to the poem "Monólogo." Vasseur writes that the would-be fiancé "cree que la Soror no se desposará jamas; y parece que esa idea lo consuela algo" (believes that Soror will never marry; and it appears that the idea consoles him somewhat).[66] Vasseur advocates on the suitor's behalf, arguing that "es el Unico con quien la Soror podria unirse—como desea la Mater—sin perder su independencia moral, ni su originalidad intelectiva. . . . Seria la única Eleccion posible digna de la Soror, del Quele, de la Mater, de la admiracion infraternal del Super" (he's the only one with whom the Soror could be united—as Mater wishes—without losing her moral independence or her intellectual originality. . . . It would be the only possible Choice worthy of Soror, of Quele, of Mater, of the unfraternal admiration of Super).[67] Vasseur goes on to reference María Eugenia's history of rejecting marriage proposals, encouraging her to change her habits: "Debe cambiar el punto de vista de los añejos *para ques*; y decirse: *¿para que no querer? ¿por que* renunciar?" (You must change the viewpoint of the old *what fors*; and say to yourself: *why* not *love?*)[68] Vasseur closes with a reference to her mother's overbearing presence: "En fin, sinó fuera porque temo que á la Mater *le disguste* mi presencia, iria a casa de la Soror—ha abogar por su felicidad!" (Anyway, if I didn't fear that my presence *would displease* Mater, I would go to Soror's house—to advocate for her happiness!)[69]

The initials A. C. M. clearly do not refer to Arturo Santa Ana or to Vasseur himself, whom biographers have mentioned as Vaz Ferreira's possible suitors. We can guess that the beau was probably Ángel Carlos Maggiolo, born in Montevideo in 1877 and a medical school graduate in 1902, who eventually became a chemistry professor. In 1892 Maggiolo collaborated with Carlos Vaz Ferreira in a high school periodical, placing him in contact with the family from a young age.[70] In the only known letter from Maggiolo to María Eugenia, dated May 29 without a year, he laments her "cruel" response to his expression of love: "Siento allí los *ecos* dolorosos de una lastimosa disonancia. Porque soy tosco é imperfecto en la exteriorización de mis sentimientos he provocado sus crueles é injustos enojos" (I sense there the painful *echoes* of an unfortunate dissonance. Because I am rough and imperfect in expressing my sentiments, I have provoked your cruel and unjust anger).[71] Maggiolo seems bewildered when he goes on to ask, "Porqué, entonces se complace en provocar tempestades peligrosas y arrancar chispas que hieren de donde no debe emanar sinó luz y armonía?" (Why, therefore, do you enjoy provoking dangerous tempests and producing sparks that injure, from where only light and harmony should emanate?).[72] Although the specific references of his poetic language are not always clear, his anguished tone suggests that the letter dates from around the same time as María Eugenia's letter to Nin Frías and Vasseur's letter to María Eugenia. At their likely time of writing, 1902 through 1904, Vaz Ferreira would have been in her late twenties.

Perhaps the most suggestive paper trail in María Eugenia Vaz Ferreira's archive is made up of notes and cards signed by "El" (He), often written with now-purple pencil on the visiting cards and personal stationary of Dr. Mario Simeto. The Foundation archive proposes that Simeto and Vaz Ferreira might have met through his sister, Cloris Simeto, who worked as a mathematics professor with Vaz Ferreira at the Universidad de Mujeres (Women's University).[73] Always brief and coded, some notes show small mutilations over part of the cards' printed name, usually scribbles or corner tears that undermine the marks of social formality, such as the title or surname. Some marks also anonymize the correspondence, suggesting that the correspondents' surroundings may have harbored prying eyes. Simeto appears to have gone unnoticed by Vaz Ferreira scholars, despite his many missives remaining in the poet's archive. In mid-1912, the poet began work at the Universidad de Mujeres and turned thirty-seven years old, and by mid-1918, Simeto was married to another woman and welcoming his first child.[74] Although we do not know when Vaz Ferreira established an independent home, we can guess that Simeto's courtship developed while she continued living with her mother, or perhaps soon after moving out in her late thirties or early forties.

Simeto seems to have been disconnected from the Montevideo literary scene, but his brief notes are cryptic and occasionally poetic, and indicate a complex relation of secrecy with the poet. Simeto called Vaz Ferreira "Margenia" or "La" (She), and called himself simply "Él," a game in which we can guess she participated. Some small calling cards, of the sort that could have arrived with a bouquet of flowers, are so brief as to say nothing but "Sí" (Yes).[75] Several notes suggest that the poet also wrote letters to Simeto, for example when Simeto appears to respond to a question that Vaz Ferreira must have asked. Others profess devotion: "Mi Margenia Mia, Pero júrote que soy bueno y que soy Tu-yo" (My Margenia of Mine, but I swear to you that I am good and I am all-yours."[76] One of the longer examples reads: "Bueno Margenia: Vengo á traerte como ofrenda de Paz, las ramas de olivo de todos los Olivares... Él" (Well Margenia: I come to bring you as a Peace offering, the olive branches of all the Olive Groves).[77] In another note: "La: nos encontramos. El" (She: We will meet. He).[78] And another: "La: Para que / Contigo / silenciosamente / en el misterio / de los naranjos!—El" (She: So that / With you / silently / in the mystery / of the orange trees!—He).[79] And finally: "Mi Margenia / Será a la hora de las estrellas. / El" (My Margenia / It will be at the hour of the stars. / He).[80] These archival traces depict an apparently clandestine courtship, with nighttime encounters in a starry landscape of orange blossoms and olive groves. The promise of "silently" would seem a tender accommodation for Vaz Ferreira's hyperacusis, as the rendezvous locations outdoors appealed to her claustrophobic nature. The conservation of the notes among her papers suggests that she appreciated Simeto's attentiveness. However, despite these indications of a rich sentimental life together, the two never married. Did she love him, and might he be reflected obliquely in the "tú" of some of her poems? The dates of their relationship are unknown, as are the causes for their separation. On these questions, like so many in Vaz Ferreira's life, the archive keeps its secrets.

BATLLISMO AND CENACULISM

We have mentioned that Vaz Ferreira lived independently of her family home thanks to employment at the Universidad de Mujeres, which was founded during an unprecedentedly progressive administration. The start of Batlle y Ordóñez's radical presidency in 1903 both resulted from a society increasingly tolerant of cultural exploration and contributed to a liberalized environment that gave writers greater leeway in Montevideo. In addition to increasing political legitimacy for radical cultural exploration and liberalism, Batlle's reforms in pursuit of a "model country" gave women new legal rights. He advanced social welfare programs aimed at eradicating poverty, enacted comprehensive education programs for both boys and girls through secondary school, and in May of 1912 founded Uruguay's Universidad de Mujeres, where Vaz Ferreira quickly found employment. He also established the first law in Latin America to legalize divorce by the sole will of the woman in September of 1913—a law inspired in part by the influential philosophies of Vaz Ferreira's older brother, Carlos—and which Agustini used when she divorced Enrique Job Reyes soon thereafter.[81] These reforms were not unlimited: historian Christine Ehrick summarizes that "the Batllista state did challenge many pillars of Spanish American orthodoxy, including those sanctioning the subordination of women, but it was never as revolutionary as its biggest champions or critics painted it to be."[82] The careers of Vaz Ferreira and Agustini nonetheless developed in a political environment that supported women's rights and professional development more than could be found in any other Latin American country at the time. Women, moreover, were not the only marginalized subjects that found themselves newly authorized to participate creatively in the arts: explicit homoeroticism made an appearance in Alberto Nin Frías's novels, and Roberto de las Carreras promulgated a "free love" philosophy that he considered a foundation of women's liberation. Fernando Aínsa organizes the literary field of Montevideo in this period into dandies and bohemians.[83]

This is not to say that all expressions of creativity were welcomed and supported in Battle y Ordóñez's Uruguay, and the most radical voices still found limits. For example, de las Carreras considered Agustini's writing to be excessive and insufficiently embodying the kind of femininity he supported. Similarly, Vaz Ferreira's older brother, the philosopher Carlos, wrote a book in favor of women's education, *Sobre feminismo* (On Feminism, 1945), based on university lectures from around 1915 to1920, in which he argued that women deserved special protections, beyond mere equality: they should be treated differently from men because they would always be fundamentally different and should not be expected to assume all the functions of men.[84] The peak years of Battle y Ordóñez reformism, roughly 1908–1914, gave way to a conservative backlash, and throughout the twentieth century, scholars of that period inadequately examined the literary-artistic production of women and other marginalized figures. As Carla Giaudrone reminds us, "la crítica tradicional sobre el *Novecientos* ha demostrado ser profundamente misógina y homofóbica" (traditional criticism of the turn of the century generation has proven to be deeply mysoginistic and homophobic).[85]

Giaudrone proposes that local political factors combined with a fascination with decadentism common to Modernism more broadly, to create the conditions for the *rareza* particular to the Uruguayan cultural scene in this period.[86] She considers the uniqueness of Uruguayan Modernismo to be its insistence on the body and a greater sexualization of the style than as seen elsewhere: "[sitúa] el cuerpo en el centro de su poética, sexualizando la escritura, mediante un proceso donde las representaciones eróticas del modernismo previo son retomadas y corregidas por medio de imágenes sexuales que con frecuencia, y con diferentes resultados, logran invertir los roles tradicionales de suejto/objeto" ([it situates] the body in the center of its poetics, sexualizing writing, by way of a process in which the erotic representations of prior Modernism are taken up again and corrected with sexual images that often, and with different results, manage to invert the traditional roles of subject/object).[87] *Rareza* in this context, then, is deviation from the socially-enforced norm; it is barely tolerated difference, often an expression of individuality marked by sex and gender expression, or "non-hegemonic forms of desire."[88] For Arturo Sergio Visca, despite the variability among the Generation of 1900 authors, the turn of the twentieth century is defined by their shared conviction that "han surgido un nuevo modo de sentir la vida y una sensibilidad nueva complejísima y refinada" (a new way to experience life has arisen, as well as a new, refined, and extremely complex sensibility).[89] *Rareza* was the language of this shared generational particularity, and heightened sensibility was their practice: "Para esos jóvenes ... ser un artista era ser un *raro*. Ser artista era sentirse exquisito y hallarse como traspasado o aguijoneado por las más extrañas sensaciones" (for those young people ... to be an artist was to be *strange*. To be an artist meant to feel oneself to be exquisite and to consider oneself to be run through with or prodded on by the strangest sensations).[90] In this way, language of *rareza* frames anecdotes and scholarship about the Generation of 1900 throughout the twentieth century, and in the case of María Eugenia Vaz Ferreira, it refers to her isolation, illnesses, peculiarity, and possible mental illness. She insisted on her sense of individuality at the expense of social acceptance, even as her isolation became unbearably painful. We resort to animal metaphors: she was a fish out of water, an *ave rara*, an odd duck. This is because, although Vaz Ferreira was part of the most innovative and significant literary generation in Uruguay up to this time, her social contact with that group was limited enough that she almost cannot be considered a participant.

A defining image of Montevideo's Generation of 1900 today is the literary cenacle, an informal club of friends who enjoyed their poetry, social activities, and high jinks, as they shared news of literary innovations abroad. One of the most influential coteries was the Consistorio del Gay Saber, broadly considered a manifestation of Montevidean Modernismo.[91] It followed the leadership of Horacio Quiroga (1878–1937), an eccentric young poet who fashioned himself as a dandy, and was very different from his later image as the Misiones recluse. Destitute after a brief trip to Paris, Quiroga settled in the capital with several friends from his hometown of Salto.[92] Consistorio members emphasized their separateness from broader society by assuming ecclesiastical titles, such as *Pontífice* (Pontiff) for Quiroga, *Arcediano* (Archdeacon) for Federico Ferrando, *Sacristano* (Sacristan) for Julio J. Jauretche, and *Campanero* (Bell-ringer) for Alberto Brignole; the crew was rounded out by the *Mónagos menores* (Alter Boys), Asdrúbal Delgado and José María Fernández Saldaña.[93] The Consistorio met first at the residence shared by Quiroga and Jaureche at Calle 25 de Mayo 118, currently 293, and moved in early 1901 to a small living space in a *conventillo*, or immigrant tenement house, at Calle Cerrito 113, shared among Quiroga, Jaureche, and Delgado.[94] The Consistorio sought innovation to such an extreme that it became, in Arturo Sergio Visca's phrasing, "un mar de extravagancias, de piruetos mentales, de actitudes clownescas más que literarias, de ebullición juevnil que producía los más delirantes vapores síquicos" (a sea of extravagances, of mental pirouetting, of attitudes more clowinsh than literary, of youthful turmoil that produced the most delirious psychic vapors).[95] In a brief 1899 text, "Aspectos del modernismo" (Aspects of Modernismo), Quiroga links his moment to a generalized "imaginación hiperestesiada" (hypersensitive imagination), insisting that "la imaginación es nuestra fuerza, y la quintaesencia, el motivo y fin de la literatura modernista" (imagination is our strength and the quientessence, motive, and purpose of Modernista literature). He viewed Modernismo as a growing "sentido refinado" (refined sense) shared among a select few at the time, but which "pronto será de la masa mediana por la precipitada extenuación de nuestro sistema nervioso" (soon will characterize the masses due to the hurried exhaustion of our nervous system).[96] In this view, the decadent tendencies and hypersensitivity of Modernismo resulted from the stresses of modernity and faced a future of continual and inevitable expansion.

Within the Consistorio, aesthetic innovation developed alongside what Aldo Mazzucchelli calls "la decadencia vivida" (lived decadence). He considers Quiroga to be "realmente decadente" (truly decadent), in the sense of poverty, drug use, and drunkenness.[97] Consistorio meetings would begin late at night, when friends trickled in from their favorite café, usually the Sarandí, and featured recitations and improvisation, debates and drunken invectives, drugs, and musical outbursts that exasperated neighbors. Friends could sleep there when drunk and even find bedmates among poor nearby "doncellas" (maidens).⁹⁸ In their shared memoir, Delgado and Brignole describe their space at the 25 de mayo address as sexually raucous:

> Los otros cuartos del vasto caserón estaban ocupados por gente de humilde clase: artesanos, empleados, proletarios. Era un pequeño mundo promiscuo, en donde las tentaciones, despertadas por la robustez de unas caderas, o por la nubilidad de unos senos, o por la guinda de una boca, en su pasaje constante y variado por patios y corredores, abundaban, no invitando precisamente a las santas abstracciones. Gemidos de batallas de amor, atravesando las puertas condenadas, venían frecuentemente a turbar el numen del "Consistorio" con ráfagas afrodisíacas. El Eros metafísico, tutelador del fuego idealista, se tornó sáfico.

> The other rooms of the vast mansion were occupied by people of humble class: artisans, employees, proletarians. It was a small, promiscuous world, in which temptations—awakened by the robustness of some hips, or by the nubility of some breasts, or by the cherry of a mouth—abounded in their constant and varied passage through patios and hallways, not inviting precisely to saintly abstractions. Moans from battles of love frequently emerged through condemned doors to disturb the inspiration of the Consistorio with aphrodisiacal gusts. The metaphysical Eros, guardian of the idealist fire, became Sapphic.⁹⁹

The young poets' creativity, sociability, and even their Modernista idealism were linked closely to their sexual access to space and to bodies. These characteristics were codified in the Consistorio's "ten commandments," which mandated, among other points, that members must: "2—Gustar del placer donde quiera que lo encontremos. 3—Satisfacer todos los deseos que pudiera ocurrírsenos. 4—No creer en el pecado. 5—Fornicar eternamente, así en el pensamiento como en la obra" (2—Enjoy pleasure wherever we might find it. 3—Satisfy all the desires that could occur to us. 4—Not believe in sin. 5—Fornicate eternally, both in thought and in deed.)¹⁰⁰ The Consistorio dissolved after Quiroga accidentally killed his best friend Ferrando on March 5, 1902, as he helped him to prepare for a duel.¹⁰¹ Of the group, only Quiroga would go on to a literary career, becoming famous for his short stories about Misiones, life in the forest, and mental illness.¹⁰²

Despite Vaz Ferreira's "fuerte presencia personal en el ambiente artístico montevideano" (strong personal presence in the artistic milieu of Montevideo), according to editorial notes on her digital archive, all members of the Consistorio were men, and the environment would have been considered wildly inappropriate for middle-class young women like Vaz Ferreira and Agustini.[103] Women's role in that space was as erotic object, and creativity was coded as a social privilege of men. One result of their exclusion is the limited access of Vaz Ferreira and Agustini to the group synergy and literary experimentation, such as the Consistorio's radical methods of collective writing based on fictional associations, rather than contiguity associations.[104] Vaz Ferreira maintained a combination of more isolated artistic extravagance alongside religious conviction and personal conservatism—for example, she took offense when a friend compared her to Sappho—and although we lack detail on her opinion of Consistorio members, her letters indicate that she considered the literary milieu in general to be artificial.[105] In a missive to Alberto Nin Frías, undated but likely from 1902 though 1904, she called it "la bulliciosa falange de los 'nuevos', en su mayoría picaflores del pensamiento, sutiles divagadores de la idea" (a boisterous phalanx of the "new ones," most of them hummingbirds of thought, subtle ramblers of ideas).[106] From this we can surmise her rejection of Montevidean literary tendencies as inconsequential and unserious, particularly among "los nuevos," or the poets associated with Modernismo.

When Julio Herrera y Reissig (1875–1910) established his own cenacle in late 1902 or early 1903, he "reinaugurated" the model of the Consistorio, which he had visited in 1901.[107] His coterie met in the Torre de los Panoramas (The Tower of Panoramas), a small watchtower on the rooftop of his family's residence at Calle Ituzaingó 235, at the corner of Reconquista.[108] Attendees entered into a rarified atmosphere as they ascended the narrow staircase, and images of famous French authors decorated the walls of the tiny room, which eventually housed a bed to accommodate Reissig's poor health. The tower provided a space for the performance and social affirmation of poet identities built on innovation and extravagance: Reissig and his close friend Roberto de las Carreras performed recent compositions for guests, and listened and offered praise and congratulations in turn as visitors read their own work. Mazzucchelli notes a high degree of group consciousness from the Torre's earliest days, observing "tanta creencia en todos de estar formando parte de *algo importante*" (so much belief from them all in forming part of *something important*).[109] Beyond Reissig's remarkable talent, it seems the most important factor in the fame of the Torre de los Panoramas was not the synergy of a creative and dynamic cohort, but rather his able branding of a socio-literary coterie, roughly styled after the Consistorio. He praised enthusiastically and avoided critique (although this praxis would change in later years), and in the Tower he managed to create a space that was simultaneously welcoming and that projected an aura of mystery and exclusivity. Montevideo was transfixed.[110]

Although this review is necessarily brief, Roberto de las Carreras (1873–1963) bears further mention before we return to Vaz Ferreira. The most audacious participant in the Generation of 1900, he advocated for free love and declared himself "Doctor of Anarchism and Voluptuousness."[111] De las Carreras linked a recognizable Modernista aestheticism—which in Uruguay included a performative sexuality, as we have seen—with a political militancy for anarchism and free love. He was an iconoclast: Marcos Wasem proposes that his exclusion from the Modernista cannon today stems at least in part from his "deliberate resistance toward integration into the literary market."[112] Blixen points out that, among his other peculiarities, Roberto de las Carreras "fue el único que creó una imagen de mujer contestataria; los otros artistas del Novecientos no imaginaron una mujer intelectual, con autonomía y capacidad de decisión. El sentimiento liberador masculino [en el resto de la generación] se pensaba o se realizaba a costa de la libertad de las mujeres" (was the only one who created the image of a contestatory woman; the other artists of the generation did not imagine an intellecutal woman with autonomy and decision-making capacity. Men's liberating sentiment [in the rest of the generation] was considered or realized at the expense of women's liberty).[113] Giaudrone nonetheless underscores the limits of de las Carreras's practical support of women, noting that he, "frente a la creación literaria de Delmira Agustini, adopta un actitud autoritaria y censora hacia una feminidad que entiende ripiosa, excesiva, descontrolada" (facing the literary creation of Delmira Agustini, adopted an authoritarian and censoring attitude toward a femininity that he considered unkempt, excessive, uncontrolled).[114] This complex cultural-political moment in Uruguay thus offered unprecedented advances for women and a certain fascination with the prospect of their creative production, even as they were firmly excluded from the spaces and mores of literary sociability.

Within this socio-literary panorama, the case of Delmira Agustini, which we considered also in the introduction, merits further examination, particularly regarding her relationship with Vaz Ferreira. Agustini's full-throated critique of Modernista misogyny has garnered significant critical attention in recent decades and is important to understanding the circumstances that shaped women writers' opportunities. Agustini was eleven years younger than Vaz Ferreira and began publishing her poetry in Montevideo periodicals around 1894. By the time of her first book publication, *El libro blanco (Frágil)* in 1907, she began to eclipse Vaz Ferreira as the best-known woman writer of Uruguay, and until her tragic death in 1914 she continued producing her brilliant and challenging verse. Her poetry is more self-consciously dense with Modernista tropes than Vaz Ferreira's, even as it challenges that literary movement with bloody, violent, and woman-centered imagery.[115]

More importantly for our purposes here, however, Agustini shared Vaz Ferreira's experience of gender-based exclusion from the spaces of sociability open to her male peers, and as a result her poetry was more individual and isolated, and not drawing on the collective experimentation of the cenacles. Indeed, her poetry was perhaps more brilliant and challenging than that of any of her male counterparts. For Blixen, "las pulsiones de eros y tánatos están entrelazadas en la poesía de Delmira de una forma más dinámica, interior y conflictiva que en las elaboradas descripciones masculinas. Su poesía—no su vida—expresa un dinamismo totalmente ajeno a las estáticas y complacientes—a pesar de no ser burguesas—imaginerías de los poetas de su época" (the impulses of Eros and Thanatos are interlaced in Delmira's poetry in a more dynamic, interior, and conflictive way than in the men's elaborate descriptions. Her poetry—not her life—expresses a dynamism totally foreign to the static and complacent—although not bourgeois—imaginaries of the [male] poets of her time).[116] Blixen emphasizes the isolation of women writers in Uruguay's turn of the century, pointing out that the men's polemics and "chisporroteo gozoso" (pleasureable sparking) are lacking in the correspondence of Vaz Ferreira and Agustini: "Tampoco revelan ningún vínculo grupal. Los hombres tenían la posibilidad social de la disidencia, las mujeres, no" (They also did not have any group links. Men had the social possibility of dissidence; women did not).[117] Blixen insists that "las mujeres no formaron nunca un grupo" (the women never formed part of a group).[118]

BANISHED

In the Uruguayan literary field shaped by cenacles and radical politics, women writers received unprecedented political support and educational and professional opportunities, even as they were strictly excluded from the sociability of the creative class's experimentation. For Pleitez Vela, the two images of the woman writer available at the time, that of the moralist and the passionate "poetisa" (poetess), were two extremes, between which Vaz Ferreira sought a third space that would permit her to be "vigorosa y apasionada pero dentro de unos términos morales que ella acoge con firme determinación" (vigorous and impassioned but within some moral terms that she embraced with firm determination).[119] Uruguay supported relatively innovative aesthetic proposals but fell short of extending the freedom of sociability as creatives to women writers. For Giaudrone, "el sujeto femenino, que había encontrado en la creación literaria su medio de expresión, continuó ocupando un lugar al margen de la institución" (the female subject, who had found her means of expression in literary creation, continued to occupy a place at the margins of the institution).[120] As isolated *raras* within a field of clubbish *raros*, women poets found little space to participate in their male peers' poetic synergy, and their vocation and self-expression marked them as pariahs with, at least according to Vaz Ferreira's poetry, no social role at all. Blixen reads this conflict as related to their illness and mental health challenges; she explains that the passivity defining women's social roles meant that "'ser uno mismo' significó alguna forma de autodestrucción: esas fueron las maneras femeninas de manifestar la excentricidad" ("being oneself" meant a sort of self-destruction: they were women's ways of manifesting eccentricity).[121] For Pleitez Vela, Vaz Ferreira became known as essentially blocked and denied her purpose; she was "un ser trágicamente marcado por un *querer* vivir frente a un *no poder* vivir" (a person tragically marked by a *desire* to live, facing an *inability* to live).[122]

Indeed, anecdotes about Vaz Ferreira's *rareza* far outnumber substantive examinations of her poetry. This chapter opened with a consideration of the tradition of *raros* in Uruguayan poetry, in which she can be considered part of the founding generation. A related tradition of the gendered *poeta rara* (strange woman poet) can also be traced within Uruguay, as well as beyond: in this regard Vaz Ferreira is a pioneer, predating her more famous sisters, including Agustini and Mistral. Her poetry was little read and eventually all but forgotten, even as her name continued to circulate in Uruguayan collective consciousness as an example of creative women's strangeness. Medical and psychological factors affected her social interactions, and her own self-representations cemented her image as a *rara avis*.

Let us consider her poem "La tempestad" (The Tempest) in closing. Apparently unpublished before Vaz Ferreira's *Poesías completas* of 1986, the sonnet traces connections between her peculiarity, creativity, and painful social exclusion:

> El diablo que me sopla harto frecuentemente
> caprichos, incoherencias, raras genialidades
> me llevó por tu lado con aire indiferente
> como entre sus vasallos cruzan las potestades.
> Regresé en el crepúsculo y te vi de repente
> entrar, grande y sonoro como las tempestades. . . .
> Más tarde la armonía de las conciliaciones
> unificó de nuevo nuestros dos corazones;
> en el quedo silencio de la desierta sala
> se fueron apagando las fórmulas postreras,

solo tu voz quedóse diciendo "Mala . . . mala,"
como queda el monótono ritmo de las goteras.

The devil that so frequently whispers to me
caprices, nonsense, strange bits of brilliance,
brought me to your side with an indifferent air,
as authorities pass among their vassals.
I returned in the twilight and I saw you suddenly
enter, great and sonorous like the tempests. . . .
Later the harmony of conciliations
brought our two hearts together again;
in the soft silence of the deserted parlor
the last formulas were turning off,
only your voice remained, saying "Bad girl. . . bad girl,"
like the lingering monotonous rhythm of drips.[123]

In "La tempestad," the unspecified "you" of Vaz Ferreira's other poems returns, a powerful figure who recalls the fantasy figure of "Holocausto." Here the distance between them is overcome when the devil of her own creativity pushes her with "caprices, nonsense, strange bits of brilliance" to seek his contact. The renewed union of two hearts nonetheless ends with recrimination, amid a monotonous solitude and rain that recalls the closing of "Los desterrados."

While for Modernista poets the sexual encounter is occasion for celebrating the poetic voice, here the poet closes by silently hearing her lover's reproach (*"Mala . . . mala"*); similarly, rhythm—that electrifying opportunity for exploration in broader Modernismo—is the domain of a dull, maddening drip. The "tú" is paradoxically more vocal and active than the poet (he is "great and sonorous like the tempests"), while she is passive and silent, only pushed to act or to speak by the "diablo" of her own creativity. "La tempestad" thus joins creative production with eroticism in the best Modernista tradition, but it suggests that celebration of the *woman* poet's voice proves all but impossible. Her gesture of disavowal recalls other women poets' conventional modesty, locating creative agency outside their own will—but here in contrast it is not a Catholic God that animates, but a Decadent, post-Nietschian *diablo*.[124] "La tempestad" thus tracks Vaz Ferreira's anguished attempt both to realize her vocation by acting on its creative-erotic mandate, and to renounce her vocation by shaping herself into the passive, silent woman that social norms demanded. Both efforts fail, and she is left alone with her writing and her solitude.

Vaz Ferreira's characterization of herself as La Rara is analogous to Agustini's performance as La Nena, the infantilized persona that so appealed to period audiences: lacking a social role for the woman poet, both represent themselves with their own marginality. The irony is that this gesture positions them as meeting, as well as any of their male peers did, the aesthetic criteria for inclusion as Modernistas—*Mi poesía es mía en mí*, wrote Darío, insisting that any modern poet must cultivate an individual style rather than imitate—even as the social criteria of the coteries excluded them. In light of this double bind, then, consider Vaz Ferreira's idea, in letter to Nin Frías, that "tan pronto me considero el primer poeta de América, como la más insoportable poetisa del Uruguay" (I would just as soon consider myself the first poet of America, as the most insufferable poetess of Uruguay).[125] One wonders whether "la poeta" might have appealed to her, but at the time available options included "el poeta" and "la poetisa." Although the social role of *el poeta* was gendered masculine, it was a role at which she could excel. The *poetisa* was always insufferable, made all the more impossible by her excellence.

CHAPTER 5

SOUVENIRS

Aurora Cáceres and the *Álbum personal* as Collection

To open an old scrapbook is to release some of the auratic spell of a collection: fragments of the past are fully available and vulnerable in the reader's hands, and also inscrutable in their specificity to another's experience. The textures and scents of brittle paper and fading ink contribute to a sense of shared space with the book's maker. A narrative takes form as we turn a page, unfold a letter, or peek behind a ribbon, following a choreography planned long ago. We observe the life of another with curiosity and sometimes frustration, as if the real story remains always just out of reach. To page through a found scrapbook is to attempt to remember what the reader has never known.

Such is the material experience of the *Álbum personal* that documents the life of the Peruvian author Zoila Aurora Cáceres (1872–1958), whose long career as a writer and feminist started on the margins of Modernismo, and who went on to campaign for women's rights across three continents.[1] The album documents her professional activity with journalistic clippings and copious correspondence spanning five languages and countless countries, with a particular emphasis on Parisian writers' circles of the early twentieth century, as well as on letters relating to her activism and research on women's movements.[2] Other items included in the album range from portrait photographs to menu cards, holiday greetings, and party invitations. Some materials track the author's travels, such as a passenger list for a transatlantic steamer that conveyed her from New York to Paris in 1906, or a ticket later that year to the World's Fair in Milan, which she visited with a commission of invited journalists, including her new husband, the Guatemalan Enrique Gómez Carrillo. The scrapbook brings together clippings of her own and her husband's published articles, alongside "social notes" commenting on their marriage and travels, from far-flung periodicals.[3] It also includes her two student identification cards at the École Sociale Superior (16 Rue de la Sorbonne, 16, Paris): one from 1901/02, for the École des Hautes Études Sociales, is still bright pink against the yellowing album pages; the other, a faded blue, is for the following year at the École de Journalisme. Housed today in the library of the Pontificia Universidad Católica of Peru, the album shows how Cáceres collected materials related to her own career as well as, for a time, her famous husband's.[4]

This chapter will read the album alongside Cáceres's other texts and writing about her, conjuring from the archive a fuller understanding of one woman's professional experience on the edges of Modernismo. We will attend to the material experience of the album as a window onto the questions of nostalgia and memory that give it meaning, resisting what Leah Price has described as "a commonsense Cartesianism [that] teaches us to filter out the look, the feel, the smell of the printed page."[5] Cáceres and her work have much to teach us about the social role of the Latin American woman writer in a pivotal period of women's professionalization, as well as about the limits of Modernista representations of femininity. My broad aim is to increase critical attention to a fascinating but understudied writer from the early twentieth century, as well as to consider Cáceres's strategies for career advancement and her involvement in and exclusion from various intellectual networks, such as that of women writers internationally, of writers residing in Paris, and of writers identified with Spanish American Modernismo.

What emerges in this chapter is a detailed view of Cáceres as a writer and public figure, working and building a memory of that work under circumstances largely hostile to women's active participation in literary creation, knowledge production, and intellectual networks. Vanesa Miseres has read Cáceres's album as "una memoria personal para la posteridad que dé cuenta de su profesión, sus relaciones intelectuales y la repercusión de su trabajo en un contexto transnacional . . . en medio del auge modernista, Cáceres patenta en el álbum un modo subjetivo, transversal y no jerarquizado de relacionarse con el movimiento, el cual se resistió al ingreso de la mujer" (a personal memoire for posterity that would account for her profession, her intellectual relationships, and the impact of her work in a transnational context . . . at the peak of Modernismo's influence, Cáceres lays out in the album a subjective, transversal, and non-hierarchical way to relate to the movement, which resisted the entry of women).[6] This chapter takes up a similar proposal, examining the scrapbook as a an artifact of material culture that documents a career and makes intellectual networks visible. My approach also reads the album as defined by a sense of nostalgia encompassing both pride and regret, as the work of an older woman reflecting on her success and the obstacles she confronted.

A WRITER AND HER ALBUM

Cáceres grew up in privilege in Peru during a time of great national upheaval. Her parents, Antonia Moreno Leyva and General Andrés Avelino Cáceres, were heroes during the War of the Pacific (1879–1883), when they brought their three young daughters on the famous La Breña Campaign (1881–1883); the youngest, Rosa Amelia, died in 1889.[7] Her father twice became president of Peru, ending in 1895 when a coup by Nicolás de Piérola sent the family into exile in Buenos Aires. There they joined other Peruvian exiles, among them the director of *Búcaro Americano*, Clorinda Matto de Turner, an accomplished journalist, editor, and fiction writer whose work in the Argentine capital is treated in Chapter 3. It was in that city and in the pages of *Búcaro* that twenty-four-year-old Cáceres launched her journalistic career under the pseudonym of Eva Angelina, which she would employ throughout her life. With her article "La emancipación de la mujer" (The Emancipation of Woman) positioned prominently in the magazine's sixth and seventh issues, Cáceres participated in the most feminist line of thought in *Búcaro*, deconstructing common arguments against women's education and predicting with brio that in South America, women "tendremos el mismo derecho que nuestras compañeras del Norte, porque la corriente del progreso en el cauce de la luz va sin detenerse" (will have the same rights as our sisters of the North, because the current of progress flows unstopping in the riverbed of light).[8] Although this early article closes optimistically regarding the possibility of improved conditions for Latin American women, the young author is clear that she and other crusaders started from a deplorable situation: "Triste, tristísima es la condición de la mujer sudamericana" (Sad, so terribly sad, is the condition of South American women).[9]

Cáceres's youthful feminist dynamism started a long career in journalism that would include publications in Spain, France, and throughout Latin America, promoting women's advancement and increased educational opportunities. In her twenties she studied in a Berlin convent and at the

Sorbonne in Paris, where she was the first Spanish-speaking woman to give a conference, "El oro del Perú" (The Gold of Peru) and to graduate with a thesis, *El feminismo en Berlín* (Feminism in Berlin).[10] This research likely contributed to her first book, the historical analysis *Mujeres de ayer y de hoy* (Women of Yesterday and of Today), which was followed by a volume of travel writing and art criticism, *Oasis de arte* (Oasis of Art, likely 1911).[11] She published two novels in 1914, the Andean-themed *Las perlas de Rosa* (The Pearls of Rosa), and the European-themed *La rosa muerta* (A Dead Rose)—recirculating today thanks to a 2007 edition by Thomas Ward and Stock Cero—which reformulates the beautiful body as an expression of female autonomy and sexual desire, rather than a passive muse to another's inspiration or an embodiment of aesthetic debate, as was more common among Modernista novelists.[12] Cáceres's varied career included co-authorship, with her father, of *La campaña de la Breña, memorias del mariscal del Perú, D. Andrés A. Cáceres* (1921).[13] She also wrote a second book of travel narrative focusing on Peru, *La ciudad del sol* (City of the Sun, 1927), and a collection of stories, *La princesa Suma Tica* (The Princess Suma Tica, 1929). Cáceres was a committed, life-long Catholic, but she enjoyed the freedoms available to modern women of her social station: she smoked, rode horses, took fencing classes, and studied in at least five countries and four languages. As a journalist, she had published in periodicals from at least six countries by 1903.[14]

Cáceres's own memoir of marriage, *Mi vida con Enrique Gómez Carrillo* (My Life with Enrique Gómez Carrillo, 1929), foregrounds the challenges of a woman writer on the edges of Modernismo. *Mi vida* recounts the author's relationship with the second famous man in her life (following her father), to whom she was briefly married in 1906 and 1907.[15] A Guatemalan Modernista journalist known as the prince of the *cronistas*, whose work we have examined in Chapter 2, Gómez Carrillo wrote travel narratives and descriptions of modernity that were eagerly reprinted throughout Latin America and reached an unprecedentedly large readership in daily newspapers. The title of *Mi vida con Enrique Gómez Carrillo* presents Cáceres's own life as narratable or worthy of memoir to the extent that it is connected to the life of a famous man. In contrast with her husband's fame, easy access to audiences, and frenetic pace of publication—what we could call his assiduous cultivation of a personal brand—her career was slower and often dedicated to the unglamorous work of building organizations and networks, both local and international, that aimed to improve the situation of women.

Cáceres founded the Centro Social de Señoras (Ladies' Social Center) in Lima in 1905, the Unión Literaria de los Países Latinos (Literary Union of Latin Countries) in Paris in 1909, and the Unión Católica de Señoras de

Lima (Catholic Union of Ladies of Lima); she also led Feminismo Peruano (Peruvian Feminism) starting in 1924, as well as the Sindicato de Telefonistas del Perú (Syndicate of Telephone-Operators of Peru), among many other organizations.[16] She organized campaigns and strikes to improve the wages and working conditions of women. Her activism contributed to the expansion of married women's rights in the 1933 constitution of Peru and, eventually, to Peruvian women's full suffrage. She also wrote about public education and produced a 1945 report associated with her role as Peruvian delegate to the Inter-American Women's Commission in Washington, DC, *Labor de armonía interamericana en los Estados Unidos de Norteamérica, 1940–1945* (Labor of Interamerican Harmony in the United States of North America, 1940–1945).[17] As late as 1945, when Cáceres was seventy-three years old, a biographer admired her continuing activity, commenting that "cualquier juicio que se emita hoy sobre Evangelina será prematuro; está en el momento de la evolución de sus inclinaciones y no sería raro que su obra en el porvenir supere aún a la que lleva realizada" (any judgement issued today about Evangelina will be premature; she is in the moment of her inclinations' evolution, and it would not be strange for her future work even to surpass what she has already done).[18]

Cáceres's early optimism observed above in "Emancipación de la mujer" resonates with her later work in women's associations, but a note of persistent sadness nonetheless echoes over decades of her publications. We have seen that in 1896 she characterized the condition of South American women as "triste, tristísima" (sad, so terribly sad). Some ten years later, frustrated with married life, she describes her own emotional state in identical terms: "He amanecido triste, tristísima, con un abatimiento tan grande que no he tenido ánimo para responderle [a Enrique]" (This morning I've been sad, terribly sad, so dejected that I haven't had the energy to respond [to Enrique]).[19] Similarly, Laura, the protagonist of *La rosa muerta*, laments, "esto es triste, tristísimo" (this is sad, terribly sad) when observing poor Parisian women and the pervasive threat of prostitution, which was one of the few self-supporting paths available to women at the time.[20]

Cáceres's echo of *triste, tristísimo* emerges at moments of frustration regarding women's societal and personal marginalization, like a verbal tic that marks the author's own, developing feminist consciousness. It suggests an enduring unhappiness with the limits placed upon women's social roles and professional opportunities. That this malaise would surface for one of the most privileged and successful women authors in Latin America at the time points to a field in which women's equal participation in public debate and professionalization was simply impossible. Her early confrontations with women's social roles on the edges of Modernismo led her both to reject the restrictions of marriage and to pursue a solo career, not as secretary and amanuensis of her husband, but rather as a feminist and reformer who both advocated for women's rights and produced her own varied body of work. In a situation all too common for women writers, her exclusion from the great literary movement of her time pushed her career toward greater individuality and idiosyncrasy. It also rendered her uncategorizable and thus, for a time, invisible in literary history.

Cáceres's *Álbum personal* fits the category of a scrapbook, or a unique, individually crafted book that assembles scraps for personal memory, including photographs, notes, tickets, and other small objects that, although generally flat, have a three-dimensionality not present for printed text.[21] Her *Álbum* is a sort of personal archive documenting travel, social connections, and a career in journalism, situating its subject within a particular cultural geography. Probably intended for her own use, the album would have also been available to display Cáceres's experiences and connections for friends and acquaintances, such that her most intimate letters are not included, for example those between herself and her husband.[22] The album is a heterogeneous, visually determined text of life writing that, by crafting a personal archive of memory, resists the neglect and oblivion that would come to define Cáceres's career as a writer and activist.

Large, leather-bound, and accented with Cáceres's name in gold on the cover, the album is in good condition given its many decades of existence. It contains materials from as early as 1892, when the author was about twenty years old and still living in her native Peru, until at least 1927, when her political activity and literary career had long been well established. Many materials are undated, and the composition date of the album itself is unknown, although we can place it roughly after 1930 due to the use of cellophane tape, a new technology at the time.[23] The album bears the stamp of Carlos Fabbri of Fabbri Hermanos, a Lima lithography and typography shop established in 1888 and recognized with gold medals at exhibitions in 1906 and 1910.[24] Many of the album's materials date from 1900 to 1907, when Cáceres spent much of her time in Paris, raising the possibility that for this author the collecting impulse emerged in exile: movement inspired a desire for fixity, and in young adulthood, that moment of forward momentum to forge a career and define a personal space in the world, the craft of memory became necessary.[25] Indeed, it was in 1906 and in Paris that her diary mentions "la caja donde guardo el pequeño archivo de mis recuerdos literarios" (the box where I save the small archive of my literary souvenirs).[26]

It seems likely that the book was purchased by early in the twentieth century, and Cáceres began collecting items by 1892, but she did not put the book together and finalize composition until several decades later. If we imagine this scene in 1940, for example, the author would have been 68 and still working actively in women's campaigns. What memories wafted up as she turned the pages and gently arranged her scraps and ribbons? The student identification cards may have inspired a sense of pride and perhaps nostalgia for a time when her career seemed unlimited. Would fragments of her failed marriage have stirred relief, regret, or a combination of these? The scrapbook's composition presented a moment to reflect upon her success and frustrations in both personal and professional terms.

The album's most substantial category of materials is received correspondence, with letters relating to Cáceres's individual, professional life, but not to personal relationships or letters she received representing an organization.[27] These letters are signed by people or institutions of note in international politics, such as the Office of the Education and Culture in the Ministry of France; the Valencian sculptor, Mariano Benlliure, who writes in February, 1902, with a distinctive letterhead showcasing some of his work, to comment on his travels and relations with governmental and cultural authorities; and the Argentine Alfredo Palacios, whose letters include a rather flirtatious one in 1902, as he began a long career as a socialist politician. Cáceres's correspondents also include periodical editors, women intellectuals, and feminists from around the world, such as Ersilia Caetani Lovatelli, the Italian archeologist and academic, and Helene Lange, the German feminist and pedagogue some forty years older than Cáceres, who joined the Hamburg parliament in 1919. Many of these letters seem to respond to surveys and requests that Cáceres likely sent in preparation for her thesis at the Sorbonne. One from Paris, dated 31 May 1903, discusses the logistics of having the thesis translated, copied, and submitted for degree completion.[28]

Of particular interest are the correspondents who situate Cáceres within an international network of writers. One such person is Emilia Serrano, a Spaniard also known as the Baronesa de Wilson, whose two letters of 1902 likely coincided with Serrano's writing of *El mundo literario americano* (The American Literary World), a book published one year later that includes Cáceres among the author profiles. The five-page note on Cáceres, accented with an engraving of the young Peruvian, imagines her at the Sorbonne: "Allí en ese centro, piensa, medita, observa y puebla de ideas nuevas la pensadora mente, una joven, casi una niña, tan noble por su belleza como por su talento" (There, in that center, a young woman, almost a girl, thinks, meditates, observes, and fills her thinking mind with new ideas, as ennobled by her beauty as she is by her talent).[29] According to Serrano, Cáceres has "una inteligencia tan despejada como sólida" (an intelligence as clear as it is solid).[30] Alongside these traditionally masculine characteristics, she bears talents then associated with femininity: "Evangelina pertence al número de aquellos talentos privilegiados que tiene estilo propio, y en sus correspondencias, en sus artículos o labores imaginativas más extensas, resalta un corte especial, reflejándose en sus trabajos literarios el espíritu observador y el sentimiento más exquisito y más puro" (Evangelina belongs to the number of those privileged talents who have their own style, and in her correspondence, in her articles or longer labors of the imagination, a special profile stands out, reflecting in her literary works an observant spirit and the most exquisite and pure sentiment).[31] As is true for Serrano herself, who was from Spain but spent many years traveling throughout Latin America, Cáceres's life bridged the Atlantic. Serrano describes her as "americana por nacimiento y europea por lo profundo y vasto de su instrucción" (American by birth and European by the depth and vastness of her education).[32] The feminist gesture of including Cáceres in her catalog of Latin American authors contributes to the building of international networks of female support to encourage women writers in this period, when national literary organizations, both formal and informal, tended to exclude them.[33]

The album's correspondence allows us to reconstruct some of the communication practices that Cáceres employed to develop her writing career, including how recommendations from influential people opened new doors for journalistic publication. For example, one letter from Darío Pérez, the editor of Spain's *El Liberal*, for whom Gómez Carrillo was a long-term correspondent, explains that the Baronesa de Wilson has shared some of Cáceres's writing. As a result, Pérez would like Cáceres to begin contributing regularly to his newspaper. From his later correspondence, we can surmise that she agreed to the request. Messages on letterhead or printed holiday cards, from Pérez and editors at other periodicals, similarly initiate or maintain professional relationships with Cáceres as a contributing journalist. The author's motivations for including these items in her scrapbook might have included a sense of pride, aesthetic appreciation for the letterpress printing, and simple recordkeeping of professional correspondence.

The album includes undated items that evince social contact with the writerly communities of Paris, which might have been collected any time during her residence in that city. She saved cards or letters from Gustave and Rachel Kahn, Jules Bois, and Lucie Paul-Margueritte, usually brief notes that confirm or modify plans for a social meeting, such as tea or a dinner. Clearly, she both engaged actively in Parisian sociability and saved the relics of that time as souvenirs. At the same time, however, she avoided the bohemian café scene of the period, which she considered toxic, particularly for her husband.[34] Social encounters could also be a burden; depressed about the state of her marriage, she writes in her autobiography of a meeting with Jules Bois: "No me creo obligada a ser amable ni tengo voluntad para sobreponerme al estado de mi espíritu; así, apenas si cambio algunas frases de estricta cortesía. Pensaría de mí que soy una tonta; no me importa" (I do not think I am obliged to be pleasant, nor do I wish to overcome my spiritual state; so, I barely exchange a few phrases of strict courtesy. He must think I am stupid; I do not care).[35]

Above all Cáceres wished to be seen as a writer, rather than as a president's daughter or a famous writer's wife. When Gómez Carrillo caught her attention by repeatedly asking to read her work, she wrote in her diary, "Qué bien principio mi carrera literaria. Quiero ser profesional y no quedarme en aficionada, que viene a ser el último gato de la procesión" (How well I am starting my literary career. I want to be professional and not stay as an amateur, which is like being the last cat in the parade).[36] She was first impressed with her future husband when he treated her as an equal, although his attitude would not remain consistent: "nadie me ha comprendido mejor que él al tratarme como a escritora y no como a señorita de sociedad, porque si algo amo en la vida es la profesión literaria, en la que es permitido pensar, sentir y decirlo todo libremente" (no one has understood me better than he did when he treated me like a writer and not a society belle, because if I love anything in life it is the literary profession, in which one may think, feel, and say everything freely).[37] Quite a few correspondents archived in Cáceres's album were fellow Latin Americans who visited or lived in what Beatriz Colombi has called the "Mecca" of Latin American culture in this period.[38]

ON THE EDGES OF MODERNISMO

It was perhaps during her 1906–1907 marriage to Gómez Carrillo that Cáceres most acutely felt her own potential and ambition colliding with the social obstacles to a woman's career. As the polyglot daughter of a former president, a young lady extensively educated abroad, and the pretty wife of a famous journalist, she was well positioned to enjoy the professional opportunities and sociability available to artists and writers living in Paris. Arancha Sanz Álvarez considers her "parte fundamental de la bohemia latinoamericana en el París de principios de siglo" (a fundamental part of the Latin American bohemian community in Paris at the beginning of the century).[39] Cáceres was even dubbed "la americana más conocida en Europa" (the American woman known best in Europe).[40] This notoriety in Europe and especially within the social spaces of Paris constituted Cáceres's most valuable social capital and supported her career opportunities. Her access to those social spaces, however, was sharply curtailed during her seven-month marriage. In her reading of Cáceres's memoire, Miseres identifies marriage as the principal limitation on Cáceres's access to the city and all that it represented: "El estar casada con un artista no aumentó su experiencia de mundo como intelectual y mujer sino que la limitó, la supeditó a la letra del otro" (Being married to an artist did not increase her world experience as an intellectual and a woman; rather, it limited her and made her subject to her husband's writing and career).[41] Respectable women were effectively barred from many of the spaces of writerly sociability.[42] Gómez Carrillo further attempted to control Cáceres's access to the space of Paris during their marriage, leading to power struggles over her mobility. He demanded that she await him at home rather than venture alone into the city, and eventually he went to the extreme of barring her from conversations with writer friends in their shared home by marking off the study as his own, exclusive space.[43]

As Cáceres's dwindling mobility meant lessened participation in the writerly sociability of Paris, her time and labor also became increasingly not her own. Although Gómez Carrillo initially addressed her as an "escritora" (writer) and an "hermana intelectual" (intellectual sister), their marriage soon prioritized his work over hers.[44] He worked obsessively, suffered from insomnia, and became increasingly unstable, especially while in Paris: his letters transcribed in *Mi vida* list doctors' concerns, including "anemia cerebral posible [y] neurastenias crónicas agudas" (possible cerebral anemia [and] chronic, acute neurasthenia).[45] Meanwhile, she supported his extreme productivity by contributing translations from French into Spanish, producing clean copies of his drafts, and helping to manage his correspondence.[46] Cáceres writes, for example, that Gómez Carrillo "está preparando un nuevo libro sobre el Japón, en el que trabaja toda la tarde, y yo con él, revisando cuartillas y haciendo traducciones, por lo que me dice que el libro lo escribimos juntos" (is preparing a new book on Japan, which he works on all afternoon, and I with him, checking pages and translating, which is why he says that we write the book together).[47] Apparently with the goal of claiming her work as his own, he went to the extreme of asking her to adopt his handwriting, to which she agrees, and his literary style, which she rejects: "mi naturaleza rechaza las imitaciones. Mala o buena, prefiero seguir mi propia inspiración" (my nature rejects immitations. Bad or good, I prefer to follow my own inspiration).[48] Later, she concludes that her husband "exige de mí un imposible: un aniquilamiento absoluto de mi voluntad" (he demands the impossible of me: an absolute annihilation of my will).[49]

Gómez Carrillo's demands resulted not only from a social system that sharply delimited different roles for men and women, but also from his sense of exceptionality as an artist. In a letter to Cáceres toward the end of their marriage, transcribed in *Mi vida*, he described what kind of wife he needed:

> pregúntate si eres capaz de la inmensa benevolencia maternal, fraternal, tierna y risueña que una mujer debe tener para un ser como yo, todo impresiones y nervios, todo capricho y fantasía. En general, las mujeres de seres así son desgraciadas y hacen desgraciados a esos seres. Sólo las mujeres superiores, capaces de perdonarlo todo y de vivir en el perpetuo sacrificio de sus [propias] existencias, consagradas a sus grandes hombres, insoportables; solo esas mujeres inteligentes y extraordinarias pueden casarse con artistas. ¿Te sientes capaz de serlo?

> ask yourself if you are capable of the immense benevolence—maternal, fraternal, tender and cheerful—that a wife must have for someone like me, all impressions and nerves, all caprice and fantasy. In general, wives of people like this are unfortunate, and they make those people unfortunate too. Only superior women, capable of pardoning everything and of living in the perpetual sacrifice of their [own] existences, dedicated to their great, unbearable men; only those intelligent and extraordinary women can marry artists. Do you feel capable of being this?[50]

Gómez Carrillo's awareness of his own limitations, combined with his generalized blaming of artists' wives for the artists' unhappiness ("and they make those people unfortunate too"), reveals the marriage as stifling and unforgiving for Cáceres, and indeed as unsatisfying for them both. In this framework, characteristics associated with decadentism, creativity, and unpredictability define the husband's personality as an artist (he is "all impressions and nerves, all caprice and fantasy"), which as a result limits the characteristics permitted of the wife, who must be stable and patient, exhibiting "immense benevolence—maternal, fraternal, tender and cheerful." An artist is never a woman nor an equal partner in marriage. He later writes to her, succinctly, "Yo necesito como mujer lo que tú llamas una cocinera: es decir una muchacha sin ideas de igualdad" (I need as a wife what you call a cook: that is, a girl without ideas of equality).[51] They harbored incompatible understandings of what marriage would entail, and eventually both were made physically ill by the stress of their union.[52]

Gómez Carrillo's decadentist-bohemian pose reflects a belief that his life was an extension of his art, which predominated over other priorities. The demands of the aesthetic benefitted from a loose relation to objective truth, and a story's style and stylistic effect took precedence over its veracity. On one occasion, Jean Moréas came to lunch and said that Gómez Carrillo had falsified a prologue from Moréas, but he did not mind: "¡Bah! Es Carrilllo" (Ah! That's Carrillo).[53] In contrast, Pachas Maceda observes Cáceres's own "rigurosidad en los datos" (rigor with detail).[54] Gómez Carrillo's life-as-art ethos is also clear in family relationships: in a letter sent to Cáceres after the couple's separation, his father convincingly refutes Enrique's story of his departure from Guatemala; he writes that the famous *cronista* "exagera las cosas y se olvida de la realidad" (exaggerates things and forgets reality).[55] Cáceres agrees with the point and commiserates with his parents. Through the international exchange of letters and her wedding ring, which Cáceres mailed to her mother-in-law, Cáceres sought solace in a sort of support group of people who felt betrayed by her husband.

Although the second half of their cohabitation perhaps marks the highest point of Cáceres's frustration with her diminished career expectations, contemporary Peruvian author Alfredo Bryce Echenique insists that her entire career was defined by adversity: Cáceres "conoció en vida todas las adversidades de un talento literario femenino en un mundo absolutamente machista, violento, desordenado y sumamente despectivo con su vocación de escritora" (saw in her life all the adversities of a talented literary woman, in an absolutely machista, violent, disordered world that supremely disdained her vocation as a writer).[56] When her husband's desire to limit her movement became unbearable, it was by reclaiming her right to the city space—specifically by going to the theater with her sister—that she asserted her autonomy and reclaimed her time and mobility as her own. The choice meant divorce, followed some fifteen years later by a church annulment, which for Cáceres was more meaningful.[57]

In May of 1907, about one month after their split, Cáceres offered this assessment of their shared professional life and her newfound resolution to write a book:

> ¿La vida al lado de Enrique? No ha sido la mía; he vivido la suya, palpitante de inquietudes, martirizada por inconscientes caprichos. Su talento literario me turbaba al punto de cohibirme y de destruír la poca fe que tengo o la falta de vigor de mi pobre alma, fuertemente sacudida y doblegada por su actividad febril. Hoy renace para mí una nueva ilusión: la esperanza que cifro de emprender una labor meritoria.

Life alongside Enrique? It has not been my own; I have lived his life, racing with worries, martyred by unconscious caprices. His literary talent disturbed me to the point that I held myself back, destroying the little faith I have, or the lack of vigor of my poor soul, strongly shaken and beaten down by his febrile activity. Today a new illusion is reborn for me: the hope that I harbor to undertake worthy work.[58]

Cáceres describes a creative reawakening here in terms of a new "illusion," suggesting hope or excitement, but with an undercurrent of doubt from the word's secondary meaning of chimera or trickery. This newborn hope must be encoded or synthesized (*la esperanza que cifro*) because it is vulnerable, dangerous, or otherwise excessive, but it grows and gains focus as a desire for worthy work, or something more deserving of her energies than serving as another's secretary. Cáceres "worthy" task would of course be a new writing project, which she exuberantly describes two pages later: "Esta noche tengo el deseo de escribir: la idea de principiar una novela me obsesiona; solo me detiene el compromiso de un corto artículo que me urge enviar a Madrid . . .; no importa. Esta noche principio mi novela" (Tonight I wish to write: the idea of starting a novel obsesses me; only the obligation of a short article that I have to send to Madrid holds me back . . .; no matter. Tonight I begin my novel).[59] This project might have become either of her 1914 novels, *La rosa muerta* or *Las perlas de Rosa*, or perhaps it became a project that honed her skills with fiction but never saw publication. It is nonetheless clear that, for Cáceres, the end of a disastrous marriage opened the door to new inspiration with pen and paper.

While this decision makes possible a later productivity in both literature and journalism, the fact remains that her writing career never seemed to take off. Cáceres's truncated success is clearest when considered alongside the achievements and renown of her male contemporaries, as Mónica Cárdenas suggests when she observes her "relación de subordinación" (relation of subordination) with respect to other journalists of the time.[60] The prolificacy and broad circulation of Gómez Carrillo and their contemporary, Rubén Darío, gave the men an immeasurably greater opportunity to shape readers' perceptions at a critical moment of Latin America's engagement in global cultural modernity. They also participated in the newsrooms, cafés, and other places of writerly sociability considered unacceptable for respectable women. Miseres reminds us that Cáceres "busca constantemente presentarse como escritora y profesional en un espacio y tiempo (el del Modernismo) que se define no sólo por aspectos estéticos, sino también de acuerdo a modos específicos de sociabilidad, de los cuales la mujer era frecuentemente excluida" (constantly seeks to present herself as a writer and a professional in a space and time [that of Modernismo] defined not only by aeshetic aspects, but also according to specific modes of sociability, from which women were frequently excluded).[61] Women's limited access to public space meant that Cáceres's experience of Paris and its writerly opportunities fell far short of those available to the period stereotypes of the young Latin American bohemian, *rastaquouère*, or student: men who enjoyed greater freedom despite economic marginalization. The writer herself understood this very clearly later in life, when she wrote, "siempre hemos considerado aquí a la mujer en un plano secundario. Nunca se ha tratado de escucharla seriamente; de tomarse en cuenta sus propósitos, por prejuicio quizá, o porque la tradición así nos lo ha trazado" (here we have always considered women on a secondary level. We have never tried to listen to her seriously; to consider her goals, due to prejudice perhaps, or because tradition has laid this path for us).[62]

Importantly, and as we see with other women writers of her period, this double standard of recognition has only become more trenchant after Cáceres's early career: the limited success she enjoyed during her lifetime was largely forgotten by the mid- to late-twentieth century. It appears that no peers, relatives, or scholars rescued her work from oblivion during her lifetime; she had no children to keep track of her papers; no collection of her journalism has been published; no examination of her fiction or travel writing offers a global account for her remarkably varied career. Quite recently it was possible to affirm—as did Fernando Carvallo in 2007—that "cuando murió [Cáceres] en Madrid en 1957 no tenía quien la leyera. Las cosas no han cambiado desde entonces" (when [Cáceres] died in Madrid in 1957, no one read her. Things have not changed since then).[63] Bryce Echenique agreed one year later: "Nadie recuerda hoy en el Perú—o en España y Francia—a Zoila Aurora Cáceres" (No one remembers Zoila Aurora Cáceres in Peru today—or in Spain or France).[64] This context of oblivion makes current critical interest in Cáceres's work all the more exciting. Sofía Pachas Maceda's 2019 book, *Zoila Aurora Cáceres y la ciudadanía femenina: La correspondencia de Feminismo Peruano* (Zoila Aurora Cáceres and Feminine Citizenship: The Correspondence of *Feminismo Peruano*), is the most extensive example of historiographical assessment of the author grounded in archival research. It answers such basic questions as the author's date of birth in 1872 (sometimes listed incorrectly as 1877) and offers the first in-depth study of her work as an activist for women's organizations in Peru.

Our best access to opinions of Cáceres and her work by her Modernista contemporaries can be found in the prologues to her published books, in which writers of import express their admiration for her writing, while voicing reservations about women writers more broadly and gesturing toward her own, more individual limitations as a writer.[65] The first of these is the most positive: Luis Bonafoux writes in 1909 that an apt title for *Mujeres de ayer y de hoy* could be simply "Feminismo" (Feminism): "Es, á mi juicio, el más completo, en lengua castellana, que se ha escrito del movimiento femenino, ó el más cabal de cuantos leí sobre el tema, y su autora honra muy mucho á las letras hispanoamericanas en general y á las peruanas particularmente" (It is, in my view, the most complete account that has been written in Spanish on the women's movement, or the most thorough of what I have read on the topic, and its author greatly honors Hispanic-American letters in general, and Peruvian letters particularly).[66] In contrast, likely just two years later, Rubén Darío's prologue to *Oasis de arte* is quite critical of the entire category of women writers: "¿de dónde proviene mi poco apego a las escritoras? Posiblemente, o seguramente, porque todas, con ciertas raras excepciones, han sido y son feas. Evangelina no se encuentra en este caso" (Where does my little affection for women writers come from? Possibly, or certainly, because they all, with certain rare exceptions, have been and are ugly. Evangelina is not among them).[67] About three years later, Amado Nervo provided a prologue for *La rosa muerta* full of confident pronouncements regarding women's nature and aptitudes—for instance, "para la mujer . . . si no es una anormal, el amor constituye el fin por excelencia de la vida" (for woman, . . . if she is not abnormal, love constitutes the purpose par excellence of life)—which he offers as support for the proposal that women writers should focus their energies on the romance novel.[68] Nervo goes on to observe that Cáceres is well known in "este París 'Meca' de nuestras ingenuas almas hispanoamericanas" (this Paris, Mecca of our naive Hispanic-American souls).[69] *La rosa muerta* also included a "comentario breve" (brief commentary) from the Spaniard Miguel de Unamuno, who opines that travel writing is the best area for women to pursue in writing, although he really does not expect much of them: "Tanto como en general me fastidian las escritoras, gusto de las mujeres que escriben como usted, amiga mía" (As much as women writers generally irritate me, I enjoy women that write like you, my friend).[70]

These performances of ambivalence by famous men in Cáceres's early career would echo in later decades. In 1924, Gómez Carrillo wrote a prologue to *La ciudad del sol*, which she published and dedicated to her former husband in 1927, soon after his death. The prologue praises Cáceres and her work in detail, but still falls short of taking her seriously when he notes her "gracia casi infantil" (almost infantile grace) and comments that "todo se convierte en poesía, cuando es un poeta quien lo evoca" (everything becomes poetry, when it is a poet who evokes it), although the archives offer no hint that Cáceres ever wrote poetry.[71] This recourse to cliché suggests that even her own, verbose ex-husband found himself struggling to discuss the oxymoron of a woman writer. The last known prologue to a Cáceres book written by an important writer of her generation is that of Manuel Ugarte, which fronts her 1929 memoir *Mi vida con Enrique Gómez Carrillo* complimentarily, with an emphasis on reminiscing about the recently deceased title character. With the exception of Ugarte's and Bonafoux's, these prologues of Cáceres's books demonstrate (or even exaggerate) a characteristic of the prologue genre in the period, which was to provide what is known colloquially as a backhanded compliment: an ironic bit of negative praise that took critical measure of the writer, while ostensibly promoting the book for commercial purposes. The fact of Cáceres's sex is a particular sore point for her illustrious prologue-writers, and those of greater literary prestige (Darío, Nervo, Unamuno) feel especially authorized to reject women's writing writ large.[72]

With these prologues we can track Cáceres's relationships with several of the most important Modernista writers residing in Paris in the first decade of the twentieth century: the names of Gómez Carrillo, Darío, and Nervo especially stand out as the movement's most influential writers at the time. It is also clear that she maintained a commitment to her career as a writer over decades of publication in both periodicals and books, and her social and educational privilege positioned her unusually well for success. Despite these factors that would mark her inclusion, however, Cáceres herself was generally not considered a Modernista writer during her lifetime, because the rhetorical systems and social practices proper to Modernismo excluded women from that social role. In Laura Kanost's reading, "the fraternity [of Modernismo] clearly did not consider her one of their own."[73] Thomas Ward expands the point convincingly when he proposes, in his 2007 introduction to *La rosa muerta*, that we might even conclude that Modernismo had no women writers.[74]

With her struggles to build a professional career adjacent to Modernismo, Cáceres allows us to reflect on the markedly homosocial, masculine nature of the movement. Peluffo has insightfully linked Modernismo's homosociability to its reluctance to expand the project of modernity, explaining that "el cosmopolitismo modernista estuvo dominado por una política homosocial de la amistad en la que los productores culturales formaron alianzas masculinas dentro de un espacio globalizado de fronteras móviles" (Modernista cosmopolitism was dominated by a homosocial politics of friendship, in which cultural producers formed alliances among men, within a globalized space of shifting borders).[75] In light of this perspective, Cáceres's story reveals the limits of Modernismo's search for the new. The movement was the most aesthetically innovative, trans-Hispanic literary phenomenon of its time—and here I refer especially to 1890–1916, the years when Cáceres was establishing her career—but that innovation was not radical enough to dislodge the Modernista woman from her position as aesthetic object and render her legible, within the logic of Modernismo, as herself a writer, subject, and equal.

CRAFTING, MEMORY, AND THE SOUVENIR

Cáceres's *Álbum personal* presents a different reading of her life and work. As a text shaped for its author's own appreciation—Jean Baudrillard considers a collection to be "a discourse addressed to oneself"—the scrapbook can also be considered a radically individualized form of life writing.[76] The gesture of fixing a souvenir into a collection assigns that object a meaning in the present that exceeds its original purpose, fixing a knot of sentiment and social relations from a specific moment, and projecting it forward through the unknown circumstances of the future. The album genre forefronts narrative fragmentation and questions of temporality, giving these a particularly subjective meaning, largely impenetrable to the reader. The readerly sense of fragmentation inspired by many scrapbooks is exacerbated in Cáceres's, because it lacks an overarching narrative voice; rather strikingly for an author who built a career on narration, she includes no captions, titles, dates, or other explanatory notes, perhaps recalling what Christa Wolf calls women's "difficulty of saying I."[77] The material frame of the book is insufficient to unify the collection as a narrative and to contain the souvenirs' multivalent and conflicting signs. The album thus seems to belong more fully to its author only, to have been crafted more for her own memory than for ours, as if a satisfying reading would only be possible with an explanatory performance by the author herself.

Although reading conventions dictate that we start at the beginning and proceed sequentially through a book, in the case of an album our pace can vary widely, as readers might linger on a page as long as interest demands. The album also resists narrative conventions by bringing together disparate scraps within a unifying frame, for example by juxtaposing items from very disparate periods in Cáceres's life. A 1906 letter scrawled by Alfredo Palacios precedes a page with two clippings from unknown newspapers—undated and titled "Condición jurídica de la mujer" (Women's Juridical Condition) and "Espíritu burlón" (Teasing Spririt), from Tacna, 1899, and both with the "Eva Angelina" byline—which is in turn followed by a 1902 letter from Darío Pérez, the editor of *El Liberal*. Several pages later, dated January 1899, Federico A. Gutiérrez writes on letterhead from the Buenos Aires magazine *Vida Social*, addressing Cáceres in Tacna, just after her departure from the Argentine capital, and inviting her contributions to the magazine; a small photograph of a young man appears alongside the letter, presumably included in an ambiguous gesture of semi-intimacy. What we are seeing, of course, is that Cáceres's scrapbook eschews the organizing logic of chronology, genre, source, or any other identifiable determinant. The graphic designer and historian Jessica Helfand proposes that what she calls "scrapbook time" is fundamentally "unmoored to the demands of the everyday" and is characterized "not so much by decorum as by a kind of tacit dislocation. The nature, scope, and relative placement of that information are entirely self-determined, requiring no external approval process—indeed no apparent formal logic at all—and therein lies its strangely captivating beauty."[78] Helfand's "scrapbook time" is subjectively determined and often follows a logic opaque to the reader. Ordered by personal associations or sentiment, or even by material or graphic qualities of the collected scraps, its logic remains unexplained.

Similarly, the scrapbook's material form draws on techniques of accumulation that depend on fragments and assemblage, which Susan Tucker, Katherine Ott, and Patricia P. Buckler frame as characteristic of modern narrative and of innovative aesthetics. "If scrapbooks can be distilled to one overarching interpretive theme," they propose, "it is that of rupture. Scrapbooks shuffle and recombine the coordinates of time, space, location, voice, and memory. What could be more emblematic of the fractured narratives of modernity than scrapbooks?"[79] In this framing, scrapbooks exhibit many of the formal experiments associated with the avant-gardes of the 1920s and 30s, or even the Boom novels of the 1960s. (We could add to this list concrete poetry, calligrams, and similarly visual forms inspired by painting and graphic design.) Earlier, the decorative excesses and almost obsessive accumulation of references and ornament apparent in Modernismo strained the limits of narrative unity, such as with the luxurious and cluttered spaces of José Asunción's Silva's novel, *De sobremesa* (After-Dinner Conversation), and Darío's "Sonatina," to name just two of the most famous examples.[80]

It is important to note, however, that the formal experiments of the scrapbook significantly predate these literary experiments. The albums examined in *Playing With Pictures: The Victorian Art of Photocollage*, for example, are aesthetically astonishing pieces for their period and clearly prefigure the ruptures and playful juxtapositions of the avant-gardes.[81] Tucker, Ott, and Buckler remind us that the scrapbook has a centuries-long history, having developed from the nostalgic collector's impulse with the seventeenth century *Wunderkammer*, "a poor family's version of the cabinet of curiosities, . . . which was the earliest recognizable version of the modern museum."[82] The aestheticization of accumulation thus emerges as a mode of cultural production that predates—and likely contributed to—gestures later enshrined in high-prestige literary currents. Cáceres's album is part of two long but under-valued traditions, that of personal collecting, and that of women's cultural production, largely excluded from the systems of prestige and recognition that differentiate high art from other forms of art in the early years of her career.[83]

Given, then, its assembly after 1930, which we suppose based on its use of cellophane tape; its aesthetic of fragmentation, collection, and assemblage; and its radically individual temporality, should we consider Cáceres's *Álbum personal* a text of the historical avant-gardes? This book proposes that a literary movement is made not only by a body of work in proximity and sharing aesthetic characteristics, but also by the writers' sense of identification as a group. According to this logic, the evidence of Cáceres's life and work might indicate proximity and shared aesthetic characteristics with both Modernismo and the avant-gardes at different moments. However, her novel's accumulation of the objects and tropes of Modernismo no more make her a Modernista than her album makes her a Vanguardista, because those movements exhibited a high degree of group identity consciousness from which she was excluded. Although she was not a member of either club, so to speak, her work and her life merit study in their own right, and her exclusion offers an opportunity to examine the functioning of group identity that made these literary movements possible.

In the now iconic essay "Unpacking My Library" (1931), Walter Benjamin reflected on the special tension between control and chaos that for him defined the work of the collector. He considered disorder to be inherent to the nostalgic instinct of any collector, proposing that "every passion borders on the chaotic, but the collector's passion borders on the chaos of memories."[84] Although the desire to define a collection, to demarcate it as a permanent and complete unit, rarely achieves its aim, for Benjamin, a compelling allure grows from the opposition of chaos and control: "The most profound enchantment for the collector is the locking of a magic circle in which they are fixed as the final thrill, the thrill of acquisition, passes over them."[85] In his essay Benjamin was considering his personal library as a collection of books and relishing the material experience of opening boxes after a move, but his thoughts wandered also to the varied terrain of scrapbooks and family albums. Indeed, his dream of composing a manuscript entirely of quotations—what we know today as the *Arcades Project*—could be read as a sort of scrapbook of historical research. Benjamin's iconic library, similarly, is his collection of souvenirs, his scraps of past reading.

More recently, the language of magic has also been useful to Susan Stewart, who considers a souvenir to be the result of a transformation, as it has been reserved in the past and brought into the present: "The souvenir is not simply an object appearing out of context, an object from the past incongruously surviving in the present; rather, *its function is to envelop the present within the past*. Souvenirs are magical objects because of this transformation."[86] Memory work lives on this magic, but holding the aura of the past is not the souvenir's only function. Stewart proposes that it has two: "The double function of the souvenir is to authenticate a past or otherwise remote experience, and, at the same time, to discredit the present. The present is either too impersonal, too looming, or too alienating compared to the intimate and direct experience of contact which the souvenir has as its referent."[87] The souvenir speaks through what she calls "a language of longing," and the scrap anchors a memory of what has been lost but is still desired.[88] For Cáceres, perhaps as she unpacked her own library of scraps from a dusty box and taped them into her long-waiting scrapbook, as she locked that ephemera in Benjamin's magical circle of the collection, what she handled were the materials of memory, the small successes and failures that made up a career.[89]

In the nineteenth century, an "album" could be many things—an anthology of poets, for example, or a periodical—but the most traditional definition of the word, a unique, hand-made memory book, might be the least familiar to scholars of the long nineteenth century in the Luso-Hispanophone: they are among the objects least examined and the hardest to find in the archives. Finding one or two albums is not difficult, but finding enough that we might produce a theory and a history of the album, is a slow and laborious process. They are scattered, irregularly catalogued, and in many cases completely lost or destroyed. They are also vulnerable to the disregard of later generations who viewed them as frivolous and unimportant, that is, as a manifestation of women's conventional sentimentality. Samantha Matthews points out this broad disdain in how the scrapbook is portrayed in historical narrative: she proposes that, although many examples from fiction "ostensibly present the album as a tame sign of conventional femininity, . . . they simultaneously reveal more complex and subtle functions for albums in the social, affective, and erotic lives of the books' female owners and their circles."[90] Any veneer of conventionality is thin for Cáceres's particular scrapbook, which quickly reveals itself as a richly textured portrait of a young writer and her professional networks.

This chapter opens with Cáceres's statement in "Emancipación de la mujer," her first known publication, that "triste, tristísima es la condición de la mujer Sudamericana" (sad, terribly sad is the condition of South American women), a statement that echoes through passages of both her memoir and her novel, *La rosa muerta*. The verbal tic marked for Cáceres a developing consciousness of women's marginalization, and offers a curious counterdiscourse to Darío's own repetition of sadness in the famous introductory verses to "Sonatina": "La princesa está triste, qué tendrá la princesa? / Los suspiros se escapan de su boca de fresa" (The princess is sad, what's wrong with the princess? / The sighs escape from her strawberry mouth). Real women on the fringes of Modernismo, such as Cáceres, as well as the imaginary women of Modernismo—like Darío's princess, Silva's Helena from *De sobremesa*, and perhaps Laura from *La rosa muerta*—bore the heavy responsibility of embodying beauty for a literary current obsessed with femininity and with idealized form, a situation that exacerbated women writers' marginalization from the social positions of literary prestige. The objectifying gaze that defined the Modernista feminine filtered through to daily life and affected real women writers in very tangible ways. Among the varied responses of women writers, Cáceres insists on drawing the relationship between the female body and beauty away from Modernista idealizations, and toward a material experience of the self from a woman's perspective. Our study of a scrapbook has allowed us to reread the life and circumstances of a professional woman, the building of a career, and the overcoming of some measure of the obstacles to these ambitions. The *Álbum personal* of Aurora Cáceres clarifies both her persistence and pleasure in building a career—the collecting of beautiful, informative, or legitimizing scraps, the souvenirs of a life's work—and the nostalgic reflection that must have tinged the process of assemblage.

MODERNISMO'S OTHERS

The final pages of Cáceres's album contain two autographed photos from Carmen Tórtola Valencia, a Spanish-British dancer who debuted in Europe in 1908 and performed extensively throughout Latin America between 1913 and 1930. She visited Peru at least twice, in 1917 and in 1925, when she premiered her acclaimed "danza incaica guerrera" (Inca warrior dance) at Lima's main theater and received a medal of honor from the Municipal

Council.[91] This "Inca" dance is depicted in the second of Valencia's autographed pictures in the album; the first shows her "danza de la serpiente" (serpent dance), which she developed around 1913.[92] Cáceres's autobiography places her in Peru in 1925, during one of Tórtola's tours that included Peru; in this time she might have been working on a piece of Andean-themed fiction, *La princesa Suma Tica*.[93] Tórtola's and Cáceres's shared language and their interest in indigenous cultures raises the possibility of their friendship. What would these pioneering women have discussed, perhaps over tea or after a performance? Would Tórtola have read Cáceres's work and asked her about current projects? They shared an interest in travel and in international careers as well. Curiously, the only dissent from positive reviews of Tórtola's serpent dance, according to Michelle Clayton, had come in 1913 in Spain's *El Liberal* and was penned by none other than Enrique Gómez Carrillo.[94] By this time Cáceres and Gómez Carrillo had long been separated, but it is nonetheless likely that Cáceres attended multiple Tórtola Valencia performances over the years. Would their conversation have broached the meandering paths of women's careers that wove around the obstacles presented by misogyny and incomprehension?

The possibility of a friendship between the two women gains credence from another item in Cáceres's album, a "Christmas Greetings" card in English, from Tórtola, and signed "Londres 1927" (London). It was likely sent around the time of Gómez Carrillo's death in late November of that year and between the dancer's third and fourth tours of Latin America. This scrap of evidence raises suggestive questions and, like many objects included in Cáceres's album, permits an alternative reading of the great cultural movements that define the trans-Hispanic cultural canon. The most legible and memorable writers for their contemporaries, and for the first generation of scholars who cemented their importance in our cultural imaginary, were far from the only significant cultural activity of their time, and the field needs more study of the alternative and sometimes contested networks that operated in different terms and produced different aesthetics. Paradoxically, concrete poetry has taught us how to read nineteenth-century scrapbooks, and the critiques of excluded women writers have taught us to read Modernismo. Continuing work on unconventional texts such as the scrapbook will render careers like Cáceres's more legible, against the oblivion that defines the roles of non-canonical figures in literary history.

CONCLUSION

The stories told in this book respond in different ways to the question of why Modernismo admitted no women unconditionally. We took as our starting point a commitment to account for women's disappearance from the literary canon as a form of gendered violence. *Las Raras* rereads Modernismo in this vein, refusing to accept women's absence as natural or unavoidable, and seeking instead to articulate the power systems and discourses that produced that void. Delmira Agustini's sonnet "El poeta y la ilusión" guided this initial framing of the issue: her empty hemistiches within the muse's dialogue pointed to the void of women's voice in Modernismo, and she revealed women's traditional role in poetry as the muse to be artificial. She was the most Modernista woman poet—in the sense that she presented a unique and innovative vision of poetry and steeped her work in the movement's favored tropes—even as she was the woman poet who most clearly critiqued the gendered violence of Modernismo's style and practices. However, her challenge was largely illegible to her contemporaries, whose strictly dichotomic imagination responded with what a queer reading defines as a form of denial. This book proposes that the misreading of her work was part of the same system that brought about her death at the hands of her ex-husband. Without being equal in violence, it was nonetheless part of the silencing practices of patriarchy.

Chapter 1 stepped back to consider Modernista imaginings of the feminine and its significance for that movement, particularly in the renderings of Rubén Darío, Manuel Gutiérrez Nájera, and Amado Nervo. For Darío, femininity is both a light, flexible style associated with beauty and youth, and an opportunity to foreground his own innovation and productivity as the creator of these. His *princesa* in "Sonatina" and the languid Carlota of

"De invierno" await his arrival in scenes of luxurious passivity, while the sleep-walking virgin of "Ite, Missa Est" waits for the erotic awakening to be inspired by his voice; indeed, the prologue to *Prosas profanas* leaves no doubt as to the importance of masculinity as the starting point of poetic subjectivity, in Darío's framing. In contrast, for Gutiérrez Nájera femininity represented modernity more directly by functioning as a cipher of the modern and of aesthetic innovation: in "La duquesa Job" and "Mis enlutadas," women make poetry possible and highlight the novelty of Modernista expression, but his later pieces in prose reveal a sharper critique of the identity shifts that accompanied Mexico's deepening engagement with globally hegemonic modernity. While Nájera played at feminine hospitality by welcoming his female reader to his house/magazine in "Al pie de la escalera," Nervo multiplied the feminine poses by writing in a series of women's voices in his newspaper series "Cartas de mujeres," inviting both humorous and critical interpretations. Later, however, his woman-annihilating fantasies of homosocial bonding revealed a deeper scorn for women and a desire for artistic production freed from the mundane concerns that he associated with them. Although these writers each engaged feminine style and representation of women differently, they share an interest in codifying writing as an activity for men whose symbolically feminine sensibilities brought innovation to trans-Hispanic literature. For Modernismo, women were readers and inspirations for poetic innovation, but never themselves writers of significance.

Chapter 2 studies Paris as a location of convergence and increased group consciousness for Modernismo, and as the place where Modernismo most directly confronted an ostensibly feminine modernity. Darío and Enrique Gómez Carrillo were among chroniclers that advanced a discourse of the feminine modern that found massive circulation in Latin American newspapers. Gómez Carrillo's theory of a feminine Paris was a discourse on aesthetics that mediated postcolonial modernity for Latin America. His *crónicas de París* celebrated women's beauty and performance of gender roles in the French capital and were famous for his "frivolous" writing style, which his contemporaries associated with the femininity of the city. Like Darío and others, Gómez Carrillo grappled with his own marginality in the space of globally hegemonic modernity by situating himself as an expert evaluator of the spectacle of Parisian modernity, in effect calling his own narration to the task of crafting a position of greater prestige and stability. As trans-Hispanic readerships looked forward, both eagerly and warily, to the new technologies, social shifts, and experiences that the twentieth century promised, Gómez Carrillo promoted a presumably feminine modernity as protection from the dangers of industrialization and increasing commercialism that he observed elsewhere.

Having sketched these key moments in the development of Modernismo's discourse of feminine style, the next three chapters of the book change course, turning instead to the responses of three women writers in close contact with the socio-aesthetic network of Modernismo. During her exile in Buenos Aires, the Peruvian novelist and journalist Clorinda Matto de Turner confronted a literary milieu very different from that of her native Peru. Her response was to build the community that she needed to make a self-reinvention possible, despite her difficult circumstances. She engaged strategically with local literary networks, such as in the Ateneo de Buenos Aires, and called on her existing contacts among trans-Hispanic writers to contribute to her new project, *Búcaro Americano*. This literary magazine joined her interests in advancing the women's cause and in promoting trans-Hispanic literature. She also drew on a tradition of women's sociability and performance as she worked to build a community of women writers in her new home. Matto de Turner's projects map emerging literary trends and traditions, particularly of women writers, as they prioritize the memory work that drew from the past and projected that community forward, into the future. Although her magazine published the work of Modernista writers, she generally kept her distance from their bohemian sociability and association with frivolity. Instead of the Modernista feminine as an idea about style and beauty, she tirelessly pursued a modernity in which women would have the right to an education and to work, to prevent the dependence or impoverishment she had experienced as a young widow.

Although María Eugenia Vaz Ferreira, of Uruguay, spent her life in Montevideo and never experienced an exile like Matto de Turner's, she was like the Peruvian in their shared proximity with a significant group of Modernistas. For Vaz Ferreira, this was the Generation of 1900 and the performative decadence of literary cenacles like the Consistorio del Gay Saber and the Torre de los Panoramas. Amid a political moment defined by the radical presidency of Batlle y Ordóñez, these groups pushed the bohemian lifestyle to an extreme that was irreconcilable with social expectations for young women at the time, contributing to Vaz Ferreira's conclusion that life as an artist was incompatible with her condition as a woman. Her need to forge a new social role took the shape of youthful idiosyncrasy and later illness, providing anecdotes of her eccentricity that would define the memory of her after death. Vaz Ferreira's poetry and correspondence, including archival materials made available recently, illustrate a poetic subjectivity of anguish, hope, and commitment to self-expression, interwoven with critiques of

Modernismo's tropes for the portrayal of women. She was also a professor and part of the first generation of Uruguayan women who achieved independence through their professional work, but she was profoundly lonely throughout her life. The chapter situates Vaz Ferreira as a pioneer in the Uruguayan tradition of *rareza*, which gained a foothold during the earliest years of the twentieth century.

Finally, in Chapter 5 we considered the life and career of another woman writer on the edges of Modernismo, the Peruvian Aurora Cáceres, who brings the study well into the twentieth century. Her autobiography and scrapbook allow us to glimpse her clear-sighted ambition as a woman writer. Cáceres's significant privilege as a well-educated and world-traveling daughter of a former president would seem to position her unusually well for success. Marriage to an influential journalist, moreover, expanded her contact with writerly networks in Paris, but she found herself stifled by the resulting lack of autonomy, both personally and professionally. She undoubtedly deserves greater scholarly attention for the merits of her work; what emerges is not only new information to fill in the gaps of literary history, however, but also a reframing of known writers and movements with which she had contact. Reading Modernismo through Cáceres's life and work dismantles and rebuilds what we thought we knew about the formation of a literary movement as both a social network and an aesthetic. Her contact with and exclusion from Modernismo are instructive both regarding Cáceres herself and regarding Modernismo. One of the broadest lessons of this book is thus that we cannot know Darío's work without knowing Agustini's, or Gómez Carrillo's without knowing Cáceres's, because part of their work's meaning is its social emplacement. A literary movement is defined as much by what it excludes as by what it claims. Alternative networks, moreover, beckon from the shadows of those canonized by literary history, inviting new readings of the literary and cultural field of their time.

A second broad lesson of this book is the failure of early- to mid-twentieth century scholars to maintain a memory of women's writing, and the continuing need to return to the archives to bring forgotten material and perspectives to light. Matto de Turner, Vaz Ferreira, and Cáceres built astonishing literary careers but nonetheless fell from cultural memory throughout the twentieth century. Their promoters dwindled after their deaths, and as notions of national literature came to dominate the field, women's writing from the previous generation was neglected. Today, a return to archives is an invaluable part of the effort to more fully reconstruct distant historical realities. Although the recuperation of Cáceres, Vaz Ferreira, and Matto de Turner has begun—most extensively for the latter, thanks to the work of

Cornejo Polar dating back to the late 1970's, and more recently Denegri and Peluffo, among others—much work remains. We must commit moreover to seeking marginalized texts, including correspondence and items such as Cáceres's scrapbook, because genres neglected by previous scholars are a treasure-trove of historically marginalized writers. At the same time, however, the familiar methods of archival work must engage in constant dialogue with new approaches. In this regard, this book's introduction considered an invitation to *queer the archive*, or to bring to the archive a sensitivity to non-normative experiences of gender and an openness to sometimes coded expressions of resistant gender identity. Indeed, this framing supported our examination of texts and writers located within Modernismo, as well as those beyond the scope of its self-definition. Digitization of archives gives scholars today unprecedented opportunities to expand and reframe our narratives of literary history; we must pursue especially the reframing made possible by centering the margins.

NOTES

INTRODUCTION

1. *Hipsipilo* is an untranslatable word. If written in Spanish with an accent, *Hipsípila* (or *Hypsipyle* in English) refers to the Greek daughter of Lemnos and an eponymous drama by Eurípides; Darío uses the word without an accent (*hipsipila*) to refer to a butterfly, which also reflects a scientific usage: *Hypsipyla* is a genus of snout-nosed moths. Agustini's use is more similar to Darío's than to the ancient Greek, but clearly is not identical.
2. All translations are my own, unless indicated otherwise in the bibliography. Modernista poetry is exceptionally difficult to translate due to its complex forms and musicality. One relevant example is "Sonatina," by Rubén Darío, which Daniel Link has considered "el poema más difícil de traducir del mundo" (the world's most difficult poem to translate). See "Rubén Darío in the US: Translation Challenges," panel video on YouTube, 7:50. Carlos F. Grigsby proposes that some of Darío's poems, including "Sonatina," are "virtuosic exercises in prosody, where it is not as important to follow the exact lexical meaning of the words as it is to achieve the overall sonorous effect of the poem." Grigsby, "Rediscovering Rubén Darío," 33. Despite the importance of prosody, in my translations here I do not attempt to recreate the rhyme and rhythm of the original texts; I focus instead on word choice and tone, and hope to achieve some musicality as well. I beg the reader's understanding with these necessary but imperfect renderings in English.
3. Agustini, *Poesías completas*, 134.
4. Agustini included many challenging muses in her poetry: gray, sad, angry, etc. For more information, see García Pinto, "El retrato."
5. Cabello Hutt, "Undisciplined Objects," 29. In another recent study, *Argentine Intimacies*, Joseph Pierce also defines queerness broadly as produced by the tension between normativity and its others. Pierce takes the family as the primary social structure under examination, underscoring that his "is not a book about queer families, but about how family is queer": it focuses "on the normative family as a productive site of queerness." Mapping this approach onto a different social structure—here, the intellectual network or literary movement, rather than the family—allows us to analyze gender as a key point of negotiation for inclusion and exclusion in group identity and prestige. Pierce, *Argentine Intimacies*, 5–6.

6. Two of the three were economically independent (Clorinda Matto de Turner and María Eugenia Vaz Ferreira); none of them had children; Vaz Ferreira never married, while Matto de Turner spent most of her adult life as a widow, and Aurora Cáceres divorced Enrique Gómez Carrillo, separating from him less than a year after their marriage.
7. Cabello Hutt similarly defines illegibility, which "comes into play when the transgression against illegibility is seen, recognized as such, but cannot be named, understood, or allowed to exist. Illegibility generates frustration, anxiety, and occasionally violence at the possibility of ways of life that threaten the dominance of heteronormative and cis-male centered ways of reading and living." Cabello Hutt, "Undisciplined Objects," 33.
8. Medina Betancourt, 89, 93.
9. Although in 1907 the two had not yet met, Darío would later provide a brief "Pórtico" (Portico) for Agustini's 1913 volume, *Los cálices vacíos* (The empty chalices). There he writes that she is a "deliciosa musa" (delicious muse), situating her as inspiration for rather than creator of poetry. He also isolated her from a women's literary tradition by insisting that it was "la primera vez que en lengua castellana aparece un alma femenina en el orgullo de la verdad de su inocencia y de su amor, a no ser Santa Teresa en su exaltación divina" (the first time in the Castilian language that a feminine soul appears in the pride of the truth of her innocence and her love, with the exception of Saint Teresa in her divine exultation). Darío, "Pórtico," 223.
10. On media coverage of Agustini's death, see Rocca, *El crimen*.
11. Women continue to be severely underrepresented in the highest strata of the trans-Hispanic literary field. They comprise seven of 39 numbered academics of the Real Academia Española, or 18 percent ("Académicos de número"); six among 46 recipients of the Premio Miguel de Cervantes, or 13 percent ("Premiados—Premio Cervantes"); three awardees among twenty, or 15 percent, for the Premio Rómulo Gallegos ("Premio Rómulo Gallegos"); three of 20 recipients, or 15 percent, of the Premio de Poesía José Lezama Lima, organized by the Casa de las Américas ("Premio de Poesía José Lezama Lima"); and eight among 31 recipients, or 26 percent, of the Premio Reina Sofía de Poesía Iberoamericana ("Premio Reina Sofía").
12. With the phrase *trans-Hispanic*, I refer to the sum of Spanish-speaking historical subjects, especially throughout Spain and the parts of Latin America and the Caribbean that primarily communicate in Spanish, a region that showed new levels of interconnectedness in the period under examination. This transnational view allows us to analyze phenomena exceeding national borders, as is necessary in studies of Modernismo. Although language of the "global Hispanophone" also provides many of the same possibilities, here I favor *trans-Hispanic* for the sake of consistency. Mass media—as with modern newspapers like *La Nación* of Buenos Aires—contributed to the creation of a trans-Hispanic discourse on the region's relationship to modernity, particularly with the work of writers of chronicles and foreign correspondents, who published their interpretations of local or far-flung cities throughout the Spanish-speaking world. Many of these newspaper writers were associated with Modernismo. See Chapter 2 for more information on this topic.
13. See especially Jrade, *Delmira Agustini*; Escaja, *Salomé decapitada*; Castillo, "Delmira Agustini"; Bruña Bragado, *Delmira Agustini*; Guerrero, "El archivo uruguayo"; Molloy, *Poses*.
14. Molloy, "Female Textual Identities," 109.
15. These books had expanded, second editions: Barcelona in 1905 for *Los raros*, and 1901 in Paris in the case of *Prosas profanas*.

16. Darío, *Obras completas*, 115, vol. 1.
17. Darío, "Prólogo," 50.
18. Schmigalle, "Introducción," 38–40.
19. Darío, cited in Schmigalle, "Introducción," 31.
20. In *The Women in the Men's Club*, Catharina Vallejo insightfully addresses the challenge of situating women writers and their innovations during Modernismo. She focuses primarily on the Cuban women poets Nieves Xenes, Mercedes Matamoros, and Juana Borrero, and aims "to show that there were, indeed, women writing in modernismo from its beginnings" (3). Vallejo defines Modernismo as "a search for a new identity, a modernizing dynamic, beauty expressed in words, consciousness of other arts, rupture with the past and search for innovation. . . . It is clear that some women fulfilled the modernista conditions to the full" (153). Where my approach differs from Vallejo's is in exploring the question of intellectual networks and their mechanisms of exclusion; in attending to a distinct geographical range, from the River Plate, Mexico, and Peru, to Paris; and applying a methodology that draws heavily on journalism, ephemera, and their collections (such as visiting cards and scrapbooks). I also have a different understanding of what is at stake in the label of "Modernista," as Chapter 1 will explain.
21. Many scholars choose not to capitalize "Modernismo" in English, maintaining instead the Spanish version. I do use a capital "M" in English to communicate my understanding that, by 1895 or 1896 and perhaps earlier, the movement's core participants had a degree of group consciousness. For a recent discussion of "modernization" and "modernity" as a discourse or rhetoric in the trans-Hispanic literary field, see Skinner, *Gender*.
22. For more on Bourdieu's terminology and its applications, see Grenfell, ed, *Pierre Bourdieu*. On the parallel frameworks proposed by Latin Americanists, see especially Moraña, *Bourdieu*.
23. Other Latin American literature specialists delving deep into Bourdieu's methodology and relevant to this study include Sánchez Prado, *Pierre Bourdieu*; Reynolds, "Bourdieu's Imposition of Form"; and Mejías-López, *The Inverted Conquest*.
24. Maíz and Fernández-Bravo, *Episodios en la formación*, 19.
25. For more information on Emilia Pardo Bazán and her rejection by the RAE, see Peluffo, "Necrofeminismo y redes."
26. Recent work such as a volume edited by Pura Fernández, *No hay nación*, indicates increasing critical attention to this issue, and builds on the earlier work of scholars including Francesca Denegri, Ana Peluffo, Francine Masiello, Carolina Alzate and Darcie Doll, among others.
27. Maíz and Fernández-Bravo, *Episodios en la formación*, 31–32.

CHAPTER 1
1. de la Barra, "Prólogo," VI, XXIV, XVIII.
2. Martínez, *Amado Nervo*, 152. Martínez extensively analyzes this topic in relation to the work of Amado Nervo and Manuel Gutiérrez Nájera but extends his considerations to include Modernismo more broadly.
3. de la Barra, "Prólogo," III.
4. de la Barra, "Prólogo," IX.
5. Scholarship on Modernista journalism has burgeoned in recent decades. See especially González, *La crónica*; Rotker, *La invención*; Ramos, *Desencuentros*; Reynolds, *The Spanish American Crónica*.

6. This shift in Modernista uses of the feminine is analogous to what Rita Felski has described in Europe. She proposes that, "whereas in sentimental and early Romantic literature the male fascination with the feminine is associated with an expressive aesthetic, providing a vehicle for the cultivation and articulation of feeling, later manifestations of this motif emphasize very different qualities of parody, style, and artifice. Femininity is now appropriated by the male artist as emblematic of the modern, rather than as standing in opposition to it. This interpretive shift brings with it a reconceptualization of the feminine as epitomizing artifice rather than authenticity, simulation and illusion rather than the authentic voice of the heart. In this new guise, femininity is increasingly appropriated as a cipher for the very self-reflexivity and self-referentiality of poetic language itself." Felski, *The Gender of Modernity*, 94.
7. Martínez, *Amado Nervo*, 33.
8. Cardwell, "Romanticism, Modernismo," 487.
9. The perceived opposition between Modernismo and the Generation of '98 has been complicated and undermined by more recent scholars. In addition to Cardwell's work, see Salgado, "Rubén Darío y la Generación"; and Jrade, "Modernism on Both Sides" and "El modernismo y la Generación," which is particularly helpful. My interest here is the gendered language that has been used to describe these groups of writers.
10. Valera, "A D. Rubén Darío," 107.
11. On "La hija" see González, "Modernismo, Journalism." On the portrayal of women in *De sobremesa* see Molloy, "Voice Snatching"; and Krause, "Placer, violencia, espiritualidad."
12. Sternbach examines novels by Pedro César Dominici (Venezuela), Augusto D'Halmar (Chile), and Enrique Larreta (Argentina). Sternbach, "The Death." See also Peluffo, "Latin American Ophelias."
13. Gwen Kirkpatrick, *The Dissonant Legacy*, 7–8. I examine a similar proposal and extend it to consider reforms of the urban space of Buenos Aires in "Modern Form."
14. Escaja, *Salomé Decapitada*, 2.
15. Kanost, "Modernismo," 23.
16. Molloy, "Female Textual Identities," 109, emphasis original.
17. Darío, "Pórtico," 223. See Moody, "Radical Metrics" for more detail.
18. "La mujer sujeto, tan distinta de la mujer fetichizada del texto modernista, es una realidad cultural—piénsese en el incipiente feminismo de la época, en la creciente intervención social de la mujer, en la influencia del anarquismo—que amenaza el sistema de representación modernista (y en particular el de Darío)," (Woman as subject, so different from the woman fetishized in Modernista texts, is a cultural reality—consider the incipient feminism of the period, the growing social intervention of women, the influence of Anarchism—that threatens the Modernista system of representation [and in particular that of Darío]). Molloy, "Lecturas de descubrimiento," 21.
19. Molloy, "Female Textual Identities," 109.
20. Ward, "Introducción," xiii–xiv.
21. For more information on women writers of trans-Hispanic Romanticism, see especially Susan Kirkpatrick, *Las Románticas*. The growing differentiation of women's and men's social roles in this period has been noted by scholars. Lee Skinner wrote recently that "over the course of the [nineteenth] century, Latin American intellectuals were increasingly preoccupied with the question of gender roles and appropriate behaviors and beliefs for both men and women." Skinner, *Gender*, 18–19.
22. Martínez, *Amado Nervo*, 168–69.
23. Martínez, *Amado Nervo*, 213.

24. Valis, "The Female Figure," 372.
25. Mapes, *L' influence francaise*, 40. See also Salinas, *La poesía de Rubén Darío*; and Paz, "El caracol y la sirena," in *Cuadrivio*.
26. Darío, *Obras completas*, 750, vol 5.
27. On Darío's concept of the "reino interior," see Gwen Kirkpatrick, "Delmira Agustini"; and Morán, "Con Hugo fuerte."
28. Darío, *Obras completas*, 764, vol. 5.
29. Darío, *Obras completas*, 762, vol. 5.
30. Darío, *Obras completas*, 775, vol. 5.
31. Darío, *Obras completas*, 793, vol. 5.
32. Peluffo, "Latin American Ophelias."
33. Paz, *Cuadrivio*, 42.
34. Paz, *Cuadrivio*, 31, 39.
35. "Sin duda el movimiento más claramente homosocial de Hispanoamérica (aunque el reciente Boom no le va en zaga), la estrecha brotherhood del modernismo—para usar el término de los prerrafaelitas tan caro a Darío—se preocupa porque no se la confunda con sus malas compañías" (Without a doubt the most clearly homosocial movement in Spanish America (although the recent Boom is not far behind), the narrow *brotherhood* of Modernismo—to use the term of the prerafaelistas so dear to Darío—is concerned that it not be confused with their unsavory company). Molloy, "Lecturas de descubrimiento," 23.
36. Gutiérrez Nájera, *Poesías*, 2:20.
37. This middle-class, urban representation innovatively reflected Mexico City's reforms and new hierarchization of public space according to social class and gender. For more information, see Figueroa Obregón, "Espacio político."
38. Gutiérrez Nájera, *Poesías*, 2:23.
39. Gutiérrez Nájera, *Poesías*, 2:179.
40. Although Sigmund Freud would popularize the notion of the unconscious with *The Interpretation of Dreams* (1899) and later texts, the idea circulated throughout the nineteenth century and even earlier. For an example of an early treatment of the topic, see the 1890 text, James, *The Principles of Psychology*.
41. Gutiérrez Nájera, *Poesías*, 2:182.
42. The direct address to a female reader was frequent in the work of both Nájera and Amado Nervo, as Martínez has studied at length in the case of the latter especially. See José María Martínez, *Amado Nervo*.
43. El Duque Job, "Al pie," 2.
44. El Duque Job, "Al pie," 2.
45. El Duque Job, "Al pie," 1.
46. El Duque Job, "Al pie," 2. Nájera elsewhere refers to the imagination as the "loca de la casa." Gutiérrez Nájera, *Cuentos completos*, 295.
47. El Duque Job, "Al pie," 2. Ellipses original.
48. Darío, *Prosas profanas*, 85-86.
49. El Duque Job, "La vida," 178.
50. Berman writes that "to be modern is to find ourselves in an environment that promises us adventure, power, joy, growth, transformation of ourselves and the world—and, at the same time, that threatens to destroy everything we have, everything we know, everything we are." Berman, *All That Is Solid*, 15. On hysteria, see especially Showalter, *The Female Malady*; and Molloy, "Voice Snatching."

51. For example, in 1882 Martí wrote in "Prólogo al poema del Niágara": "La elaboración de un nuevo estado social hace insegura la batalla por la existencia personal y más recios de cumplir los deberes diarios que, no hallando vías anchas, cambian a cada instante de forma y vía, agitados del susto que produce la probabilidad o vecindad de la miseria. Partido así el espíritu en amores contradictorios e intranquilos; alarmado a cada instante el concepto literario por un evangelio nuevo; desprestigiadas y desnudas todas las imágenes que antes se reverenciaban; desconocidas aún las imágenes futuras, no parece posible, en este desconcierto de la mente, en esta revuelta vida sin vía fija, carácter definido, ni término seguro" (The elaboration of a new social state makes the battle for personal existence more insecure, and the daily obligations more intense to complete, which, not finding a broad path, change their form and direction at every instant, agitated by the fright that the probability or proximity of poverty produces. The spirit split in this way among contradictory or agitated loves; the literary concept always alarmed by a new gospel; disparaged and naked all the images that used to be revered; unknown still the future images; defined character and certain terms do not seem possible, in this bewilderment of the mind, in this mixed up life without a set path). Martí, *Ensayos y crónicas*, 63.
52. El Duque Job, "La vida," 178.
53. Darío, *Escritos dispersos*, 2:81.
54. El Duque Job, "La vida," 178, ellipses original.
55. El Duque Job, "La vida," 178.
56. El Duque Job, "La vida," 177.
57. El Duque Job, "La vida," 178–79.
58. El Duque Job, "La vida," 179.
59. Pineda Franco, *Geopolíticas*, 107–8.
60. Irwin, *Mexican Masculinities*, 100.
61. Sánchez Prado, "Nación y castración," 283. Molloy builds on her proposals considered earlier, arguing that "la mujer como vacío es gesto constante en Nervo. . . . La mujer es, ante todo, carencia de mujer y la condición para amarla está en relación directa con su ausencia, su alejamiento, su silencio o su muerte" (woman as a void is a constant gesture in Nervo. . . . Woman is, above all, the lack of woman and the condition for loving her is in direct relation with her absence, her distance, her silence, or her death). Molloy, "Sentimentalidad," 268.
62. Martínez, *Amado Nervo*, 214–15.
63. Martínez, *Amado Nervo*, 214–15, my emphasis.
64. Molloy, "Sentimentalidad," 268.
65. Conway, "Troubled," 475.
66. Conway, "Troubled," 462.
67. The column was in the daily *El Mundo*, one of the Rafael Reyes Spíndola newspapers of Mexico City. For more information on the significance of these modernizing periodicals, see Bunker, *Creating Mexican Consumer Culture*, 81–88.
68. Quirarte, "Presentación," 11.
69. Nervo, *Cartas*, 43.
70. Kurz, "La transformación," 34–35.
71. Martínez, "El público femenino del modernismo: Las lectoras," 393.
72. For more information on Nervo's "autofiguración histérica" (self-portrayal as hysterical), see Molloy, "Sentimentalidad," 265–66.
73. Márquez Acevedo, "Estudio preliminar," 17.
74. Nervo, *Cartas*, 78.

75. Nervo, *Obras completas*, 97–98, vol. 25.
76. Nervo, *Obras completas*, 98 vol. 25.
77. Nervo, *Obras completas*, 99, vol. 25.
78. Nervo, *Obras completas*, 169, vol. 25.
79. Nervo, *Obras completas*, 169, vol. 25.
80. Nervo, *Obras completas*, 170, vol. 25.
81. Nervo, *Obras completas*, 170, vol. 25, emphasis original.
82. Nervo, *Obras completas*, 171, vol. 25.
83. For Molloy, "es desde y a través de este femenino expropiado que Nervo postula otra comunidad, la apasionada, sentimental fraternidad entre hombres que marca tantas de sus páginas" (it is from and through this expropriated femininity that Nervo postulates another community, the impassioned, sentimental fraternity among men that marks so many of his pages). "Sentimentalidad," 272.

CHAPTER 2

1. Cáceres, *Mi vida*, 17.
2. Nervo, cited in Cáceres, *Mi vida*, 36.
3. García Calderón, "La frivolidad," XV.
4. García Calderón, "La frivolidad," XIX.
5. García Calderón, "La frivolidad," XXII.
6. García Calderón, "La frivolidad," XXII.
7. García Calderón, "La frivolidad," XVIII.
8. The prologue was reprinted in García Calderón, *Semblanzas*.
9. Blanco-Fombona, *Letras y letrados*, 91.
10. Blanco-Fombona, *Letras y letrados*, 92.
11. Ehrlicher analyzes a partial list, including *La Revista de América*, *Cosmópolis*, *Revista Azul*, and *Las Tres Américas*. See Ehrlicher, "Enrique Gómez Carrillo," 48–49.
12. Reynolds, "Difference as Fashion," 110.
13. For recent scholarship on Gómez Carrillo, see Siskind, *Cosmopolitan Desires* (especially chapter 5) and "The Spectacle"; Reynolds, "Difference as Fashion" and *The Spanish American Crónica* (especially chapters 3 and 4); Ehrlicher, "Enrique Gómez Carrillo"; LaGreca, *Erotic Mysticism* (especially chapter 5) and "Intertextual Sexual Politics"; Vilella, "Of Bayaderas"; and Outes-León, "La barbarie refinada."
14. Benjamin, "Paris." For more on the image and importance of Paris in the nineteenth century see also Hazan, *The Invention of Paris*; and Prendergast, *Paris*.
15. Schwartz, *Writing Paris*, 13.
16. Streckert, "Latin Americans," 182.
17. Colombi, *Viaje intelectual*, 185.
18. Colombi, *Viaje intelectual*, 186.
19. Streckert, "Latin Americans," 186–87.
20. Weiss, *The Lights*, 8.
21. Colombi, "Camino."
22. Darío's first chronicle in *La Nación*—"Desde Valparaíso. Llegada de la Argentina y del Almirante Barrozo. Recepción y festejos de Omeyko" (From Valparaíso. Arrival of the Argentina and of the Admiral Barrozo. Reception and Festivities of Omeyko)—appeared in February 15, 1889, before he moved to Buenos Aires in 1893. On Darío's time in Buenos Aires, see Chapter 3.
23. Siskind, *Cosmopolitan Desires*, 192.

24. Darío, *Autobiografía*, in *Obras completas*, 102, vol. 1.
25. Darío, *Obras completas*, 460, vol. 1. Other Modernistas also compared Paris to an illness. On the "imaginario epidémico" associated with the city, see Colombi, *Viaje intelectual*, 190–91.
26. Darío, *Obras completas*, 380, vol. 3.
27. Darío, *Obras completas*, 398, vol. 3.
28. See, for example, "Año Nuevo: 'Artículos de París,'" in Darío, *Crónicas desconocidas*, 195–206.
29. "La catástrofe del Metropolitano," in Darío, *Crónicas desconocidas*, 320.
30. "París y los escritores extranjeros," in Darío, *Obras completas*, 468, vol. 3.
31. Here Darío quotes Tulio M. Cestero. Darío, *Obras completas*, 467–68, vol. 3.
32. Ugarte, *Escritores iberoamericanos*, 25. Ugarte's clarity here surely relates to the fact that since his youth he had, according to Colombi, "rechazado la faz decadente y afrancesada del modernismo" (rejected the decadent and French-influenced surface of Modernismo). Colombi, *Viaje intelectual*, 177.
33. Colombi, "Camino," 546.
34. Darío, *Obras completas*, 1, 463.
35. A similar example can be found in "La exposición: los hispanoamericanos" (The Exposition: the Spanish-Americans). Darío writes, "La vida intelectual es difícil y áspera. Nuestros jóvenes de letras que sueñan con París deben saber que la vorágine es inmensa. Se nos conoce apenas. La literatura nueva de América ha llamado algo de atención en algunos círculos, como en el Mercure de France, pero como nadie sabe castellano, salvo rarísimas excepciones, se nos ignora de la manera más absoluta" (The intellectual life is difficult and harsh. Our literary youth who dream of Paris must know that the maelstrom is immense. We are barely known. New literature from America has gotten a bit of attention in a few circles, such as the Mercure de France, but because nobody knows Castilian, with very rare exceptions, we are ignored in most absolute way). Darío, *Escritos dispersos*, 2:69.
36. Colombi, *Viaje intelectual*, 190.
37. Darío, *Obras completas*, vol. 1, 464.
38. Darío, *Crónicas desconocidas*, 339.
39. Darío, *Crónicas desconocidas*, 350–51.
40. Darío, *Crónicas desconocidas*, 350–51.
41. Darío, *Crónicas desconocidas*, 353–54.
42. Ugarte's negative view of Paris, which he considers "[l]a ciudad de las lágrimas" (the city of tears), begins with his arrival there, contrasting with Darío's initial euphoria. Ugarte, *Paisajes parisienses*, 38. His memoir notes, "no pude sacudir . . . durante varias semanas la primera impresión de tristeza que puso en mí la capital monstruosa" (I could not shake . . . for several weeks the first impression of sadness that the monstrous capital made on me). Ugarte, *Escritores iberoamericanos*, 23. For a more thorough treatment of Ugarte's early writing about Paris, see Moody, "Women of Paris."
43. Darío, "Historia de un sobretodo," 35.
44. Darío, *Obras completas*, 465, vol. 1.
45. On the sometimes-contentious relationship between Darío and Gómez Carrillo, see Phillips, "Sobre Rubén Darío"; and López-Calvo, "Estrategias de poder."
46. Darío, "Snobs y bobos," 50.
47. Darío, "Snobs y bobos," 49.
48. Darío, "Snobs y bobos," 50.

49. For more detail on Darío's disappointment with Parisian knowledge of world literature and of Spanish-American letters, see Grigsby, "El Fracaso."
50. Darío, "Cabezas: Enrique" (Busts: Enrique). Darío tells an earlier version of the story in "Historia de un sobretodo" (Story of an Overcoat). Darío's portrayal of his own paternalism toward Carrillo may have reflected his own biases more than historical accuracy. Ehrlicher points out that in going to Paris, Gómez Carrillo "no hizo más que regresar a una tradición cultural todavía muy presente en el entorno familiar" (did nothing more than return to a cultural tradition that was still very present in his family home). Ehrlicher, "Enrique Gómez Carrillo," 46.
51. Colombi, *Viaje intelectual*, 189.
52. Siskind, *Cosmopolitan Desires*.
53. "Como el insecto que toma el color de la planta en que vive, así el espíritu del hombre. Gómez Carrillo es un parisiense." Cortón, in Gómez Carrillo, *El alma encantadora*, 21.
54. Darío, *Obras completas*, 464, vol. 1.
55. González, *La crónica*, 166.
56. Bastos, "La crónica," 87. Today, Gómez Carrillo's style can sound trite and has relegated his work to near oblivion. Bastos opens her article by affirming that today, "nadie lee las obras de Enrique Gómez Carrillo" (no one today reads the work of Enrique Gómez Carrillo). Bastos, "La crónica," 65.
57. Rodríguez Ortiz, "Presentación," 7.
58. Gómez Carrillo, *Treinta años*, 191.
59. Gómez Carrillo, *Treinta años*, 186.
60. Gómez Carrillo, *Vistas de Europa*, 7.
61. Gómez Carrillo, *Vistas de Europa*, 13. On Gómez Carrillo's travel writing, see Siskind, *Cosmopolitan Desires*, 223–60.
62. For example, Ugarte argues that the fast pace of Parisian life ensures superficial prose, because no writer can dedicate himself at length to any one topic. "¿Cómo encadenar su atención a un asunto, cuando en el hervor de las conversaciones saltan mil ecos y noticias de última hora? . . . Por eso es París la ciudad más difícil para el cronista extranjero" (How can we chain our attention to just one topic, when thousands of echoes and last-minute updates jump into the boil of conversations?). Ugarte, *Crónicas del bulevar*, 58.
63. Ugarte, *Crónicas del bulevar*, 62.
64. Colombi, "Peregrinaciones," 8.
65. Molloy, *La diffusion*, 28.
66. Gómez Carrillo, "El bulevar."
67. For more information on the development of a beauty industry and culture in France throughout the nineteenth and early twentieth centuries, see Grout, *The Force of Beauty*. On the shifts in the representation of women's social roles in Spanish America in this period, see Masiello, *Between Civilization*; and LaGreca, *Rewriting Womanhood*.
68. Gómez Carrillo, "El bulevar."
69. Bornay, *Las hijas*, 89.
70. Dijkstra, *Idols of Perversity*.
71. Highlights in this deep scholarly field include Molloy, "Too Wilde for Comfort," "Sentimentalidad," and "Voice Snatching"; Masiello, *Between Civilization*; and Jrade, *Delmira Agustini*.
72. *Psicología* was first published as a stand-alone book, then included in *El libro de las mujeres* (1909), which I cite here, and later reprinted in *Obras completas*, vol. XII (1920). I treat Cáceres in greater depth in Chapter 5.

73. Díaz-Marcos, "El arte," 89.
74. Gómez Carrillo, *El libro*, 261.
75. Susan Kirkpatrick, *Mujer, modernismo*, 191.
76. Gómez Carrillo, *El libro*, 212.
77. Gómez Carrillo, *El libro*, 239.
78. Gómez Carrillo, 2 *El libro*, 41. For Díaz-Marcos, in this piece "la mujer moderna cuya actitud vital—exteriorizada a través de un estilo deportivo, falda más corta y pelo a lo *garçon*—se percibe como un delito contra la estética y contra las expectativas de género" (modern woman whose attitude toward life—exteriorized through a sporty style, a shorter skirt, and a boyish haircut—is perceived as an infraction against aesthetics and against gender expectations). Díaz-Marcos, "El arte," 95.
79. Paul Adam, quoted in Gómez Carrillo, *El libro*, 224.
80. Reynolds, "Difference as Fashion," 114.
81. Gómez Carrillo, *El libro*, 290.
82. Ugarte, *Crónicas del bulevar*, 59.
83. Ugarte, *Crónicas del bulevar*, 63.
84. Jacovkis, "El desafío," 5.
85. Hajjaj, "Crónica y viaje," 32.
86. Gómez Carrillo, *El encanto*, 24.
87. For more information on Buenos Aires's remodeling and the influence of Parisian style, see Adrián Gorelik, *La grilla* and Moody, "Poetic Form."
88. Gómez Carrillo, *El encanto*, 27.
89. Gómez Carrillo, *El encanto*, 47.
90. "Buenos Aires . . . ha ido á inspirarse á Francia, y de Francia, país de medida, de armonía, de elegancia sobria, ha traído estas líneas puras que dan á la avenida de Mayo su gracia severa de gran bulevar parisiense" (Buenos Aires . . . has sought inspiration in France, and from France, country of measure, of harmony, of sober elegance, it has brought these pure lines that give the May Avenue its severe grace of a great Parisian boulevard). Gómez Carrillo, *El encanto*, 29.
91. Gómez Carrillo, *El encanto*, 53.
92. They have "una fealdad urbana innegable é insuperable" (an undeniable and insuperable ugliness). Gómez Carrillo, *El encanto*, 39.
93. Gómez Carrillo, *El encanto*, 47.
94. Gómez Carrillo, *El encanto*, 38.
95. "[L]a palma de la monotonía urbana debían llevársela nuestros lejanos abuelos los conquistadores al inventar é imponer en todo el nuevo mundo la teoría siniestra del damero con sus cuadros paralelos. ¡Ah, las manzanas, las odiosas manzanas de las Américas!" (The prize for urban monotony should go to our distant grandfathers the conquistadors, for inventing and imposing in all the New World the sinister theory of the grid with its parallel blocks. Ah, the blocks, the hateful blocks of the Americas!). Gómez Carrillo, *El encanto*, 39.
96. Gómez Carrillo, *El encanto*, 50–51.
97. Gómez Carrillo, *El encanto*, 203.
98. Gómez Carrillo, *El encanto*, 208.
99. Gómez Carrillo, *El encanto*, 205–6.
100. Gómez Carrillo, *El encanto*, 207.
101. Martí studied a cultural incompatibility and opposition between the United States and "Latin" culture, for example in "Nuestra América" (Our America), "La verdad sobre los

Estados Unidos" (The Truth about the United States), "Coney Island," "El Puente de Brooklyn" (The Brooklyn Bridge), etc. Rodó's work opposed "Arielist," Latin culture (of French, Italian, or Roman tradition) to "Calibanesque" culture of North America in *Ariel*.
102. For Ehrlicher, "en los años inmediatamente después de la Primera Guerra Mundial, la obra modernista de ambos gozaba de un reconocimiento público semejante" (in the years immediately after World War One, the Modernista work by both of them enjoyed similar public recognition). Ehrlicher, "Enrique Gómez Carrillo," 44.
103. Bastos, "La crónica," 66.

CHAPTER 3

1. Matto de Turner, "Las obreras," 7.
2. Matto de Turner, "Las obreras," 7.
3. Matto de Turner, "Las obreras," 13.
4. Matto de Turner included this essay in her 1902 book, *Boreales*, 246–66. The Red Interdisciplinaria de Estudios Latinoamericanos-RIEL Peru XIX de la Pontificia Universidad Católica del Perú digitally hosts some numbers of *Búcaro*, including the first: http://red.pucp.edu.pe/riel/clave-biblioteca/bucaro-americano/. For a more detailed analysis of Matto de Turner's rhetorical strategies in this speech and in the magazine more broadly, see Moody, "Latin American Women."
5. Fundamental scholarly work on Matto's career in Peru include Peluffo, *Lágrimas andinas*; and Denegri, *El abanico*.
6. See Argentina's 1895 census: Argentina and Fuente, *Segundo censo*, cuadro V.
7. Matto and other Peruvian women were also known in the Buenos Aires periodical press prior to her arrival. See Vicens, "Lectoras de patria grande."
8. Matto states the new magazine's two aims thusly: "*Búcaro Americano*, como su nombre lo deja comprender, recogerá toda la flora literaria exuberante hoy en América, para ofrecerla á los lectores. Pero, no es la literatura el único objetivo; hay algo más trascendental en el fondo de nuestros ideales: la educación de la mujer en el rol que le depara el movimiento del progreso universal para que pueda cumplir satisfactoriamente los deberes que esa misma corriente evolutiva le señala, no solo como á madre y esposa, cargos fáciles de desempeñar porque el corazón los dirige, [sino también] la mujer como suegra, como madrastra, como nuera, como cuñada, como amiga, tiene delate escollos difíciles de salvar si no es el cerebro ilustrado y la voluntad educada los que vienen á tomar parte directa en su modo de ser" (*Búcaro Americano*, as its name communicates, will gather all the exuberant literary flora today in America, to offer it to readers. But, literature is not the only objective; there is something more transcendental behind our ideals: the education of woman in the role given to her by the movement of universal progress, so that she can satisfactorily carry out her obligations indicated by that same evolutionary current, not only as a mother and wife—responsibilities easy to carry out because the heart directs them—[but also,] woman as a mother-in-law, as step-mother, as daughter-in-law, as sister-in-law, and as friend, faces hurdles difficult to overcome, if what contributes directly to her way of being is not her learned brain and her educated will). Matto de Turner, "Bautismo," 3.
9. Matto's letters to Ricardo Palma indicate that she started work in the Escuela Normal de Profesoras about four months after launching *Búcaro*, and in the Escuela Comercial de Mujeres some months later. See Matto de Turner, *Su afectísima discípula*, 129–30. These positions were possible in part thanks to her earlier work in the field of pedagogical theory, such as her 1884 manual for women's education, *Elementos de literatura*; see

Briggs, *The Moral Electricity*, 114–17. Matto's financial recovery is apparent in her ability to bequeath funds at the time of her death to her family and to a hospital in Lima; see Denegri, *El abanico*, 167–68.

10. Darío arrives during a state of martial law that lasted from July 28 to August 25, a politically turbulent context that merits further study. The alarm was enough to partially halt Ateneo activity during 1893. See Giusti, *Momentos*, 72–73. On the technical modernization of *La Nación*, see Mogillansky, "Modernización literaria."
11. Darío, *Obras completas*, 123, vol. 1. Darío recounts in his autobiography, for example, that in the restaurant "Las 14 Provincias" (The 14 Provinces) he dictated an improvised "poemita" (little poem), which a friend wrote "a falta de papel, en unos cuantos sobres" (on a few envelopes, because we had no paper). Darío, 113, vol. 1. "Pasaba, pues, mi vida bonaerense escribiendo artículos para *La Nación*, y versos que fueron más tarde mis *Prosas profanas*, y buscando por la noche el peligroso encanto de los paraísos artificiales" (So I spent my Buenos Aires life writing articles for *La Nación*, and verses that were later my *Profane Proses*, and looking through the night for the dangerous charm of artificial paradises). Darío, *Obras completas*, 116, vol. 1.
12. Darío, *Obras completas*, 129, vol. 1. These magazines include the *Revista de América* (Magazine of America, 1894), which Darío founded with Bolivian Ricardo Jaimes Freyre; *La Biblioteca* (The Library, 1896–1898), founded by Franco-Argentine Paul Groussac; and *El Mercurio de América* (The Mercury of America, 1898–1900), founded by Argentine Eugenio Díaz Romero, after Darío had left Buenos Aires. For more information, see Pineda Franco, *Geopolíticas*; Carter, *La Revista*; Fernández Moreno, "Las revistas literarias."
13. Payró, *Evocaciones*, 63–4.
14. Giusti, *Momentos*, 59–60.
15. Giusti, *Momentos*, 74.
16. Giusti, *Momentos*, 74. In February of 1893, the Ateneo announced an art exposition that opened on May 15, the first of five that would eventually lead to the founding of the Museo de Bellas Artes (Fine Arts Museum) in the location at Florida and Córdoba. Giusti, *Momentos*, 70. Prior to this location, the Ateneo was also housed briefly at the Nuevo Banco Italiano (New Italian Bank) on the Plaza de Mayo, at Rivadavia and Reconquista.
17. For more information on the renovation of Buenos Aires and its significance for cultural production in the period, see Gorelik, *La grilla*; and Moody, "Poetic Form." On Matto's own experience of the federalized city of immigrants and modernization projects, as well as her teaching and participation in the community of Peruvian exiles, see Moody, "Clorinda Matto de Turner en la Cosmópolis;" and Moody, "Clorinda's Cosmopolis."
18. Malosetti Costa, *Los primeros modernos*, 351.
19. On the professionalization of the literary field in this period, see Rama, *Rubén Darío*; and Ramos, *Desencuentros*.
20. For more information on the Ateneo's history, see Giusti, *Momentos* (especially 53–89); Laera, "El Ateneo"; and Malosetti Costa, *Los primeros modernos* (especially Chapter 9).
21. For example, Darío describes his adventures in the city with Ricardo Jaimes Freyre and his father, Julio Lucas Jaimes (who used the pseudonym Brocha Gorda), without mentioning his friend's mother, Carolina Freyre, who was herself an accomplished novelist and journalist. Darío, *Obras completas*, 126, vol. 1. For Darío, who would later comment of women writers that "todas con ciertas raras excepciones, han sido y son feas" (all, with certain rare exceptions, have been and are ugly), a friendship with a woman

journalist from Peru is unthinkable, due to an incompatibility of interests and temperament. Darío, "Aurora," 72.
22. Auza, *Periodismo y feminismo*, 95.
23. Similarly, at the Ateneo's first meeting "concurrió tout Buenos Aires" (all Buenos Aires attended); Giusti names many male spectators, but no women. Giusti, *Momentos*, 54, 64. The Ateneo hosted many non-literary events as well, particularly in music and painting, and here women's exclusion was not as complete. The pianist Fanny de Martinoli performed, and many women painters participated in the first Salón de Pintura del Ateneo (Ateneo Painting Salon, 1893), including Sofía Posadas and Eugenia Belín Sarmiento. Giusti, *Momentos*, 66–72. See also Malosetti Costa, *Los primeros modernos*.
24. The main exception was a speech by another exiled Peruvian, Margarita Práxedes Muñoz. Vicens explains that *Búcaro* "no menciona ninguna otra conferencia ofrecida por una escritora en este ámbito y apenas hemos encontrado referencias en esta línea en la prensa de la época" (mentions no other conference offered by a woman writer in this environment, and we have barely found these sorts of references in the press of the period). Vicens, "Clorinda Matto de Turner," 53.
25. 25 May 1896. Matto de Turner, *Su afectísima discípula*, 132.
26. 17 July 1897. Matto de Turner, *Su afectísima discípula*, 136.
27. Matto de Turner, "Carlos," 460.
28. Matto de Turner, "Carlos," 460.
29. Matto de Turner, "Nuestras miniaturas: Carlos."
30. The "Nuestras miniaturas" section profiles *letrados* from both Athenian currents, among them Estanislao Zeballos, Martiniano Leguizamón, Norberto Piñeiro, Ernesto Quesada, Ricardo Jaimes Freyre, and Carlos Baires. Matto also includes many Peruvians and Uruguayans, in addition to a variety of Mexicans, Venezuelans, Chileans, etc. Profiles of women are frequent, including Laura Méndez de Cuenca, the Uruguayan sisters Dorila and Adela Castell, and the United States Normalist Sara Eccleston, among others. Many such notes, including the one on Guido y Spano, are reprinted in the "Miniaturas" section of Matto de Turner, *Boreales*. For information on the visual portraits, see Ariza and Gluzman, "Mujeres virtuosas."
31. Matto de Turner, "Carlos," 460.
32. Migoya García quoted in Matto de Turner, "Carlos," 460.
33. The phrase appears in a commentary on a novel by Eugenio de Castro, who had been the subject of an Ateneo address by "el Príncipe Azul." Matto adds a rare footnote to clarify that she refers to Rubén Darío. Matto de Turner, "Bibliografía," 314.
34. 9 June 1895. Matto de Turner, *Su afectísima discípula*, 121. In her memoir of Chile, Matto prints a negative opinion of Romanticism and an indictment of Modernismo and Darío's imitators, in the form of a quotation by an unnamed friend: the former are "imitaciones europeas que han dado tan ruines becquerianas aun que [sic] no tan malas como las rubendariacas que propinan los neófitos de la escuela" (European imitations that have produced such terrible copies of Bécquer, although not as bad as the awful Rubén Darío imitations that the neophites inflict upon us). Matto de Turner, *Boreales*, 80.
35. Matto de Turner, "La mujer en el Ateneo," 77.
36. Matto argued many times that the Americas were the space of literary and cultural modernity. See Miseres, *Mujeres en tránsito*, 187–98. On the international outcry by women in response to Pardo Bazán's rejection by the Academy, see Peluffo, "Necrofeminismo."
37. Matto de Turner, "La mujer en el Ateneo," 74.

38. Vicens, "La fantasía porteña," 87. This article examines the self-reinvention and disappointments of Matto de Turner, Mercedes Cabello de Carbonera, and Carolina Freyre de Jaimes in Buenos Aires between 1880 and 1910.
39. Peluffo, "Comunidades de sentimiento," 474.
40. Matto de Turner, cited in del Monte, "Social," February 1, 1896, 17–22.
41. Frederick, "In Their Own Voice," 284, 287.
42. Del Monte, "Social," February 1, 1896, 18. It appears that Larrosa's husband had syphilis, which likely infected her as well. Matto writes that he was "víctima del mal que arrastró al sepulcro la gloriosa existencia de Guy de Maupassant" (victim of the disease that dragged the glorious existence of Guy de Maupassant to the grave). Matto de Turner, quoted in del Monte, "Social," February 1, 1896, 18.
43. See the first number of *El Álbum de Señoritas*, 1854, 2. See also Coromina, "El Álbum," 181.
44. Matto de Turner, quoted in del Monte, "Social," February 1, 1896, 18. In a later speech at the same event, María Emilia Passicot explains that the Society's mission is "protejer la inteligencia [y] alentar los talentos femeninos especialmente" (to protect women's intelligence [and] especially to encourage their talents). María Emilia Passicot, quoted in del Monte, "Social," February 15, 1896, 46. Passicot also provides more information in a future article; see Passicot, "Sociedad Proteccionista Intelectual," February 15, 1897; Passicot, "Sociedad Proteccionista Intelectual," March 15, 1897.
45. Matto de Turner, quoted in del Monte, "Social," February 1, 1896, 19.
46. Matto de Turner, quoted in del Monte, "Social," February 1, 1896, 18.
47. Vicens, "Clorinda Matto de Turner," 50, emphasis original.
48. Matto de Turner, quoted in del Monte, "Social," February 1, 1896, 18.
49. Del Monte, "Social," February 15, 1896, 45.
50. Peluffo, "Comunidades de sentimiento," 473. Peluffo proposes the phrase "comunidades de sentimiento" (communities of sentiment) as a more period-appropriate version of "emotional communities," which she draws from the work of Rosenwein, *Emotional Communities*.
51. Often while traveling, a writer would describe meeting a colleague and new friend as a thrilling moment of mutual understanding that provided an opportunity to discuss their professional accomplishments in the terms of friendship and even sisterhood. These texts portray intimate scenes of identification and sisterly affection between two women. They bear some similarity to the performative eulogy we have examined by Matto de Turner, in that a rhetoric of sentiment and affirmation of a woman's qualities are publicized. Vicens, "Por una tradición," 373.
52. My proposal in this chapter, alongside those of Peluffo and Vicens, focuses on the turn of the twentieth century, but an interesting point of comparison is found in Vicky Unruh's study of the 1920s and 30s in Latin America. Unruh asks, "where did women who wanted to be writers rather than muses build their intellectual homes? In a cultural arena that still regarded their presence as uncommon or even forbidding, how did they fashion their writing personas, and what did they understand their artistic missions to be? For the women in this book, one answer lies in the striking fact that their access to the artistic world derived in part from public performance: theatre, poetry declamation, song, dance, oration, witty display, or bold journalistic self-portraiture." Unruh, *Performing Women*, 2.
53. On Gorriti's veladas, see Gorriti, *Veladas literarias*; Denegri, *El abanico* (especially chapter 4); and Peluffo, "Comunidades de sentimiento." On Matto's *veladas*, see Sotomayor Martínez, *Pensar en público*.
54. Denegri, *El abanico*, book subtitle.

55. Tauzin Castellanos, "La narrativa femenina," 167. On the veladas' variety of activities, see Batticuore, *El taller*, 20.
56. Schneider, "Prólogo," 10.
57. Del Águila, "Afiliaciones femeninas," 49. Del Águila employs Edward Said's theory of affiliation in her analysis, proposing "el excesivo abuso del tema de la familia como mecanismo compensador para su realidad personal de parias y de su disfuncionalidad individual.... [Son] relaciones que permiten a estas mujeres escapar de un lugar inferior—social y familiar—asignado por el esquema vertical del sistema patriarcal imperante" (the excessive use of the family theme as a compensatory mechanism for their personal reality as outcasts and their individual dysfunction. These relationships allow these women to escape from an inferior place in social and family terms, assigned by the vertical scheme of the prevailing patriarchal system). Del Águila, "Afiliaciones femeninas," 46.
58. Peluffo, "Comunidades de sentimiento," 476.
59. Bronfen, *Over Her Dead Body*, xi. Peluffo reads Latin American literature alongside Bronfen's book, analyzing several Modernistas in depth (Casal, Darío, Gutiérrez Nájera, Martí, Nervo, Silva). Peluffo, "Latin American Ophelias."
60. Bronfen, *Over Her Dead Body*, xii.
61. Secret, *The Politics and Pedagogy*, 104.
62. For a foundational study of women's writing in nineteenth-century Argentina that sheds light on this dynamic, see Masiello, *Between Civilization*.
63. Matto de Turner, "Bautismo," 2.
64. Matto de Turner, "Bautismo," 2.
65. The article suggests that these "godmothers"—Argentine María Colman de Blanco, Peruvian Julia Moreno de Moreno, and Uruguayan Margarita V. de Cometti—hosted Matto in their homes when she first arrived in Buenos Aires. La Dirección, "Nuestras madrinas," 77-9.
66. For more analysis of this article, see Moody, "Latin American Women."
67. Del Monte, "Social," February 1, 1896, 22.
68. On this community of Peruvian writers exiled in Buenos Aires, see de Lucía, "Positivismo y exilio"; Vicens, "La fantasía porteña"; and Miseres, "Transiciones."
69. For example, #9, 179-80.
70. Eight (15 January 1897), nine (15 February 1897), ten (15 March 1897), and eleven (15 April 1897). Additional texts by Cáceres in *Búcaro* include Angelina, "Ley social" (Social Law) February 15, 1899; Angelina, "Ley social," April 15, 1899; Angelina, "Ley social," September 15, 1899.
71. ZAC, "Al paso del tren," February 15, 1897, 175.
72. ZAC, "Al paso del tren," March 15, 1897, 190.
73. Peluffo's analysis of "sororophobic" episodes—largely limited to the intimacy of correspondence rather than public events—examines negative sentiment among women writers, including envy, jealousy, rivalry, and conflict. Two famous examples involve debates between Juana Manuela Gorriti and Teresa González de Fanning, and between Matto de Turner and Mercedes Cabello de Carbonera, in which disputes over differing political or aesthetic programs were carried out somewhat publicly. See Peluffo, "Comunidades de sentimiento"; and chapter 7 of Peluffo, *Lágrimas andinas*.
74. Pachas Maceda, *Zoila Aurora Cáceres*, 48. Cáceres was appointed president for life. Following her absence during a trip to Europe, señorita Zuzunaga, the acting president, refused to cede the position. A dispute ensued, until Cáceres abandoned the endeavor and founded a new organization, Feminismo Peruano Zoila Aurora Cáceres, in 1930. Pachas Maceda, 47-48.

75. A program from the 1924 event is held at the National Library of Peru in Lima, in a folder catalogued as "Papeles de la Sociedad Femenina Peruana, Lima, oct 1938 (1925–1938)," E 1975, 20000970.

76. Author unknown, untitled, unpaginated. See Cáceres, *Álbum personal*. Given Cáceres's habit of saving her own work in the album, she is likely the author of the article.

77. Matto de Turner, "Nuestras miniaturas: Doctor," 684.

78. Matto de Turner "no comenta en sus bibliografías ninguna de las grandes obras darianas o de los otros modernistas significativos" (does not comment in her bibliographies on any of the great works by Darío or other significant Modernistas). Zanetti, "Búcaro Americano," 272.

79. My emphasis. Zanetti, "Búcaro Americano," 272.

80. To these projects shared by Matto and the Modernistas, Vicens adds "la crítica al avance del lujo y el mercantilismo" (the critique of the advance of luxury and mercantilism). Vicens, "Clorinda Matto de Turner," 48.

81. On the aesthetic importance of women and ornamentation in *Prosas profanas*, see Chapter 1; and Moody, "Poetic Form." For a discussion of frivolity as a productive concept in Modernismo, especially for Enrique Gómez Carrillo, see Bastos, "La crónica modernista."

82. Zanetti, "Búcaro Americano," 267.

83. Matto de Turner, "Nuestras miniaturas: Laura," 575.

84. My emphasis. Martínez, Elia M., "Las mujeres frívolas," 137.

85. Matto de Turner, "La mujer moderna," 726.

86. Josefina, "De todas partes," 475.

87. Matto de Turner, "La mujer trabajadora," 478.

88. Matto de Turner, "La mujer trabajadora," 478.

89. Matto de Turner, "La mujer trabajadora," 479.

90. Miseres, *Mujeres en tránsito*, 175.

91. Miseres, *Mujeres en tránsito*, 175.

92. "El verdadero objeto de su análisis [de París] será el comportamiento de la mujer parisina.... Matto concibe que la educación del mundo europeo es algo digno de ser imitado, siempre que esto esté acompañado por los valores primarios de la familia y el ejercicio de la maternidad como centro del hogar. De lo contrario, aquella mujer educada que se deja arrastrar completamente por los códigos modernos, queda reducida a una 'hembra,' es decir, a un sujeto animalizado" (The true object of her analysis [of Paris] will be the Parisian woman's behavior.... Matto conceives that the education of the European world is somewhat worthy of immitation, as long as it is accompanied by the primary values of the family and the exercise of motherhood as the center of the home. Otherwise, that educated woman who allows herself to be completed absorbed by modern codes, ends up reduced to a 'female,' that is, an animalized subject). Miseres, *Mujeres en tránsito*, 200.

93. See Miseres, *Mujeres en tránsito*, 190–93.

94. Matto de Turner, "Despedida," 1006.

95. Curiously, Matto is the only woman with a byline in the issue, although initials mask authorship in some cases; this does not necessarily indicate abandonment of women writers, as the previous issue includes several.

96. Both muses are passive and persistently frustrated with their surroundings: in "Pálida como un lirio," Emma is a beautiful actress, but "bajo el vermellón está la palidez melancólica" (beneath the rouge is the melancholy pallor). Like the princess of "Sonatina," Emma is more complex than meets the eye, functioning as a sign of feminine mystery to the poet who appears in the closing of both texts. In "Pálida" Darío comments that

"La desesperación está en el fondo de esa delicada y dulce calma, ¡Pobrecita! ¿En qué sueña? No lo podría yo decir" (Desperation is in the depths of that delicate and sweet calm, poor thing! What is she dreaming about? I couldn't say). In the end, both these texts reveal their true focus on the writer who conjures her: "Te irás muy lejos, pasarás como una vision rápida, y no sabrás nunca que has tenido cerca un soñador que ha pensado en ti y ha escrito una página á tu memoria, quizá enamorado de esa palidez de cera, de esa melancolía, de ese encanto de tu rostro enfermo" (You will go very far, you will pass like a rapid vision, and you will never know that you have had nearby a dreamer who has thought of you and written a page in your memory, maybe in love with that waxy pallor, with that melancholy, with that charm of your ill countenance). Darío, "Pálida como un lirio," 1007.

97. For Miseres, exile explains how Matto fell off the map of literary history at the end of her life. "El trascender fronteras parece dejarla fuera de lugar dentro del universo literario hispanoamericano: al abandonar el Perú, su obra ya no es considerada 'peruana' y su paso por la Argentina, a pesar de haber ingresado sin mayores objeciones a *la ciudad letrada*, tampoco le garantiza la entrada al canon nacional de este país.... escapa a cualquier lectura 'fundacional' de la literatura" (Going beyond borders seems to leave her out of place in the Spanish American literary universe: upon leaving Peru, her work is no longer considered "Peruvian," and her travel through Argentina, in spite of entering without great objections into the *lettered city*, also does not guarantee her entry into the national cannon of this country.... She escapes all "foundational" readings of literature). Miseres, *Mujeres en tránsito*, 172.

CHAPTER 4

1. Rama, *Cien años de raros*.
2. Molloy, "Dos lecturas," 57.
3. Litvan and Uriarte, "Prefacio," 11.
4. Molloy, "Too Wilde for Comfort," 199.
5. The title of the Consistorio del Gay Saber refers to Nietzsche's 1882 book *The Gay Science*, which itself refers to poetry and poetics. It was translated into Spanish as *El Alegre Saber* or *La Gaya Ciencia*. For Leonardo Garet the Montevideo club "no es Nietzsche más que en la superficie" (is not Nietzschian beyond the surface). Garet, *El Consistorio*, 13.
6. Blixen, *El desván*, 16. For further information on shifting gender roles in Uruguay around the turn of the twentieth century, see Barrán, *Intimidad, divorcio* and *Historia de la sensibilidad*.
7. For more information on girls' education in the Southern Cone, see Lavrín, *Women, Feminism* (especially chapter 3); Carlson, *¡Feminismo!* (especially chapter 3); and Masiello, *Between Civilization* (especially chapter 2).
8. Rodríguez Monegal, "La generación," sec. III.
9. Fornaro Bordolli, "María Eugenia," 33.
10. Vaz Ferreira, "F. 9r.," 2. The letter is likely from 1902–1904, as it mentions a book Nin Frías is preparing. He wrote about Vaz Ferreira's planned but unpublished first book, *Fuego y mármol* (Fire and Marble). Titled "Ensayo sobre las poesías de María Eugenia Vaz-Ferreira" (Essay on the poems of María Eugenia Vaz-Ferreira), this text appears to be published twice: as an article in *Vida Moderna* in 1903, and as a book chapter, "María Eugenia Vaz Ferreira: Presentación" (María Eugenia Vaz Ferreira: Introduction). Nin Frías, *Nuevos ensayos*.
11. Montero Bustamante, *El parnaso*, 308.

12. Moreira, *Aproximación*, 30–33.
13. Achugar, "Me muestro siempre," 7–8.
14. Crispo Acosta, *Motivos de crítica*, 186.
15. Agustini, quoted in Rosenbaum, *Modern Women Poets*, 50. Agustini began writing this column in *La Alborada*, titled "Legión etérea" (Ethereal Legion) in August of 1903, signing "Joujou." Pleitez Vela notes that "en esa columna se ocupó de hacer retratos de las muchachas montevideanas que sobresalían en lo cultural y lo social, y se trata de siluetas excesivamente ornamentales del más puro gusto modernista" (in that column she sketched portraits of the young ladies of Montevideo that stood out in the cultural or social world, and they were excessively ornamental silhouettes, of the purest Modernista taste). Pleitez Vela, "Debajo estoy yo," 147.
16. "Enmascaró su delicada sensibilidad tras una postura irónica, una frivolidad exterior que se convirtió en su mejor coraza" (she masked her delicate sensibility behind an ironic posture, an exterior frivolity that became her best shield). Pleitez Vela, "Debajo estoy yo," 55.
17. Blixen, *El desván*, 45.
18. If *una poetisa* was conceptually dangerous, *una poeta* was impossible. Here grammar reminds us of changing social acceptance over time. Today the latter phrasing is preferred, because it better avoids the saccharine or infantile overtones of the more traditional *poetisa*.
19. This fetishizing of strangeness dominated scholarly treatment of Agustini, whose legacy has largely been shaped by the sensationalistic newspaper accounts of her death in 1914, although her work has received important new attention since the 1990s. At the age of twenty-seven Agustini was shot and killed by her lover and ex-husband, Enrique Job Reyes. The local press treated the incident in depth, including gory pictures of the crime scene and the victim's lifeless body, and sparked a debate over the relative legitimacy of Agustini's and Reyes's actions. See Rocca, *El crimen*.
20. Vaz Ferreira, "F. 21r.," 2.
21. Blixen, *El desván*, 7.
22. For a fresh and well-researched reading of Mistral's methods when fashioning herself as a renowned transnational figure despite her exclusion, see Cabello Hutt, *Artesana de sí misma*.
23. Pleitez Vela, "Debajo estoy yo," 60.
24. Lockhart and Costa, *Vida y obra*, 19.
25. Lockhart and Costa, *Vida y obra*, 18.
26. Crispo Acosta, *Motivos de crítica*, 185. The verse from Darío's poem to which I refer is a sort of refrain, repeated with slight variations: "Con sus ojos lindos y su boca roja, / la divina Eulalia ríe, ríe, ríe" (With her pretty eyes and ruby mouth, / the divine Eulalia laughs, laughs, laughs). Darío, *Obras completas*, vol. 5, 765.
27. Moreira, *Aproximación*, 33–34.
28. When Vaz Ferreira moved out of the family home is unknown, but financial independence would have been unlikely before she began working in 1912. Her correspondence and archive include references to addresses at Calle Yí and Calle Treinta y Tres 1290. Echevarría, "Guía cronológica," 24. These are both more centrally located than her family home and that of her brother Carlos, with Calle Treinta y Tres situated about three blocks from the Teatro Solís and two blocks from the Rambla in Montevideo's Ciudad Vieja. A letter dated "192 . . ." (or in the 1920s) cites Cerrito 210 as her address, at the corner with Francisco Maciel, again in the Ciudad Vieja. Vaz Ferreira to Bertrani, "F. 1r.," 1.

29. Echevarría, "Guía cronológica," 23. Vaz Ferreira's father moved to Brazil for business in 1884, and she never saw him again. He died in 1894.
30. Vaz Ferreira, *Poesías completas*, 157.
31. Vaz Ferreira, *Poesías completas*, 157.
32. See Chapter 4, note 11.
33. Vaz Ferreira, "F. 12r.," 1.
34. Vaz Ferreira, "F. 12r.," 1.
35. See Echevarría, "Guía cronológica," 24; and Pleitez Vela, "Debajo estoy yo," 75.
36. The poet mentions hyperacusis in a letter to Nin Frías, a lexical choice that suggests she had received a medical diagnosis. In exchange for his essay about her, she jokingly offers her friend a gift of pretty fish, with "sutil silencio, la deliciosa consolación de los pescados" (subtle silence, the delicious consolation of fish"). Vaz Ferreira, "F. 21r.," 2.
37. Fornaro Bordolli, "María Eugenia," 46.
38. Biographers including Pleitez Vela and Achugar indicate that her mental health deteriorated notably starting in 1922.
39. A nephrologist noted her cause of death as septicemia. Echevarría, "Guía cronológica," 24.
40. Verani, in editorial notes to Vaz Ferreira, *Poesías completas*, 8.
41. Scholars disagree as to the dominant tendency of her poetry. For example, Moreira dubs her a *modernista*, while for Pleitez Vela she is a *posmodernista* (Post-Modernist). Moreira, *Aproximación*, 29; and Pleitez Vela, "No soy," 132.
42. Verani first locates "La Berceuse" in Montevideo's press on May 20, 1896, on the front page of the newspaper *La Razón*. Verani, in editorial notes to Vaz Ferreira, *Poesías completas*, 31.
43. Vaz Ferreira, *Poesías completas*, 30.
44. Vaz Ferreira, *Poesías completas*, 30.
45. Vaz Ferreira, *Poesías completas*, 30.
46. Vaz Ferreira, *Poesías completas*, 30.
47. Vaz Ferreira, "Carta a María Esther," 2.
48. Vaz Ferreira, "F. 17r.," 1.
49. For example, the digital archive co-organized by the Fundación Vaz Ferreira-Raimondi and the Biblioteca Nacional del Uruguay says that "en ningún momento comulgó con el perfil de poetisa erótica" (never did she display the profile of an erotic poet). "Archivo María Eugenia."
50. Vaz Ferreira, *Poesías completas*, 109.
51. Elsewhere in the poem, she compares herself to "Ahasvero / siempre triste y solitaria, soñando con las quimeras / y las divinas palabras" (Ahasvero / always sad and solitary, dreaming with the chimeras / and the divine words). Vaz Ferreira, *Poesías completas*, 109.
52. Vaz Ferreira, *Poesías completas*, 110.
53. Achugar, "Me muestro siempre," 21.
54. Vaz Ferreira, *Poesías completas*, 131. The title refers evidently to the flames of passion, and not the Holocaust of Nazi Germany. Verani notes that the poem was first published in the periodical press in 1910: in *Caras y Caretas* of Buenos Aires in January, and in *Vida Moderna* of Montevideo in November (see Verani's editorial notes to Vaz Ferreira, 131). It also appears in *La isla de los cánticos*.
55. Vaz Ferreira, *Poesías completas*, 131.
56. For more information on Agustini's metrics and their commentary on Modernista tradition, see Moody, "Radical Metrics."

57. She writes to Nin Frías, quoting Darío's poem "Divagación" (1894), published in *Prosas profanas*: "He versificado con preferencia, una melancolía medio neurótica, medio coqueta; (coquetería del espíritu), un amor que me recuerda al chistoso paréntesis Rubeniano: '... ó un amor alemán? (que no han sentido jamás los alemanes)'" (I've preferred to write verses, a melancholy half neurotic, half coquettish; (a coquettishness of the spirit), a love that reminds me of the joking Rubénian parenthesis, "or a German love? [Which the Germans have not ever felt]"). Vaz Ferreira, "F. 9r.," 1.
58. Vaz Ferreira, *Poesías completas*, 195.
59. Difficult to date, the poem was apparently unpublished before the Verani edition of Vaz Ferreira's *Poesías completas*.
60. Vaz Ferreira, *Poesías completas*, 138.
61. On this topic see Gwen Kirkpatrick's *The Dissonant Legacy*, particularly chapter 6, focused on Herrera y Reissig.
62. Santa Ana was a journalist close to Batlle y Ordóñez (who later became president) and became representative for Artigas Department in 1899, one year before his death; a letter from Domingo Arena characterizes Santa Ana's affections as unrequited by Vaz Ferreira. Santa Ana to Vaz Ferreira, "Carta de Arturo." Vasseur was a poet who lived in Buenos Aires from 1895 to 1900, where he was connected to Eugenio Díaz Romero's Modernista magazine *El Mercurio de América* (1898–1900). Often publishing under the pseudonym Américo Llanos, Vasseur was likely the connection that fomented Vaz Ferreira's publication there, as well as one source of her information on poetry trends. Vasseur's sole preserved letter to her, while affectionate and detailed, focuses on his advice regarding another beau. Vasseur to Vaz Ferreira, "Carta de Armando Vasseur."
63. The Quinta (Villa) maintains the archives of both the philosopher and his poet sister, including her received correspondence, notebooks, paintings, musical compositions, etc. Although she never lived in the house, upon her death her papers passed to Carlos. His descendants Sara and Cristina Echevarría, along with other relatives, have maintained the site and fostered its transition to National Monument status. The Quinta's designation in 1975 as a Uruguayan national patrimony, along with the more recent opening of María Eugenia's digital archive online through a collaboration with the Uruguayan National Library, make possible a deeper study of the poet's life and artistic process. See "Quinta Vaz Ferreira."
64. Agustini also dedicated a poem to Vaz Ferreira, "¡Artistas!" (Artists!, 1903), which comments on the envy and slander that followed Vaz Ferreira, closing with some reassuring advice: "Mas, burlaos de sus iras; ¡nada pueden! y el artista/ Tiene un arma irresistible para ellas: ¡el desprecio!" (Yet, mock their ire; they can do nothing! and the artist / has a weapon irresistible for them: desdain!). Agustini, *Poesías completas*, 72. The two also exchanged letters and had a "cordial amistad" (cordial friendship). Pleitez Vela, "Debajo estoy yo," 60–61.
65. Achugar, "Me muestro siempre," 5.
66. Vasseur to Vaz Ferreira, "Carta de Armando Vasseur," 2.
67. Vasseur to Vaz Ferreira, 2R.
68. Vasseur to Vaz Ferreira, 2V.
69. Vasseur to Vaz Ferreira, 2V. This letter appears to be the only one from Vasseur in María Eugenia's archive, leaving little foundation for scholars' proposal that he might have been her suitor. Much existing scholarship on her life was produced before some archival materials became available.
70. Visca, "Ángel C. Maggiolo," 95.

71. Maggiolo to Vaz Ferreira, "Carta de A. C. Maggiolo," 1r–2r.
72. Maggiolo to Vaz Ferreira, 3r.
73. Simeto, "Cartas de Mario."
74. Simeto was born to Italian parents in Montevideo in 1882, graduated from medical school in 1907, and became Subdirector of the Radiology Institute, before dying in 1930 of "contusión de tórax" (thoracic contusion). He married Aída Percovich Bosch, who was twenty-five when their first child was born in July 1918. Turnes, "Mario C. Simeto," 1–2.
75. Simeto to Vaz Ferreira, "Folio 18," 1.
76. Simeto to Vaz Ferreira, "Folio 7," 1.
77. Simeto to Vaz Ferreira, "Folio 1," 1.
78. Simeto, "Cartas de Mario," undated visiting card, 1.
79. Simeto to Vaz Ferreira, "Folio 4," 1.
80. Simeto, "Cartas de Mario," undated visiting card, 2.
81. Giaudrone, *La degeneración*, 21. The Uruguayan divorce law was instituted in 1907, but its 1913 reform expanded protections for women. For Asunción Lavrín, it was "one of the most advanced in the world and put Uruguay at the cutting edge of gender legislation." Lavrín, *Women, Feminism*, 231.
82. Ehrick, *The Shield*, 2.
83. Aínsa, "Dandis y Bohemios."
84. On Carlos Vaz Ferreira as a proponent of "compensatory feminism," in which he focused on "the differences that gender made for women and the injustices it could mean for them," see Lavrín, *Women, Feminism*, 38–40.
85. Giaudrone, *La degeneración*, 31.
86. "Muchas de las 'rarezas' o particularidades que ofrece el ejemplo uruguayo (específicamente la visibilidad y expresión de formas no hegemónicas del deseo) responden por un lado, a una amplificación de la propia cosmovisión del modernismo continental (cautelosamente abierto a formas marginales de sensibilidad a través del decadentismo europeo) y, por otro, a la atmósfera tolerante que promovió en sus primeros años la política comprensiva de José Batlle y Ordóñez" (Many of the "eccentricities" or particularities offered by the Uruguayan example [specifically the visibility and expression of non-hegemonic forms of desire] respond, on the one hand, to a broadening of continental Modernism's own cosmovision [cautiously open to marginal forms of sensibility through European Decadentism] and, on the other hand, to the tolerant atmosphere promoted by the comprehensive politics of the early José Batlle y Ordóñez years). Giaudrone, *La degeneración*, 8.
87. Giaudrone, *La degeneración*, 13.
88. Giaudrone, *La degeneración*, 8.
89. Visca, *Antología*, viii.
90. Visca, *Antología*, x.
91. According to Garet, "nadie discute la pertenencia del Consistorio como tal y de sus integrantes, al movimiento Modernista" (nobody disputes that the Consistorio as such and its members belong to the Modernista movement). Garet, *El Consistorio*, 10.
92. The friend group, called the "Three Musketeers," had worked previously on the *Revista del Salto* (1899–1900). Upon closing the magazine in March of 1900, Quiroga traveled briefly to Paris, where he met Darío, Gómez Carrillo, Manuel Machado, and others. His *Diario de viaje a París* (Travel Diary to Paris) notes that the city was a great disappointment: "No tengo fibra de bohemio. . . . Para llevar esa vida se necesita no hacer caso de

insultos y sonreír de alegría cuando le tiran una moneda" (I'm not a natural Bohemian. ... To live that life, one needs to ignore insults and smile with joy when they throw you a coin). Quiroga, *Diario*, 133.
93. Garet, *El Consistorio*, 12.
94. Garet, *El Consistorio*, 9, 47. Giaudrone has analyzed Montevideo's cenacles of this period as heterotopes, building on Michel Foucault's work, defining this as "espacios excepcionales que existen en todas las culturas y civilizaciones, 'lugares reales' que funcionan como contra-sitios en los que otros espacios concretos aparecen simultáneamente representados, cuestionados e invertidos" (exceptional spaces that exist in all cultures and civilizations, "real places" that function as counter-sites in which other concrete spaces appear simultaneously represented, questioned, and inverted). Giaudrone, "La esbeltez," 190.
95. Visca, *Antología*, XXXIV.
96. Quiroga, "Aspectos del modernismo," 87.
97. Mazzucchelli, *La mejor*, 152.
98. Visitors had "acceso fácil a las doncellas de los cuartos contiguos ... lo que naturalmente se les convirtió en venéreo hábito y agregó un atractivo simple y directo a la convocatoria del cenáculo" (easy access to the maidens of contiguous rooms, ... which naturally became a venereal habit for them and added a simple and direct attraction to the cenacle's meetings). Mazzucchelli, *La mejor*, 153–54.
99. Delgado and Brignole, *Vida y obra*, 123.
100. Garet, *El Consistorio*, 13.
101. Visca, *Antología*, XL.
102. Illness presents an interesting commonality between Vaz Ferreira and Quiroga. After *Diario de viaje a París* (1900), Quiroga's next book was *Los arrecifes de coral* (The Coral Reefs, 1901), in which the protagonist kills his love interest. Arturo Sergio Visca considers *Los arrecifes* to be both "la decantación de los principios estéticos y vitales de los componentes del *Consistorio*" (the decantation of the aesthetic and vital principles of the Consistorio members), and "un libro deliberadamente enfermizo" (a deliberately perverse book). Visca, *Antología*, XXXII.
103. "Archivo María Eugenia."
104. See Giaudrone, *La degeneración*, 194.
105. "Pensar que Vd., por quien siento una grande y sincera estimación, supusiera que a mi se me podia hablar de Safo (apenas sé de ella que tenía genio y se portaba mal) me causó un gran dolor" (To think that you, for whom I feel a great and sincere esteem, would suppose that someone could speak to me of Sappho [I barely know of her that she was a genius and she behaved badly], pained me greatly). Vaz Ferreira, "F. 7r.," 2. On her religious conviction, see Pleitez Vela, "Debajo estoy yo," 71.
106. Vaz Ferreira, quoted in Moreira, *Aproximación*, 89. Sixteen letters from Vaz Ferreira to Alberto Nin Frías have long been available in published articles (Vaz Ferreira, María Eugenia, "Correspondencia: Cartas"), and are now more accessible on the website of the collaboration between the Archivo Vaz Ferreira and the Uruguayan Biblioteca Nacional. "Archivo María Eugenia." The other side of this correspondence—his letters to her—became available only recently at the Quinta Vaz Ferreira in Montevideo, where eleven letters and three notes are held. They are also accessible through the website.
107. Mazzucchelli, *La mejor*, 154.
108. The patrician family fell on hard times and moved to this address, with five adult children including Julio, not long before the coterie's founding. The time coincided with

the beginning of José Batlle y Ordóñez's presidency, whose political enemy was Julio Herrera y Reissig's uncle (and perhaps father), Julio Herrera y Obes. Mazzucchelli, *La mejor*, 14, 101.
109. Mazzucchelli, *La mejor*, 236. Emphasis in original.
110. Reissig's cultivation of a public image is also apparent in a full-page profile in the Argentine illustrated magazine *Caras y Caretas*, published in 1907. It features a scandalous photograph of the disheveled poet in his bedroom and injecting morphine into his arm. He had used morphine regularly to manage illness, following an apparent heart attack in February of 1900. See, for example, Mazzucchelli, *La mejor*, 97, 291.
111. Visca, *Antología*, xviii.
112. Wasem, *El amor libre*, 12.
113. Blixen, *El desván*, 14.
114. Giaudrone, *La degeneración*, 25.
115. Books by Tina Escaja and Cathy Jrade are foundational for this chapter. See especially Escaja, *Salomé Decapitada*; and Jrade, *Delmira Agustini*.
116. Blixen, *El desván*, 13.
117. Blixen, *El desván*, 7.
118. Blixen, *El desván*, 9.
119. Pleitez Vela, "Debajo estoy yo," 85.
120. Giaudrone, *La degeneración*, 25.
121. Blixen, *El desván*, 8.
122. Pleitez Vela, "Debajo estoy yo," 70.
123. Vaz Ferreira, *Poesías completas*, 199.
124. For one of many possible examples, see Romantic poet Gertrudis Gómez de Avellaneda's discourse of divine creativity in "Respuesta a una señorita."
125. Vaz Ferreira, "F. 9r.," 1.

CHAPTER 5

1. Some scholars incorrectly note a birthdate of 1877. Pachas Maceda reviewed documents that resolve these doubts. Pachas Maceda, *Zoila Aurora Cáceres*, 28.
2. The letters' languages are Spanish, French, German, English, and Italian, and those noting a location of origin are from France, Peru, Argentina, Spain, Italy, and Germany.
3. These include *El Liberal* (Barcelona), *Álbum Literario, Penumbras* (La Serena, Chile), *América Literaria, Literatura y Arte* (La Paz), *El Pensamiento Latino* (Santiago de Chile), *El Mundo Latino* (Madrid), and *Prisma* (Lima). Many clippings are unidentified and undated.
4. I consulted the album in 2015. It has since become available online, which I use for citations.
5. Price, "Introduction," 12.
6. Miseres, "Solicitudes de amistad," 11.
7. See her parents' memoirs for more information about this period: Cáceres and Cáceres, *La campaña de la Breña: Memorias del mariscal del Perú, D. Andrés A. Cáceres* (The Campaign of La Breña: Memories of Marshall Don Andrés A. Cáceres), and Moreno de Cáceres, *Recuerdos de la campaña de la Breña: Memorias* (Memories of the Campaign of La Breña).
8. Angelina, "La emancipación," 107. Here I cite Cáceres in Glickman's *Vestales del templo azul*. The essay appeared in issues 1.6 and 1.7 of *Búcaro Americano* (15 May and 1 June, 1896, 117–19 and 127–30) and is available online through RIEL: Red Interdisciplinaria de

Estudios Latinoamericanos—Perú XIX (http://red.pucp.edu.pe/riel/). Cáceres also contributed to *Búcaro Americano* travel narrative; stories including "Flor del aire" (Flower of the Air), "Las teolocales" (The teolocales), and "Morfínicas" (Morphinics); an essay titled "Ley social" (Social Law), spread across three issues (February 15, April 15, and September 15, 1899); and a social column signed ZAC. See Chapter 3 for more information.

9. Angelina, "La emancipación," 104.
10. For information on Cáceres's time in Berlin, see the last third of Cáceres, *Oasis de arte*. I have been unable to locate her thesis. Her album includes correspondence about its translation into French before approval, suggesting cataloging under a title in French. In response to my inquiries, librarians in Paris reported that it might have been destroyed during the Nazi occupation of Paris.
11. Scholars cite different publication dates for *Mujeres*. I suggest 1909, because its prologue by Luis Bonafoux is signed July 1909. Ronald Briggs analyzes this collection in *The Moral Electricity*, 90–92.
12. For additional recent scholarship on *La rosa muerta*, see LaGreca, "Intertextual Sexual Politics" and chapter 4 of *Erotic Mysticism*; Grau-Lleveria, "La insurrección"; Kanost, "Modernism"; Morales-Pino, "Moribundas habladoras"; and Bottaro, "Feminism's Unruly Temporalities."
13. The library of the Pontificia Universidad Católica of Peru in Lima holds three "libretas" (notebooks) recorded by "una amiga" (a female friend), in which the former president Andrés Avelino Cáceres ostensibly refutes his own biography, which he had co-authored with his daughter Aurora Cáceres.
14. Miseres, "Modernismo puertas adentro," 175. According to Pachas Maceda, "antes de 1903 tenía publicados artículos en *La Ilustración Sud Americana* (Argentina), *Revista Arte y Literatura* (Bolivia), *El Pensamiento Latino* (Chile), *El Grito del Pueblo* (Ecuador), *La Alborada* (Uruguay) y *Mundo Latino* (España)" (before 1903 she had articles published in *Illustrated South America* [Argentina], *Magazine of Art and Literature* [Bolivia], *Latino Thought* [Chile], *The People's Cry* [Ecuador], *The Dawn* [Uruguay], and *Latino World* [Spain]). Pachas Maceda, *Aurora Cáceres "Evangelina*," 27. Her studies included time at a Berlin convent before 1906, at Williams College (USA) in the 1940s, and at Brigton School (UK). See Los Editores Rosay Hermanos, "Mujeres de América," 9; Pachas Maceda, *Aurora Cáceres "Evangelina*," 25.
15. The couple married in Paris on 6 June 1906 with Darío serving the groom as a witness, having known each other about two months, and by early November they were discussing separation. Cáceres sought a civil annulment in April 1907 at her father's insistence, but waited until 1922 to request a religious annulment, which for her was more meaningful. Cáceres, *Mi vida*, 69, 251, 275.
16. For information on Cáceres's many organizations and memberships, see Araujo, *Dignos de su arte*, 169; Pachas Maceda, *Zoila Aurora Cáceres*; Los Editores Rosay Hermanos, "Mujeres de América."
17. Her memoir *Mi vida* advertises additional books in progress: *Perfiles literarios* (Literary Profiles), *Cuentos peruanos* (Peruvian Stories), *Instrucción cívica* (Civic Instruction), and *Historia de arte pictórico peruano* (History of Peruvian Pictoral Art). She also wrote *Renacimiento* (Renaissance), the novel *Lunar de Plata* (perhaps Flaw of Silver), and was preparing the novel *Memorias de una loca* (Memoire of a Crazy Woman) and *La magia del talento* (The Magic of Talent), according to a note appended to her 1946 report. Los Editores Rosay Hermanos, "Mujeres de América," 3, 6. I have been unable to locate these titles.

18. Uribe Muñoz, quoted in Los Editores Rosay Hermanos, "Mujeres de América," 2.
19. The quotation is from Cáceres's diary entry dated 10 July 1906, which she transcribes in her 1929 memoir. Cáceres, *Mi vida*, 95.
20. Cáceres, *La rosa*, 41.
21. For more information on the scrapbook genre, see Garvey, *Writing with Scissors*; Helfand, *Scrapbooks*. Studies of the trans-Hispanic scrapbook tradition include Miseres, "Solicitudes de amistad"; Acevedo Rivera, "Of Frivolous Female Collectors" and "Would You Write Something."
22. To learn about Cáceres's relationship with Gómez Carrillo, see the memoirs they each published. Cáceres's draws heavily on her diary and received correspondence, although the original diary now appears to be lost. Cáceres, *Mi vida*; Gómez Carrillo, *Treinta años*. Also helpful are the recent articles LaGreca, "Intertextual Sexual Politics"; and Miseres, "Modernismo puertas adentro."
23. Helfand, *Scrapbooks*, 11.
24. Carlos Fabbri was an artist and designer at *El Perú Ilustrado* during Clorinda Matto de Turner's time as editor. For more information, see Pachas Maceda, "De Italia al Perú."
25. As a Latin American collecting in Europe, Cáceres could be productively analyzed with the framework of María Mercedes Andrade in her edited volume *Collecting from the Margins: Material Culture in a Latin American Context*. Andrade writes that "the purpose of this anthology is precisely to counter the usual narrative and the *division of labor* that assigns Europe the role of collector and labels other subaltern cultures, such as that of Latin America, as purveyors of collectible, 'exotic' objects." Andrade, "Introduction," 4, emphasis original. Four of ten articles in the volume included treat Modernistas (if we are to include Delmira Agustini among them), suggesting a heightened interest in collection in that literary movement. Like the works analyzed therein—by Gómez Carrillo, Darío, José Asunción Silva, and Agustini—Cáceres's scrapbook reverses the usual flow of objects in collecting history, as Andrade describes above.
26. Cáceres, *Mi vida*, 17.
27. Her organizations' correspondence can be accessed in the Peruvian National Library and in Pachas Maceda, *Zoila Aurora Cáceres*.
28. Although scholars offer varied dates for her study at the Sorbonne, these letters allow us to date her thesis approval to around June of 1903.
29. Wilson, *El mundo literario americano*, vol. 2, 200.
30. Wilson, *El mundo literario americano*, 201.
31. Wilson, *El mundo literario americano*, 201.
32. Wilson, *El mundo literario americano*, 202.
33. Numerous scholars have examined women's mutual citation practices and their development of professional support networks. See especially the edited volume Fernández, *No hay nación*, as well as Denegri, *El abanico*; Peluffo, "Comunidades de sentimiento"; Vicens, "Por una tradición"; and Martin, "Nation Building."
34. She complains, for example, about "esa gente ordinaria y pervertida del café" (those coarse and perverted people from the café) and tries to take Gómez Carrillo out of Paris, "lejos de esa atmósfera envenenada con la bebida y el tabaco. Llegamos a París y tú te sentiste atraído por esos individuos, a quienes les hacías falta para pagarles lo que beben" (far from that atmosphere poisoned with drink and tabacco. We arrived in Paris and you felt attracted by those people, who needed you to pay for their drinks). Cáceres, *Mi vida*, 236.
35. Cáceres, *Mi vida*, 213.

36. Cáceres, *Mi vida*, 16.
37. Cáceres, *Mi vida*, 31.
38. For more information on Latin Americans in Paris in these years, see Chapter 2.
39. Sanz Álvarez, "La Bohemia Latinoamericana," 523.
40. Los Editores Rosay Hermanos, "Mujeres de América," 5.
41. Miseres, "Una anti-crónica," 240.
42. Cáceres longed to experience Montmartre, one of the famously fun neighborhoods of bohemian Paris that her husband was known to frequent. "Es cierto lo que Manuel Machado ha escrito [sobre Enrique]: 'Hay en sus ojos una tristeza vaga y larga . . . que no se disipa ni con el champaña, ni con las chicas de Montmartre'. Me parece que un hombre del talento de Enrique se cansa de esa vida y no le haga feliz. Con todo me gustaría conocer Montmartre; debe ser muy divertido" (What Manuel Machado has written [about Enrique] is true: "There is a vague and long sadness in his eyes . . . which does not dissipate with champagne or with the girls of Montmartre." I think that a man of Enrique's talent becomes tired of that life, and it does not make him happy. Anyway I would like to see Montmartre; it must be very fun). Cáceres, *Mi vida*, 38.
43. Cáceres, *Mi vida*, 107.
44. Cáceres, *Mi vida*, 39.
45. Cáceres, *Mi vida*, 51.
46. Cáceres, *Mi vida*, 131, 197.
47. Cáceres, *Mi vida*, 116. *Mi vida* describes some of Cáceres's secretarial work for Gómez Carrillo. She transcribes a letter to her husband from Vicente Blasco Ibáñez in Madrid. Cáceres, *Mi vida*, 212. Similarly, Max Nordau and Gustave Kahn comment on recent publications by Gómez Carrillo. Cáceres, *Mi vida*, 29, 49.
48. Cáceres, *Mi vida*, 98.
49. Cáceres, *Mi vida*, 179.
50. Cáceres, *Mi vida*, 219–20.
51. Cáceres, *Mi vida*, 231.
52. Gómez Carrillo's possibly non-normative sexuality might have been an additional point of contention. In her analysis of the couple's autobiographies, Lucía Fox Lockert writes that Cáceres's diary "encubre un secreto y no dice nada sobre la homosexualidad de Enrique, . . . su reprimida sexualidad que él llama androginismo" (covers up a secret and says nothing about Enrique's homosexuality, . . . his repressed sexuality that he called androgynism); she notes that "en la narración que sigue él sucumbe a su represión" (in the narration that follows he succumbs to his repression). Fox Lockhart, "Dialéctica," 411. Despite the challenges of a changing lexicon for such topics over the last century, a queer reading of Gómez Carrillo's life would be possible with further research. Nancy LaGreca mentions Gómez Carrillo's "alleged bisexuality." LaGreca, *Erotic Mysticism*, 121.
53. Quoted in Cáceres, *Mi vida*, 213. See also Fox Lockert, "Dialéctica," 412.
54. Pachas Maceda, *Aurora Cáceres "Evangelina*," 33.
55. Quoted in Cáceres, *Mi vida*, 247, 258–59.
56. Bryce Echenique, "La hija del héroe," 64.
57. Cáceres's deeply felt Catholicism led her to arrange a permanent separation rather than a divorce from her husband, but her father rejected this plan: "me obliga a pedir el divorcio, que en Francia equivale a la nulidad civil; mas yo, en este caso, me consideraré casada cumpliendo con el precepto religioso en lo que de mí dependa. Debí ceder y conformarme, pero mi conciencia me dice otra cosa; seguiré los deberes de la Iglesia y jamás pensaré en volver a contraer nuevo matrimonio" (he obliges me to ask for divorce, which in France is the same as civil annulment; but I, in this case, will consider myself

married and meet the religious obligation, as far as I'm concerned. I had to give in and resign myself, but my conscious tells me something else; I will follow the mandates of the Church and I will never consider marrying again). Cáceres, *Mi vida*, 251. In 1921 and 1922 she spoke with church authorities in Lima, Rome, and Paris to finalize their annulment within the church. Cáceres, *Mi vida*, 272–75. She did not remarry, but he did, twice. She had earlier been engaged to a fiancé who died in Peru, whom she still grieved when she first met Gómez Carrillo. Cáceres, *Mi vida*, 37.

58. Cáceres, *Mi vida*, 254.
59. Cáceres, *Mi vida*, 256.
60. Cárdenas Moreno, "Zoila Aurora Cáceres," 2.
61. Miseres, "Modernismo puertas adentro," 400.
62. Cáceres, quoted in Los Editores Rosay Hermanos, "Mujeres de América," 4.
63. Carvallo, "Zoila Aurora Cáceres," 78.
64. Bryce Echenique, "La hija del héroe," 64.
65. For more positive, largely non-Modernista writers' reactions to Cáceres, see the lengthy praise section appended to her 1927 novel. Cáceres, *La ciudad*, 169–93. The material matches an archival pamphlet in the library of the Universidad Nacional Mayor de San Marcos, in Lima. Garnier Hermanos and Cáceres, *Juicios y opiniones* (Judgements and opinions). For Pachas Maceda, this praise reflects *Mujeres de ayer y de hoy* as Cáceres's "inicio oficial como intelectual" (official start as an intellectual). Pachas Maceda, *Zoila Aurora Cáceres*, 36.
66. Bonafoux, "Unas palabritas . . .," ix, xiv. The journalist Luis Bonafoux (1855–1918) was a French-born Spaniard raised in Puerto Rico, who in this period worked in Paris as a foreign correspondent for several Spanish newspapers.
67. Darío, "Aurora Cáceres," 72.
68. Nervo, "Prólogo," xxxi.
69. Nervo, "Prólogo," xxxiii.
70. Unamuno, "Comentario breve," 75.
71. Gómez Carrillo quoted in Cáceres, *La ciudad*, 12.
72. In Laura Kanost's phrasing, "the prologues by Darío and Nervo suggest a link to the *modernismo* movement, but are carefully worded to keep Cáceres in her place in the margins." Kanost, in editorial notes to Cáceres, *A Dead Rose*, 27.
73. Kanost, in editorial notes to Cáceres, *A Dead Rose*, 27.
74. Ward, "Introducción," xiii–xiv.
75. She goes on to note, "lo que se puede inferir de las observaciones de Darío es que, para la élite cultural modernista, el feminismo fue, junto con el anarquismo y el socialismo, uno de los disturbios sociales que agitaron las aguas del proyecto modernizador" (What we can infer from Darío's observations is that, for the Modernista cultural elite, feminism was, along with anarchism and socialism, one of the social disturbances that agitated the waters of the modernizing project). Peluffo, "Rizomas, redes," 210.
76. Baudrillard, *The System of Objects*, 105.
77. The phrase appears repeatedly in Wolf, *The Quest for Christa T.*
78. Helfand, *Scrapbooks*, 2.
79. Tucker, Ott, and Buckler, *The Scrapbook*, 16. Jeremy Braddock makes a similar proposal when he argues, in his study of US-based Modernism, that "a 'collecting aesthetic' can be identified as a paradigmatic form of modernist art." Braddock, *Collecting*, 2.
80. On ornamentation and accumulation in Modernista poetics, see Gwen Kirkpatrick, *The Dissonant Legacy*, 7–8; and Moody, "Poetic Form." Shelley Garrigan reads Delmira Agustini's accumulation of Modernista referents as a kind of collecting. Garrigan, "Delmira Agustini, Gender."

81. Siegel et al., *Playing with Pictures*.
82. Tucker, Ott, and Buckler, *The Scrapbook*, 6. The history of the album could take us even farther back to ancient Rome, with the Latin *albus* (white) and *album* (a blank tablet for recording information), or the *album amicorum* (book of friends), a predecessor of the nineteenth-century "friendship book." For more information on the album in nineteenth-century Spain and Latin America, see Miseres, "Solicitudes de amistad"; Acevedo Rivera, "Of Frivolous Female Collectors" and "Would You Write Something."
83. Huyssen's *After the Great Divide* comes to mind here, particularly the chapter "Mass Culture as Woman: Modernism's Other," which argues that "the universalizing ascription of femininity to mass culture always depended on the very real exclusion of women from high culture and its institutions." Huyssen, *After the Great Divide*, 13.
84. Benjamin, "Unpacking," 60.
85. Benjamin, "Unpacking," 60.
86. Stewart, *On Longing*, 150, my emphasis.
87. Stewart, *On Longing*, 139.
88. Stewart, *On Longing*, 135. Stewart might object to my treatment of the scrapbook as a collection. In her view, collections are fully aestheticized and are fundamentally different from souvenirs, which retain a use value; are more similar to autobiography; and include such objects as "scrapbooks, memory quilts, photo albums and baby books." Stewart, *On Longing*, 139.
89. Kathleen Cairns and Eliane Silverman read collecting as a process of self-creation: "Every woman's story is a story of creating herself. The act of keeping a particular thing is always an act of self-definition in which the object represents both an aspect of the self and a way into self-knowledge. Who was I? Who am I now? . . . An object anchors its owner in time and place, and positions her as a member of a community or a network of relationships." Cairns and Silverman, *Treasures*, 1.
90. Matthews, "Albums, Belongings," 109.
91. Clayton, "Touring History," 46.
92. Clayton, "Touring History," 34–35.
93. Cáceres, *Mi vida*, 288.
94. Clayton writes that Gómez Carrillo "complained—to Tórtola's great frustration, but arguably with some justification—that the presence of 'Oriental' dances in her program hindered the proper evolution of Spanish dance." Clayton, "Touring History," 37.

BIBLIOGRAPHY

"Académicos de número." Real Academia Española. Accessed 26 Sept. 2022. https://www.rae.es/academicos/academicos-de-numero.

Acevedo Rivera, Jeannette. "Of Frivolous Female Collectors and Manipulative Male Contributors: The Depiction of the Nineteenth-Century Album in Essays on Social Customs." *Nineteenth Century Studies* 29 (2015-2016): 17-36.

———. "'Would You Write Something in My Album?' Social Customs and Their Literary Depiction in Nineteenth-Century France and Spain." PhD diss, Duke University, 2015.

Achugar, Hugo. "'Me muestro siempre en mi obscuridad': María Eugenia Vaz Ferreira (1875-1924)." In *María Eugenia Vaz Ferreira: "Me muestro siempre en mi obscuridad."* Montevideo: Fundación Vaz Ferreira-Raimondi, 2013, 5-22.

Águila, Rocío del. "(A)filiaciones femeninas: Gorriti y la genealogía de la escritura en Lima." *Decimonónica: Journal of Nineteenth Century Hispanic Cultural Production* 10, no. 1 (2013): 45-62.

Agustini, Delmira. *Poesías completas*. Edited by Magdalena García Pinto. Letras hispánicas; 372. Madrid: Cátedra, 1993.

Aínsa, Fernando. "Dandis y Bohemios en el Uruguay del 900: Una relectura contemporánea." *RILCE: Revista de Filología Hispánica* 15, no. 1 (1999): 201-14.

Alzate, Carolina and Darcie Doll. *Redes, alianzas y afinidades: Mujeres y escritura en América Latina*. Bogotá: Ediciones Uniandes, 2014.

Andrade, María Mercedes. "Introduction." In *Collecting from the Margins: Martial Culture in a Latin American Context*, edited by María Mercedes Andrade, 1-11. London: Bucknell University Press, 2016.

Angelina, Eva. "La emancipación de la mujer." In *Vestales del templo azul: Notas sobre el feminismo hispanoamericano en la época modernista*, 104-7. Toronto: Canadian Academy of the Arts, 1996.

———. "Ley social." *Búcaro Americano: Periódico de las Familias* 4, nos. 30-31 (February 15, 1899), 461-63.

———. "Ley social." *Búcaro Americano: Periódico de las Familias* 4, nos. 32–33 (April 15, 1899), 491–93.

———. "Ley social." *Búcaro Americano: Periódico de las Familias* 4, nos. 34–35 (September 15, 1899), 513–15.

Araujo, Kathya. *Dignos de su arte: sujeto y lazo social en el Perú de las primeras décadas del siglo XX*. Nuevos hispanismos. Madrid, Frankfurt, Santiago de Chile: Iberoamericana, Vervuert, 2009.

Archivo María Eugenia Vaz Ferreira. "María Eugenia Vaz Ferreira: Presentación." Fundación Vaz Ferreira-Raimondi, Biblioteca Nacional de Uruguay, accessed May 24, 2021. http://archivomariaeugenia.bibna.gub.uy/omeka/.

Argentina, and Diego Gregorio de la Fuente. *Segundo censo de la República Argentina, mayo 10 de 1895, resúmenes definitivos: población nacional y extranjera, urbana y rural*. Buenos Aires: Juan A. Alsina, 1897. https://catalog.hathitrust.org/Record/100423503.

Ariza, Julia, and Georgina Gluzman. "Mujeres virtuosas e ilustradas: Los retratos de Búcaro Americano. Periódico de las Familias (1896–1908)." In *Atrapados por la imagen: Arte y política en la cultura impresa argentina*, edited by Laura Malosetti Costa and Marcela Gené, 75–107. Buenos Aires: Edhasa, 2013.

Auza, Néstor Tomás. *Periodismo y feminismo en la Argentina, 1830–1930*. Buenos Aires: Emecé Editores, 1988.

Barra, Eduardo de la. "Prólogo." In *Azul . . .*, by Rubén Darío, 1st ed., Valparaíso: Imprenta y litografía Excelsior, 1888, iii–xxxiv. http://www.bibliotecanacionaldigital.gob.cl/visor/BND:8301.

Barrán, José Pedro. *Historia de la sensibilidad en el Uruguay*, vol. 2, El disciplinamiento (1860–1920). Montevideo: Ediciones de la Banda Oriental: Facultad de Humanidades y Ciencias, 1990.

———. *Intimidad, divorcio y nueva moral en el Uruguay del Novecientos*. Montevideo: Ediciones de la Banda Oriental, 2008.

Bastos, María L. "La crónica modernista de Enrique Gómez Carrillo o la función de la trivialidad." *Revista Sur*, nos. 350–351 (December 1, 1982): 65–88.

Batticuore, Graciela. *El taller de la escritora: Veladas literarias de Juana Manuela Gorriti, Lima-Buenos Aires (1876/7–1892)*. Rosario, Argentina: Beatriz Viterbo Editora, 1999.

Baudrillard, Jean. *The System of Objects*. New York: Verso, 1996.

Benjamin, Walter. "Paris: Capital of the Nineteenth Century." *Perspecta* 12 (1969): 165–72. https://doi.org/10.2307/1566965.

———. "Unpacking My Library: A Talk about Book Collecting." In *Illuminations*, edited by Hannah Arendt, translated by Harry Zohn, 59–67. New York: Harcourt Brace Jovanovich, 1968.

Berman, Marshall. *All That Is Solid Melts into Air: The Experience of Modernity*. New York: Simon and Schuster, 1982.

Blanco-Fombona, Rufino. *Letras y letrados de Hispano-América*. Paris: Sociedad de ediciones literarias y artísticas, 1908.

Blixen, Carina. *El desván del novecientos: mujeres solas*. Montevideo, Uruguay: Ediciones del Caballo Perdido, 2002.
Bonafoux, Luis. "Unas palabritas . . ." In *Mujeres de ayer y de hoy*, by Zoila Aurora Cáceres, Paris: Garnier Hermanos, n.d., vii–xiv.
Bornay, Erika. *Las hijas de Lilith*. Madrid: Cátedra, 1990.
Bottaro, Mayra. "Feminism's Unruly Temporalities: *Démodé* Aesthetics in Aurora Cáceres's *La Rosa Muerta* (1914)." *Revista de Estudios Hispánicos* 56, no. 1 (March 2022): 3–28.
Bouzaglo, Nathalie. *Ficción adulterada: Pasiones ilícitas del entresiglo venezolano*. Rosario: Beatriz Viterbo Editora, 2016.
Braddock, Jeremy. *Collecting as Modernist Practice*. Baltimore, MD: Johns Hopkins University Press, 2012.
Briggs, Ronald. *The Moral Electricity of Print: Transatlantic Education and the Lima Women's Circuit, 1876–1910*. Nashville, TN: Vanderbilt University Press, 2017.
Bronfen, Elisabeth. *Over Her Dead Body: Death, Femininity, and the Aesthetic*. New York: Routledge, 1992.
Bruña Bragado, María José. *Delmira Agustini: Dandismo, género y reescritura del imaginario modernista*. New York: P. Lang, 2005.
Bryce Echenique, Alfredo. "La hija del héroe: Evangelina en el infierno." *Etiqueta Negra*, no. 63 [Lima], September 18, 2008.
Bunker, Steven B. *Creating Mexican Consumer Culture in the Age of Porfirio Díaz*. Albuquerque: University of New Mexico Press, 2012.
Cabello Hutt, Claudia. *Artesana de sí misma: Gabriela Mistral, una intelectual en cuerpo y palabra*. West Lafayette, IN: Purdue University Press, 2018.
———. "Undisciplined Objects: Queer Women's Archives." *Revista Hispánica Moderna* 74, no. 1 (2021): 27–36. https://doi.org/10.1353/rhm.2021.0006.
Cáceres, Zoila Aurora. *A Dead Rose*. Translated by Laura Kanost. Doral, FL: Stockcero, 2018.
———. *Álbum personal de Zoila Aurora Cáceres*. Pontificia Universidad Católica del Perú archives [Lima], Date unknown. https://repositorio.pucp.edu.pe/index/handle/123456789/64206.
———. *La ciudad del sol*. Lima: Libería francesa científica y casa editorial E. Rosay, F. y E. Rosay, 1927.
———. *La rosa muerta*. Edited by Thomas Ward. Buenos Aires: Stockcero, 2007.
———. *Mi vida con Enrique Gómez Carrillo*. Madrid: Renacimiento, 1929.
———. *Oasis de arte*. París: Casa Editorial Garnier Hermanos, 1910.
Cáceres, Zoila Aurora, and Andrés Avelino Cáceres. *La campaña de la Breña, memorias del mariscal del Perú, D. Andrés A. Cáceres*. Lima: Imp. Americana, 1921.
Cairns, K. V., and E. L. Silverman. *Treasures: The Stories Women Tell about the Things They Keep*. Calgary: University of Calgary Press, 2004. https://doi.org/10.2307/j.ctv6gqwmn.

Cárdenas Moreno, Mónica. "Zoila Aurora Cáceres, ¿escritora moderna?" 2017. HAL Id: hal-01694319. https://hal.science/hal-01694319.

Cardwell, Richard A. "Romanticism, Modernismo and Noventa y Ocho: The Creation of a Poesía Nacional." *Bulletin of Spanish Studies* 82, no. 3–4 (May 2005): 485–507. https://doi.org/10.1080/1475382052000342789.

Carlson, Marifran. *¡Feminismo!: The Woman's Movement in Argentina from Its Beginnings to Eva Perón*. Chicago: Academy Chicago, 1988.

Carter, Boyd. *La "Revista de America" de Rubén Darío y Ricardo Jaimes Freyre*. [Managua]: Publicaciones del Centenario de Rubén Darío, 1966.

Carvallo, Fernando. "Zoila Aurora Cáceres, del Sagrado Corazón a la Belle Epoque." *Cuadernos Hispanoamericanos* 688 (October 10, 2007): 73–78.

Castillo, Jorge Luis. "Delmira Agustini o el modernismo subversivo." *Chasqui: Revista de Literatura Latinoamericana* 27, no. 2 (November 11, 1998): 70–84. https://doi.org/10.2307/29741438.

Clayton, Michelle. "Touring History: Tórtola Valencia between Europe and the Americas." *Dance Research Journal* 44, no. 1 (Summer 2012): 28–49. https://doi.org/10.1017/S0149767711000362.

Colombi, Beatriz. "Camino a la meca: Escritores hispanoamericanos en Paris (1900–1920)." In *Historia de los intelectuales en América Latina I: La ciudad letrada, de la conquista al modernismo*, vol. 1, ed. Jorge Myers, 544–66. Buenos Aire; Katz, 2008.

———. "Peregrinaciones parisinas: Rubén Darío." *Orbis Tertius* 2, no. 4 (1997): 1–9.

———. *Viaje intelectual: Migraciones y desplazamientos en América Latina (1880-1915)*. Rosario: Beatriz Viterbo, 2004.

Conway, Christopher. "Troubled Selves: Gender, Spiritualism and Psychopathology in the Fiction of Amado Nervo." *Bulletin of Spanish Studies* 85 no. 4 (June 2008): 461–76.

Coromina, Irene Susana. "El Álbum de Señoritas y la emancipación de la mujer." *Dialogía: Revista de lingüística, literatura y cultura* 3 (2008): 169–86.

Crispo Acosta, Osvaldo. *Motivos de crítica: Juan Zorrilla de San Martín, Julio Herrera y Reissig, María Eugenia Vaz Ferreira*. Montevideo: Palacio del Libro, 1929.

Darío, Rubén. "Aurora Cáceres." In *La rosa muerta*, by Aurora Cáceres, edited by Thomas Ward, 71–74. Buenos Aires: Stock Cero, 2007.

———. "Cabezas: Enrique Gómez Carrillo." *Mundial Magazine*, June 1912.

———. *Crónicas desconocidas, 1901–1906*. Edited by Günter Schmigalle. Managua: Academia Nicaragüense de la Lengua; Berlin: Edition Tranvía, 2006.

———. *Escritos dispersos de Rubén Darío (recogidos de periódicos de Buenos Aires)*. Edited by Pedro Luis Barcia. vol. 2. 2 vols. La Plata: Universidad Nacional de la Plata, Facultad de Humanidades y Ciencias de la Educación, 1977.

———. "Historia de un sobretodo." In *25 cuentos de Rubén Darío*, edited by Carola Brantome and Fernando Solís B., 31–35. Managua: MINED, 2009. https://www.mined.gob.ni/biblioteca/wp-content/uploads/2018/08/25_Cuentos_Ruben_-Dario.pdf.

———. *Obras completas*. 5 vols. Madrid: A. Aguado, 1950.
———. "Pálida como un lirio." *Búcaro Americano: Periódico de las Familias* 8, no. 65 (May 15, 1908) 1,006-7.
———. "Pórtico." In *Poesías completas*, by Delmira Agustini, edited by Magdalena García Pinto, 223. Madrid: Cátedra, 2006.
———. "Prólogo a la primera edición." In *Azul . . ., de Rubén Darío*, edited by Günther Schmigalle, 49-50. Berlin: Ediciones Tranvía, Verlag Walter Frey, 2015.
———. *Prosas profanas y otros poemas*. Edited by Ignacio Zuleta. Madrid: Clásicos Castalia, 1987.
———. "Snobs y bobos de la moda." In *El archivo de Rubén Darío*, edited by Alberto Ghiraldo, 49-50. Buenos Aires: Editorial Losada, 1943.
Delgado, José María, and Alberto J. Brignole. *Vida y obra de Horacio Quiroga*. Biblioteca Rodó. Montevideo: C. García y Cía., 1939.
Denegri, Francesca. *El abanico y la cigarrera: La primera generación de mujeres ilustradas en el Perú*. 1st ed. Lima: Flora Tristán Centro de la Mujer Peruana, 1996.
Díaz-Marcos, Ana María. "El arte por excelencia: Psicología de la moda femenina (1907) de Enrique Gómez Carrillo." *Monographic Review/Revista Monográfica* 25 (2009): 89-104.
Dijkstra, Bram. *Idols of Perversity: Fantasies of Feminine Evil in Fin-de-Siècle Culture*. New York: Oxford University Press, 1986.
Echevarría, Cristina. "Guía cronológica." In *María Eugenia Vaz Ferreira: "Me muestro siempre en mi obscuridad,"* edited by Hugo Achugar and Marita Fornaro, 23-24. Montevideo: Fundación Vaz Ferreira-Raimondi, 2013. http://www.autoresdeluruguay.uy/biblioteca/Maria_Eugenia_Vaz_Ferreira/lib/exe/fetch.php?media=catalogo_expo_maria_eugenia_vaz_ferreira.pdf.
Ehrick, Christine. *The Shield of the Weak: Feminism and the State in Uruguay, 1903-1933*. Albuquerque: University of New Mexico Press, 2005.
Ehrlicher, Hanno. "Enrique Gómez Carrillo en la red cosmopolita del modernismo." *Iberoamericana* 15, no. 50 (2015): 41-60.
El Duque Job. "Al pie de la escalera." *Revista Azul*, May 6, 1894.
———. "La vida artificial." *Revista Azul*, July 22, 1894.
Escaja, Tina. *Salomé Decapitada: Delmira Agustini y la estética finisecular de la fragmentación*. Amsterdam: Rodopi, 2001.
Felski, Rita. *The Gender of Modernity*. Cambridge, MA: Harvard University Press, 1995.
Fernández Moreno, Cesar. "Las revistas literarias en la Argentina." *Revista Hispánica Moderna* 29 (1963): 46-54.
Fernández, Pura, ed. *No hay nación para este sexo: La Re(d)pública trasatlántica de las Letras: escritoras españolas y latinoamericanas (1824-1936)*. 1st ed. Frankfurt am Main: Iberoamericana Editorial Vervuert, 2015.
Figueroa Obregón, Rodrigo. "Espacio político en 'La duquesa Job' de Manuel Gutiérrez Nájera." *Decimonónica: Journal of Nineteenth Century Hispanic Cultural Production* 16, no. 1 (Winter 2019): 1-15.

Fornaro Bordolli, Marita. "María Eugenia Vaz Ferreira y la música: Las invisibilidades múltiples." In *María Eugenia Vaz Ferreira: "Me muestro siempre en mi obscuridad,"* ed. Hugo Achugar and Marita Fornaro, 33–48. Montevideo: Fundación Vaz Ferreira-Raimondi, 2013. http://www.autoresdeluruguay.uy/biblioteca/Maria_Eugenia_Vaz_Ferreira/lib/exe/fetch.php?media=catalogo_expo_maria_eugenia_vaz_ferreira.pdf

Fox Lockert, Lucía. "Dialéctica en la subversión de los sexos en la autobiografía de Aurora Cáceres." In *Mujeres que escriben en América Latina*, edited by Sara Beatriz Guardia, 409–15. Lima, Peru: Centro de Estudios La Mujer en la Historia de América Latina (CEHMAL), 2007.

Frederick, Bonnie. "In Their Own Voice: The Women Writers of the Generación Del '80 in Argentina." *Hispania: A Journal Devoted to the Teaching of Spanish and Portuguese* 74, no. 2 (May 5, 1991): 282–89. https://doi.org/10.2307/344802.

García Calderón, Ventura. "La frivolidad de Gómez Carrillo." In *El libro de las mujeres*, ix–xxviii. Paris: Garnier Hermanos, 1909.

———. *Semblanzas de America*. Biblioteca Ariel. Madrid: La Revista Hispano-Americana "Cervantes," 1920.

García Pinto, Magdalena. "El retrato de una artista joven: La musa de Delmira Agustini." *Revista Iberoamericana* 64, no. 184–85 (December 7, 1998): 559–71. https://doi.org/10.5195/REVIBEROAMER.1998.6127.

Garet, Leonardo. *El Consistorio del Gay Saber: Horacio Quiroga, Federico Ferrando, Alberto J. Brignole, José María Fernández Saldaña y Asdrúbal E. Delgado y Julio J. Jaureche*. Salto: Intendencia Municipal de Salto, 2004.

Garnier Hermanos, and Zoila Aurora Cáceres. *Juicios y opiniones de la prensa y de notables escritores*, n.d.

Garrigan, Shelley. "Delmira Agustini, Gender, and the Poetics of Collecting." In *Collecting from the Margins: Martial Culture in a Latin American Context*, edited by María Mercedes Andrade, 115–40. London: Bucknell University Press, 2016.

Garvey, Ellen Gruber. *Writing with Scissors: American Scrapbooks from the Civil War to the Harlem Renaissance*. New York: Oxford University Press, 2012.

Giaudrone, Carla. *La degeneración del 900: modelos estético-sexuales de la cultura en el Uruguay del Novecientos*. Montevideo, Uruguay: Ediciones Trilce, 2005.

———. "'La esbeltez de los barcos que están casi en el aire': El cenáculo y el barco como heterotopías en el 900." *Cuadernos LIRICO: Revista de la red interuniversitaria de estudios sobre las literaturas rioplatenses contemporáneas en Francia*, no. 5 (January 1, 2010): 189–204. https://doi.org/10.4000/lirico.411.

Giusti, Roberto Fernando. *Momentos y aspectos de la cultura argentina*. Buenos Aires: Editorial Raigal, 1954.

Gómez Carrillo, Enrique. *El alma encantadora de París*. España: Maucci, 1911.

———. "El bulevar día por dia." *Suplemento Semanal Ilustrado: La Nación*, January 29, 1903.

———. *El encanto de Buenos Aires: Obras completas, tomo XIX*. Madrid: Mundo Latino, 1921.

———. *El libro de las mujeres*. Paris: Garnier Hermanos, 1909.

———. *Treinta años de mi vida; el despertar del alma*. Madrid: Mundo Latino, 1918.

———. *Vistas de Europa*. Madrid: Mundo Latino, 1919.

González, Aníbal. *La crónica modernista hispanoamericana*. Madrid: J. Porrúa Turanzas, 1983.

———. "Modernismo, Journalism, and the Ethics of Writing: Manuel Gutiérrez Nájera's 'La hija del aire.'" In *The Contemporary Mexican Chronicle: Theoretical Perspectives on the Liminal Genre*, edited by Ignacio Corona, Beth E. Jörgensen, and Beth Ellen, 157–79. Albany: State University of New York Press, 2002.

Gorelik, Adrián. *La grilla y el parque: Espacio público y cultura urbana en Buenos Aires, 1887–1936*. Buenos Aires: Universidad Nacional de Quilmes, 1998.

Gorriti, Juana Manuela. *Veladas literarias de Lima 1876–1877*. Buenos Aires: Imprenta Europea, 1892. http://catalog.hathitrust.org/api/volumes/oclc/4626018.html.

Grau-Lleveria, Elena. "La insurrección de la bella muerta en *La rosa muerta* de Aurora Cáceres." *Latin American Literary Review* 45, no. 89 (June 1, 2018): 36–44. https://doi.org/10.26824/lalr.32.

Grenfell, Michael. *Pierre Bourdieu: Key Concepts*. 2nd ed. Abingdon, Oxon; Routledge, 2014.

Grigsby, Carlos F. "El Fracaso de París: Ruben Darío's Modernista Campaign in France." *Modern Language Review* 114, no. 4 (October 1, 2019): 720–39.

———. "Rediscovering Rubén Darío through Translation." PhD diss, Oxford University, 2019.

Grout, Holly. *The Force of Beauty: Transforming French Ideas of Femininity in the Third Republic*. Baton Rouge: Louisiana State University Press, 2015.

Guerrero, Javier. "El archivo uruguayo de los muertos: Delmira Agustini, materialidad y sobrevida sintética." *Hispanic Review* 88, no. 4 (Autumn 2020): 395–428.

Gutiérrez Nájera, Manuel. "Ama aprisa." Cuidad Seva, accessed August 7, 2021. https://ciudadseva.com/texto/ama-aprisa/.

———. *Cuentos completos y otras narraciones*. Edited by Erwin K. Mapes. Mexico: Fondo de Cultura Ecponómica, 1984.

———. *Poesías de Manuel Gutiérrez Nájera*. Vol. 2. 2 vols. Paris: Librería de la Vda de Ch. Bouret, 1929.

Hajjaj, Karima. "Crónica y viaje en el Modernismo: Enrique Gómez Carrillo y 'El encanto de Buenos Aires.'" *Anales de Literatura Hispanoamericana* 23 (January 1, 1994): 27–41.

Hazan, Éric. *The Invention of Paris: A History in Footsteps*. New York: Verso, 2010.

Helfand, Jessica. *Scrapbooks: An American History*. New Haven, CT: Yale University Press, 2008.

Huyssen, Andreas. *After the Great Divide: Modernism, Mass Culture, Postmodernism*. Bloomington: Indiana University Press, 1986.
Irwin, Robert McKee. *Mexican Masculinities*. Minneapolis: University of Minnesota Press, 2003.
Jacovkis, Vera Helena. "El desafío de (d)escribir París: 'La crónica en Francia,' de Ugarte, y 'París,' de Sarmiento." *Espéculo: Revista de Estudios Literarios* 42 (October 7, 2009).
James, William. *The Principles of Psychology*. New York: Dover Publications, 1950.
Josefina. "De todas partes." *Búcaro Americano: Periódico de las Familias* 4, nos. 30–31 (February 15, 1899), 475–76.
Jrade, Cathy L. *Delmira Agustini, Sexual Seduction, and Vampiric Conquest*. New Haven, CT: Yale University Press, 2012.
———. "El modernismo y la generación del 98': Ideas afines, creencias divergentes." *Texto Crítico* 14, no. 38 (Jan.–June 1988): 15–29.
———. "Modernism on Both Sides of the Atlantic." *Anales de la Literatura Española Contemporánea* 23, nos. 1–2 (1988): 181–96.
Kanost, Laura. "Modernismo and the Audacious Illness Narratives of Aurora Cáceres and María Luisa Garza." *Hispanófila* 186 (June 6, 2019): 23–34.
Kirkpatrick, Gwen. "Delmira Agustini y el 'reino interior' de Rodó y Darío." In *¿Qué es el modernismo? Nueva encuesta, nuevas lecturas*, edited by Richard A. Cardwell and Bernard McGuirk, 295–306. Boulder: Soc. of Spanish and Spanish-American Studies, 1993.
———. *The Dissonant Legacy of Modernismo: Lugones, Herrera y Reissig, and the Voices of Modern Spanish American Poetry*. Berkeley: University of California Press, 1989.
Kirkpatrick, Susan. *Las Románticas: Women Writers and Subjectivity in Spain, 1835–1850*. Berkeley: University of California Press, 1989.
———. *Mujer, modernismo y vanguardia en España: 1898–1931*. Translated by Jaqueline Cruz. Madrid: Cátedra, 2003.
Krause, Edith H. "Placer, violencia, espiritualidad: Las mujeres y el protagonista atormentado en De sobremesa, de José Asunción Silva." *Crítica Hispánica* 33, no. 1–2 (2011): 79–100.
Kurz, Andreas. "La transformación de estereotipos femeninos en el modernismo mexicano a raíz de una adaptación de *El retrato de Dorian Gray*." *Literatura Mexicana* 22, no. 2 (2011): 29–43.
La Dirección. "Nuestras madrinas." *Búcaro Americano: Periódico de las Familias* 1, no. 4 (March 15, 1896), 77–79.
Laera, Alejandra. "El Ateneo de Buenos Aires. Redes artísticas y culturales en el fin de siglo." In *Primeros modernos en Buenos Aires, 1876–1896*, edited by Laura Malosetti Costa, 18–25. Buenos Aires, 2007.
LaGreca, Nancy. *Erotic Mysticism: Subversion and Transcendence in Latin American Modernista Prose*. Chapel Hill: University of North Carolina Press, 2016.

---. "Intertextual Sexual Politics: Illness and Desire in Enrique Gómez Carrillo's *Del amor, del dolor y del vicio* and Aurora Cáceres's *La rosa muerta*." *Hispania: A Journal Devoted to the Teaching of Spanish and Portuguese* 95, no. 4 (December 12, 2012): 617–28. https://doi.org/10.1353/hpn.2012.0141.

---. *Rewriting Womanhood: Feminism, Subjectivity, and the Angel of the House in the Latin American Novel, 1887–1903*. University Park: Pennsylvania State University Press, 2009.

Lavrín, Asunción. *Women, Feminism, and Social Change in Argentina, Chile, and Uruguay, 1890–1940*. Lincoln: University of Nebraska Press, 1995.

Litvan, Valentina, and Javier Uriarte. "Prefacio: Raros uruguayos, nuevas miradas." *Cuadernos LIRICO Revista de la red interuniversitaria de estudios sobre las literaturas rioplatenses contemporáneas en Francia*, no. 5 (2010): 11–14.

Lockhart, Washington, and Juan Francisco Costa. *Vida y obra de María Eugenia Vaz Ferreira*. Montevideo: Academia Nacional de Letras, 1995.

López-Calvo, Ignacio. "Estrategias de poder en el campo cultural del modernismo: La escabrosa relación entre Rubén Darío y Enrique Gómez Carrillo." In *Rubén Darío: Cosmopolita arraigado*, edited by Jeffrey Browitt and Werner Mackenbach, 294–321. Managua, Nicaragua: Instituto de Historia de Nicaragua y Centroamérica, Universidad Centroamericana (IHNCA-UCA), 2010.

Los Editores Rosay Hermanos. "Mujeres de América, por Bernardo Uribe Muñoz: Zoila Aurora Cáceres (Evangelina)." In *Labor de armonía interamericana en los Estados Unidos de Norte América 1940–1945*, edited by Zoila Aurora Cáceres. Washington: Comisión Interamericana de Mujeres, 1946.

Lucía, Daniel Omar de. "Positivismo y exilio: Liberales peruanos en Buenos Aires en la transición entre los siglos XIX y XX." *Pacarina del Sur*, accessed March 19, 2021. http://www.pacarinadelsur.com/home/huellas-y-voces/201-positivismo-y-exilio-liberales-peruanos-en-buenos-aires-en-la-transicion-entre-los-siglos-xix-y-xx.

Maggiolo, A. C. Letter to María Eugenia Vaz Ferreira. "Carta de A. C. Maggiolo." Fundación Vaz Ferreira-Raimondi, Biblioteca Nacional de Uruguay, accessed June 1, 2021. http://archivomariaeugenia.bibna.gub.uy/omeka/items/show/151.

Maíz, Claudio, and Álvaro Fernández-Bravo. *Episodios en la formación de redes culturales en América Latina*. Buenos Aires: Prometeo Libros, 2009.

Malosetti Costa, Laura. *Los primeros modernos: Arte y sociedad en Buenos Aires a fines del siglo XIX*. Buenos Aires: Fondo de Cultura Económica, 2001.

Mapes, Erwin Kempton. *L'influence française dans l' oeuvre de Rubén Darío*. Paris: Librairie Ancienne Édouard Champion, 1925.

Márquez Acevedo, Sergio. "Estudio preliminar." In *Cartas de mujeres*, by Amado Nervo, 13–22. Mexico: UNAM, Instituto de Investigaciones Bibliográficas, 2004.

Martí, José. *Ensayos y crónicas*. Edited by José Olivio Jiménez. Madrid: Cátedra, 2004.

Martin, Leona S. "Nation Building, International Travel, and the Construction of the Nineteenth-Century Pan-Hispanic Women's Network." *Hispania: A Journal Devoted to the Teaching of Spanish and Portuguese* 87, no. 3 (September 9, 2004): 439–46. https://doi.org/10.2307/20063026.

Martínez, Elia M. "Las mujeres frívolas." *Búcaro Americano: Periódico de las Familias* 1, no. 7 (June 1, 1896), 137–38.

Martínez, José María. *Amado Nervo y las lectoras del modernismo*. Madrid: Editorial Verbum, 2015.

———. "El público femenino del modernismo: Las lectoras pretendidas de Amado Nervo." In *Actas del XIV Congreso de la Asociación Internacional de Hispanistas, IV: Literatura hispanoamericana*, edited by Isaías Lerner, Robert Nival, and Alejandro Alonso, 389–96. Juan de la Cuesta Hispanic Monographs. Newark, DE, 2004.

Masiello, Francine. *Between Civilization & Barbarism: Women, Nation, and Literary Culture in Modern Argentina*. Lincoln: University of Nebraska Press, 1992.

Matthews, Samantha. "Albums, Belongings, and Embodying the Feminine." In *Bodies and Things in Nineteenth-Century Literature and Culture*, edited by Katharina Boehm, 107–29. New York: Palgrave Macmillan, 2012.

Matto de Turner, Clorinda. "Bautismo." *Búcaro Americano: Periódico de las Familias* 1, no. 1 (February 1, 1896), 2–3.

———. "Bibliografía." *Búcaro Americano: Periódico de las Familias* 2, no. 18 (November 15, 1897), 313–15.

———. *Boreales, Miniaturas y porcelanas*. Buenos Aires: Imp. de J.A. Alsina, 1902.

———. "Carlos Guido y Spano." *Búcaro Americano: Periódico de las Familias* 4, nos. 30–31 (February 15, 1899), 459–61.

———. "Despedida." *Búcaro Americano: Periódico de las Familias* 8, no. 65 (May 15, 1908), 1,006.

———. "La mujer en el Ateneo argentino." *Búcaro Americano: Periódico de las Familias* 1, no. 4 (March 15, 1896), 74–77.

———. "La mujer moderna." *Búcaro Americano: Periódico de las Familias* 6, no. 49 (September 15, 1906), 726–27.

———. "La mujer trabajadora." *Búcaro Americano: Periódico de las Familias* 4, nos. 32–33 (April 15, 1899), 478–79.

———. "Las obreras del pensamiento en la América del Sur." *Búcaro Americano: Periódico de las Familias* 1, no. 1 (February 1, 1896), 5–14.

———. "Nuestras miniaturas: Carlos Guido y Spano." *Búcaro Americano: Periódico de las Familias* 4, nos. 34–35 (September 15, 1899), 502–4.

———. "Nuestras miniaturas: Doctor Carlos Pellegrini." *Búcaro Americano: Periódico de las Familias* 6, no. 47 (August 1, 1906), 683–84.

———. "Nuestras miniaturas: Laura Méndez de Cuenca." *Búcaro Americano: Periódico de las Familias* 5, no. 39 (October 20, 1900), 575–76.

———. *Su afectísima discípula, Clorinda Matto de Turner: Cartas a Ricardo Palma, 1883–1897*. Edited by Francesca Denegri and Ana Peluffo. Lima: Pontificia Universidad Católica del Perú, Fondo Editorial, 2020.

Mazzucchelli, Aldo. *La mejor de las fieras humanas: Vida de Julio Herrera y Reissig*. Pensamiento. Montevideo: Taurus, 2010.

Medina Betancort, Manuel. "Prólogo (El libro blanco, Frágil)." In *Poesías completas*, by Delmira Agustini, 89–93. Madrid: Cátedra, 1993.

Mejías-López, Alejandro. *The Inverted Conquest: The Myth of Modernity and the Transatlantic Onset of Modernism*. Nashville, TN: Vanderbilt University Press, 2009.

Miseres, Vanesa. "Modernismo puertas adentro: Género, escritura y experiencia urbana en *Mi vida con Enrique Gómez Carrillo* de Aurora Cáceres." *MLN* 131, no. 2 (March 3, 2016): 398–418. https://doi.org/10.1353/mln.2016.0019.

———. *Mujeres en tránsito: Viaje, identidad y escritura en Sudamérica (1830–1910)*. Chapel Hill: University of North Carolina Press, 2017.

———. "Solicitudes de amistad: El uso del álbum como red de sociabilidad y práctica de escritura femeninas." *Arizona Journal of Hispanic Cultural Studies* 22, no. 1 (2018): 9–27. https://doi.org/10.1353/hcs.2018.0002.

———. "Transiciones del discurso femenino en *La Filosofía Positiva* (Buenos Aires, 1898)." *Mundo Nuevo* 8, no. 18 (2016): 17–41.

———. "Una anti-crónica de Francia: Mi vida con Enrique Gómez Carrillo de Aurora Cáceres." In *Miradas recíprocas entre Perú y Francia. Viajeros, escritores y analistas (siglos XVIII-XX)*, 229–42. Lima: Universidad Ricardo Palma/Université Michel de Montaigne, 2015.

Mogillansky, Gabriela. "Modernización literaria y renovación técnica: La Nación (1882–1909)." In *Rubén Darío en La Nación de Buenos Aires, 1892–1916*. Buenos Aires: EUDEBA, 2004.

Molloy, Sylvia. "Dos lecturas del cisne: Rubén Darío y Delmira Agustini." In *La sartén por el mango: Encuentro de escritoras latinoamericanas*, edited by Patricia Elena González and Eliana Ortega, 57–69. Río Piedras, PR: Huracán, 1984.

———. "Female Textual Identitites: The Strategies of Self-Figuration." In *Women's Writing in Latin America*, edited by Sarah Castro-Klarén, Sylvia Molly, and Beatriz Sarlo, 107–24. Boulder, CO: Westview, 1991.

———. *La diffusion de la littérature hispano-américaine en France au XXe siècle*. Paris: Presses universitaires de France, 1972.

———. "Lecturas de descubrimiento: La otra cara del fin de siglo." In *Actas Irvine-92: [Actas de XI Congreso de la Asociación Internacional de Hispanistas]*, vol. 1, Asociación Internacional de Hispanistas, 1984, 17–28. https://dialnet.unirioja.es/servlet/articulo?codigo=1701246.

———. "Sentimentalidad y género: Notas para una lectura de Nervo." In *Entre hombres: Masculinidades del siglo XIX en América Latina*, Frankfurt: Vervuert Verlagsgesellschaft, 2010, 263–74.

———. "Too Wilde for Comfort: Desire and Ideology in Fin-de-Siecle Spanish America." *Social Text*, no. 31/32 (1992): 187–201. https://doi.org/10.2307/466225.

———. "Voice Snatching: De Sobremesa, Hysteria, and the Impersonation of Marie Bashkrtseff." *Latin American Literary Review* 25, no. 50 (December 7, 1997): 11–29.

———. *Poses de fin de siglo: Desbordes del género en la modernidad*, 1st ed. Buenos Aires: Eterna Cadencia Editora, 2012.

Monte, Azul del. "Social." *Búcaro Americano: Periódico de las Familias* 1, no. 1 (February 1, 1896), 16–23.

———. "Social." *Búcaro Americano: Periódico de las Familias* 1, no. 2 (February 15, 1896), 43–47.

Montero Bustamante, Raúl. *El parnaso oriental antología de poetas uruguayos; con un prólogo y notas crítico-biográficas*. Montevideo, 1905. http://resolver.iai.spk-berlin.de/IAI0000586B00000000.

Moody, Sarah. "Clorinda Matto de Turner en la Cosmópolis moderna: Espacio urbano y comunidad intelectual en Buenos Aires." In *Clorinda Matto en el siglo XXI*, edited by Francesca Denegri and Ana Peluffo, 329–58. Lima: Fondo Editorial of the Pontificia Universidad Católica de Perú, 2022.

———. "Clorinda's Cosmopolis: Crisis, Reinvention, and the Birth of *Búcaro Americano*." In *The Palgrave Handbook of Transnational Women's Writing in the Long Nineteenth Century*, edited by Claire Emilie Martin and Clorinda Donato, 323–38. London: Palgrave Macmillan, 2024.

———. "Latin American Women Writers and the Periodical Press, 1890–1910." *Letras Femeninas* 36, no. 2 (Winter 2010): 141–57.

———. "Poetic Form and City Form in the Fin de Siglo: Ornamentation and Regularity in Rubén Darío and Buenos Aires." *Latin American Literary Review* 42, no. 83 (June 1, 2014): 75–96.

———. "Women of Paris, World Literature, and a Counter-Mythology of the Metropolis in Manuel Ugarte's Early Literary Work." *Bulletin of Hispanic Studies* 93, no. 9 (October 10, 2016): 995–1008.

Moody, Sarah T. "Radical Metrics and Feminist Modernism: Agustini Rewrites Darío's *Prosas Profanas*." *Chasqui: Revista de Literatura Latinoamericana* 43, no. 1 (May 5, 2014): 57–67.

Moody, Sarah Tamsen. "Modern Form in the Periphery: Poetics, Urban Space, and Gender in Buenos Aires and Rio de Janeiro, 1880–1915." PhD diss., University of California, Berkeley, 2010.

Morales-Pino, Luz Ainaí. "Moribundas habladoras: Contestaciones al ideario patriarcal en *El Conspirador* (1892), *Incurables* (1905) y *La rosa muerta* (1914)." *LETRAS (Lima)* 92, no. 135 (2021): 125–45.

Morán, Francisco. "'Con Hugo fuerte y con Verlaine ambiguo': El reino interior o los peligrosos itinerarios del deseo en Rubén Darío." *Revista Iberoamericana* 72, no. 215–216 (September 4, 2006): 481–95. https://doi.org/10.5195/REVIBEROAMER.2006.93.

Moraña, Mabel. *Bourdieu en la periferia: Capital simbólico y campo cultural en América Latina*. Ensayo/Estudios culturales. Santiago de Chile: Editorial Cuarto Propio, 2014.

Moreira, Rubinstein. *Aproximación a María Eugenia Vaz Ferreira*. Montevideo: Montesexto, 1976.

Moreno de Cáceres, Antonia. *Recuerdos de la campaña de La Breña: Memorias*, 1st ed. Lima: C. Milla Batres, 1974.

Nervo, Amado. *Cartas de mujeres*. Edited by Sergio Márquez Acevedo and María del Carmen Ruiz Castañeda. México, DF: Universidad Nacional Autónoma de México, Instituto de Investigaciones Bibliográficas, 2004.

———. *Obras completas de Amado Nervo*. Edited by Alfonso Reyes. 28 vols. Madrid: Biblioteca Nueva, 1920.

———. "Prólogo de Amado Nervo." In *La rosa muerta*, by Zoila Aurora Cáceres, xxxi–xxxiii. Buenos Aires: Stock Cero, 2007.

Nin Frías, Alberto. *Nuevos ensayos de crítica literaria y filosófica*. Montevideo: Imprenta de Dornaleche y Reyes, [1904?]. Accessed May 24, 2021. http://bdh-rd.bne.es/viewer.vm?id=0000132363.

Outes-León, Brais D. "La Barbarie Refinada: The Crisis of European Modernity in Gómez Carrillo's Chronicles of the First World War." *Revista Canadiense de Estudios Hispánicos* 38, no. 3 (Spring 2014): 503–27.

Pachas Maceda, Sofía. *Aurora Cáceres "Evangelina": Sus escritos sobre arte peruano*, 1st ed. Lima: Seminario de Historia Rural Andina, Universidad Nacional Mayor de San Marcos, 2009.

———. "De Italia al Perú. La obra litográfica de Carlo Fabbri." *Revista del Instituto Riva-Agüero* 3, no. 1 (December 12, 2018): 137–61.

———. *Zoila Aurora Cáceres y la ciudadanía femenina: La correspondencia de Feminismo Peruano*, 1st ed. Lima: Universidad Nacional Mayor de San Marcos, 2019.

Passicot, María Emilia. "Sociedad Proteccionista Intelectual." *Búcaro Americano: Periódico de las Familias* 2, no. 9 (February 15, 1897), 171–72.

———. "Sociedad Proteccionista Intelectual." *Búcaro Americano: Periódico de las Familias* 2, no. 10 (March 15, 1897), 185–87.

Payró, Roberto Jorge. *Evocaciones de un porteño viejo [Bartolomé Mitre, Miguel Cané, Fray Mocho, Rubén Darío, José Ingenieros, Horacio Quiroga]*. Buenos Aires: Ed. Quetzal, 1952.

Paz, Octavio. *Cuadrivio: Darío, López Velarde, Pessoa Cernuda*. Mexico: Editorial de Joaquín Moritz, 1965. https://libroschorcha.files.wordpress.com/2018/04/cuadrivio-octavio-paz1.pdf.

Peluffo, Ana. "Comunidades de sentimiento: Cartografías afectivas de las redes sororales del siglo XIX." *Revista de Estudios Hispánicos* 53, no. 2 (June 2019): 473–90.

———. *Lágrimas andinas: Sentimentalismo, género y virtud republicana en Clorinda Matto de Turner*. Pittsburgh, PA: Instituto Internacional de Literatura Iberoamericana, Universidad de Pittsburgh, 2005.

———. "Latin American Ophelias: The Aesthetisation of Female Death in Nineteenth-Century Poetry." *Latin American Literary Review* 32, no. 64 (2004): 63–78.

———. "Necrofeminismo y redes de indignación en Gertrudis Gómez de Avellaneda y Emilia Pardo Bazán." *Revista Hispánica Moderna* 73, no. 1 (June 6, 2020): 61–75.

———. "Rizomas, redes y lazos transatlánticos: América Latina y España (1890–1920)." In *No hay nación para este sexo: La Re(d)pública transatlántica de las letras: Escritoras españolas y latinoamericanas (1824–1936)*, edited by Pura Fernández, 207–24. Madrid: Iberoamericana, 2015.

Phillips, Allen W. "Sobre Rubén Darío y Gómez Carrillo: Sus relaciones literarias y amistosas." In *Homenaje a Luis Alberto Sánchez*, edited by Robert G. Mead Jr. and Víctor M. Berger, 407–41. Madrid: Insula, 1983.

Pierce, Joseph M. *Argentine Intimacies: Queer Kinship in an Age of Splendor, 1890–1910*. Albany: State University of New York Press, 2019.

Pineda Franco, Adela Eugenia. *Geopolíticas de la cultura finisecular en Buenos Aires, París y México: Las revistas literarias y el modernismo*. Pittsburgh, PA: Instituto Internacional de Literatura Iberoamericana, Universidad de Pittsburgh, 2006.

Pleitez Vela, Tania. "'Debajo estoy yo,' formas de la (auto)representación femenina en la poesía hispanoamericana (1894–1954): María Eugenia Vaz Ferreira, Delmira Agustini, Alfonsina Storni y Julia de Burgos." PhD diss., Universitat de Barcelona, Departament de Filologia Hispànica, 2009.

———. "'No soy la que procuras': Relectura de arquetipos en la poesía de María Eugenia Vaz Ferreira." *Meridional: Revista Chilena de Estudios Latinoamericanos*, no. 7 (2016): 131–54.

"Premiados—Premio Cervantes." Accessed September 26, 2022. https://www.cultura.gob.es/cultura/libro/premios-literarios/listado-de-premios/cervantes/presentacion.html.

"Premio de Poesía José Lezama Lima." Accessed 26 September 2022. https://es.wikipedia.org/wiki/Premio_de_Poesía_José_Lezama_Lima.

"Premio Reina Sofía de Poesía Latinoamericana." Accessed September 26, 2022. https://www.patrimonionacional.es/concurso/xxx-premio-reina-sofia-de-poesia-iberoamericana.

"Premio Rómulo Gallegos." Ministerio de Cultura de Venezuela. Accessed March 25, 2024. https://mincultura.gob.ve/noticias/el-premio-de-novela-romulo-gallegos-ha-proyectado-labor-de-grandes-escritores/.

Prendergast, Christopher. *Paris and the Nineteenth Century*. Cambridge, MA: Blackwell, 1992.

Price, Leah. "Introduction: Reading Matter." *PMLA* 121, no. 1 (January 2006): 9–16.

"Quinta Vaz Ferreira." Fundación Vaz Ferreira, accessed May 24, 2021. http://www.quintavazferreira.org.uy/.

Quirarte, Vicente. "Presentación." In *Cartas de mujeres*, by Amado Nervo, 9–11. Mexico: UNAM, Instituto de Investigaciones Bibliográficas, 2004.

Quiroga, Horacio. "Aspectos del modernismo." In *La prosa modernista hispanoamericana: Introducción crítica y antología*, edited by José Olivio Jiménez and Carlos Javier Morales, 86–87. Madrid: Alianza Editorial, 1998.

———. *Diario de viaje a París*. Edited by Emir Rodríguez Monegal. 1st ed. Buenos Aires: Losada, 1999.

Rama, Ángel. *Cien años de raros*. Montevideo: Arca, 1966.

———. *Rubén Darío y el modernismo (circunstancia socioeconómica de un arte americano)*. [Caracas]: Ediciones de la Biblioteca de la Universidad Central de Venezuela, 1970.

Ramos, Julio. *Desencuentros de la modernidad en América Latina: Literatura y política en el siglo XIX*. México: Fondo de Cultura Económica, 1989.

Reynolds, Andrew. "Bourdieu's Imposition of Form and Modernismo: The Symbolic Power of a Literary Movement." In *Pierre Bourdieu in Hispanic Literature and Culture*, edited by Ignacio M. Sánchez Prado, 17–43. London: Palgrave Macmillan, 2018.

———. "Difference as Fashion: Enrique Gómez Carrillo and Modernista Chic." *Monographic Review/Revista Monográfica* 25 (2009): 105–19.

———. *The Spanish American Crónica Modernista, Temporality, and Material Culture: Modernismo's Unstoppable Presses*. Lewisburg, PA: Bucknell University Press; 2012.

Rocca, Pablo. *El crimen de Delmira Agustini*. Montevideo: Estuario Editora, 2014.

Rodríguez Monegal, Emir. "La generación del 900." Biblioteca Virtual Miguel de Cervantes, accessed July 31, 2021. https://www.cervantesvirtual.com/nd/ark:/59851/bmcn3o0do.

Rodríguez Ortiz, Óscar. "Presentación." In *La vida parisiense*, by Enrique Gómez Carrillo, 5–9. Caracas: Ayacucho, 1993.

Rosenbaum, Sidonia Carmen. *Modern Women Poets of Spanish America: The Precursors, Delmira Agustini, Gabriela Mistral, Alfonsina Storni, Juana de Ibarbourou*. New York: Hispanic Institute in the United States, 1945.

Rosenwein, Barbara H. *Emotional Communities in the Early Middle Ages*. Ithaca, NY: Cornell University Press, 2006.

Rotker, Susana. *La invención de la crónica*. Buenos Aires: Ediciones Letra Buena, 1992.

"Rubén Darío in the US: Translation Challenges." YouTube. ND College of Arts and Letters, posted November 11, 2021. https://www.youtube.com/watch?v=HJdoqXqBsdU.

Salgado, María A. "Rubén Darío y la Generación del 98: Personas, peronajes y máscaras del fin de siglo español." *Hispania* 82, no, 4 (Dec. 1999), 725–32.

Salinas, Pedro. *La poesía de Rubén Darío (ensayo sobre el tema y los temas del poeta)*. Buenos Aires: Editorial Losada, S.A., 1948.

Sánchez Prado, Ignacio M., ed. *Pierre Bourdieu in Hispanic Literature and Culture*. London: Palgrave Macmillan, 2018.

Sánchez Prado, Ignacio M. "Nación y castración." In *Entre hombres: Masculinidades del siglo XIX en América Latina*, edited by Ana Peluffo and Ignacio M. Sánchez Prado, 275–88. Frankfurt, Madrid: Vervuert Verlagsgesellschaft, 2010.

Santa Ana, Arturo. Letter to María Eugenia Vaz Ferreira. "Carta de Arturo Santa Ana." Fundación Vaz Ferreira-Raimondi, Biblioteca Nacional de Uruguay, accessed June 1, 2021. http://archivomariaeugenia.bibna.gub.uy/omeka/items/show/142.

Sanz Álvarez, Arancha. "La Bohemia Latinoamericana en París: Aurora Cáceres, Voyeurista." In *Viajeras entre dos mundos*, edited by Sara Beatriz Guardia and Losandro Antonio Tedeschi, 513–24. Dourados, Brazil: Editora UFGD, 2012.

Schmigalle, Günther. "Introducción." In *Los Raros*, by Rubén Darío. Berlin: Tranvía, 2015.

Schneider, Luis Mario. "Prólogo." In *Aves sin nido por Clorinda Matto de Turner*, 7–46. New York: Las Americas, 1968.

Schwartz, Marcy E. *Writing Paris: Urban Topographies of Desire in Contemporary Latin American Fiction*. Albany: SUNY Press, 1999.

Secret, Timothy. *The Politics and Pedagogy of Mourning: On Responsibility in Eulogy*. New York: Bloomsbury, 2015.

Showalter, Elaine. *The Female Malady: Women, Madness, and English Culture, 1830–1980*. New York: Pantheon Books, 1985.

Siegel, Elizabeth, Patrizia Di Bello, Marta Rachel Weiss, and Miranda Hofelt, eds. *Playing with Pictures: The Art of Victorian Photocollage*. Chicago and New Haven, CT: Art Institute of Chicago and Yale University Press, 2009.

Silva, José Asunción 1865–1896. *De sobremesa*. Bogotá: Universidad de los Andes, Universidad EAFIT, Universidad Nacional de Colombia, 2018. http://www.digitaliapublishing.com/a/60775/.

Simeto, Mario. "Cartas de Mario C. Simeto." Fundación Vaz Ferreira-Raimondi, Biblioteca Nacional de Uruguay, accessed July 27, 2021. http://archivomariaeugenia.bibna.gub.uy/omeka/items/show/134.

Simeto, Mario C. Letter to María Eugenia Vaz Ferreira. "Folio 1." Fundación Vaz Ferreira-Raimondi, Biblioteca Nacional de Uruguay, accessed June 1, 2021. http://archivomariaeugenia.bibna.gub.uy/omeka/files/show/1185.

———. Letter to María Eugenia Vaz Ferreira. "Folio 4." Fundación Vaz Ferreira-Raimondi, Biblioteca Nacional de Uruguay, accessed June 1, 2021. http://archivomariaeugenia.bibna.gub.uy/omeka/files/show/1188.

———. Letter to María Eugenia Vaz Ferreira. "Folio 7." Fundación Vaz Ferreira-Raimondi, Biblioteca Nacional de Uruguay, accessed June 1, 2021. http://archivomariaeugenia.bibna.gub.uy/omeka/files/show/1192.

———. Letter to María Eugenia Vaz Ferreira. "Folio 18." Fundación Vaz Ferreira-Raimondi, Biblioteca Nacional de Uruguay, accessed June 1, 2021. http://archivomariaeugenia.bibna.gub.uy/omeka/files/show/1214.

Siskind, Mariano. *Cosmopolitan Desires: Global Modernity and World Literature in Latin America*. Evanston, IL: Northwestern University Press, 2014.

———. "The Spectacle of War at a Distance: Latin American Modernistas in World War I." *MLN* 130, no. 2 (March 3, 2015): 234–55. https://doi.org/10.1353/mln.2015.0013.

Skinner, Lee Joan. *Gender and the Rhetoric of Modernity in Spanish America, 1850–1910*. Gainesville: University Press of Florida, 2016.

Sotomayor Martínez, Evelyn Noelia. *Pensar en público: Las veladas literarias de Clorinda Matto en la Lima de la posguerra (1887–1891)*. Lima: BNP, Biblioteca Nacional del Perú, 2017.

Sternbach, Nancy Saporta. "The Death of a Beautiful Woman: The Femme Fatale in the Spanish-American 'Modernista' Novel (Dominici, Venezuela; Halmar, Chile; Larreta, Argentina)." PhD diss., University of Arizona, 1984. https://repository.arizona.edu/handle/10150/187804.

Stewart, Susan. *On Longing: Narratives of the Miniature, the Gigantic, the Souvenir, the Collection.* Durham, NC: Duke University Press, 1993.

Streckert, Jens. "Latin Americans in Paris, 1870–1940: A Statistical Analysis." *Jahrbuch Für Geschichte Lateinamerikas* 49, no. 1 (2012): 181–204.

Tauzin Castellanos, Isabelle. "La narrativa femenina en el Perú antes de la guerra del Pacífico." *Revista de Crítica Literaria Latinoamericana* 21, no. 42 (1995): 161–87. https://doi.org/10.2307/4530830.

Tucker, Susan, Katherine Ott, and Patricia P. Buckler. *The Scrapbook in American Life.* Philadelphia, PA: Temple University Press, 2006.

Turnes, Antonio L. "MARIO C. SIMETO (1882–1930)." In *Historia de la medicina en Uruguay*, 1–36. Montevideo: Sindicato Médico del Uruguay. Accessed July 28, 2021. https://www.smu.org.uy/dpmc/hmed/historia/articulos/simeto.pdf.

Ugarte, Manuel. *Crónicas del bulevar.* Edited by Claudio Maíz and Marcos Olalla. Buenos Aires: Ediciones Biblioteca Nacional, 2010.

———. *Escritores iberoamericanos de 1900: Comentarios y recuerdos alrededor de Delmira Agostini [sic] Francisco Contreras, José Santos Chocano [y otros].* Santiago de Chile: Editorial Orbe, 1943.

———. *Paisajes parisienses.* Paris: Garnier Hermanos, 1901.

Unamuno, Miguel de. "Comentario breve de Miguel de Unamuno." In *La rosa muerta*, by Aurora Cáceres. Buenos Aires: Stock Cero, 2007.

Unruh, Vicky. *Performing Women and Modern Literary Culture in Latin America: Intervening Acts.* Austin: University of Texas Press, 2006.

Valera, Juan. "A D. Rubén Darío." In *Azul . . ., Cantos de vida y esperanza*, by Rubén Darío, edited by José María Martínez, 103–22. Madrid: Cátedra, 2006.

Valis, Noël M. "The Female Figure and Writing in Fin del siglo Spain." *Romance Quarterly* 36, no. 3 (1989): 369–81.

Vallejo, Catharina. *The Women in the Men's Club: Women Modernistas Poetas in Cuba (1880–1910).* New Orleans: University Press of the South, 2012.

Vasseur, Armando. Letter to María Eugenia Vaz Ferreira. "Carta de Armando Vasseur." Fundación Vaz Ferreira-Raimondi, Biblioteca Nacional de Uruguay, accessed June 1, 2021. http://archivomariaeugenia.bibna.gub.uy/omeka/items/show/208.

Vaz Ferreira, María Eugenia. "Carta a María Esther (probablemente Ferrer)." Fundación Vaz Ferreira-Raimondi, Biblioteca Nacional de Uruguay, accessed June 1, 2021. http://archivomariaeugenia.bibna.gub.uy/omeka/items/show/141.

———. "Correspondencia: Cartas a Nin Frías." Introduction by Arturo Sergio Visca. *Revista de la Biblioteca Nacional* [Montevideo, Uruguay], no. 12 (1 feb. 1976), pp. 71–90. http://bibliotecadigital.bibna.gub.uy:8080/jspui/handle/123456789/28939.

———. Letter to Orisini Bertrani. "F. 1r. Cartas a Orsini Bertani." Fundación Vaz Ferreira-Raimondi, Biblioteca Nacional de Uruguay, accessed July 28, 2021. http://archivomariaeugenia.bibna.gub.uy/omeka/files/show/1936.

———. "F. 7r. Cartas a Alberto Nin Frías." Fundación Vaz Ferreira-Raimondi, Biblioteca Nacional de Uruguay, accessed June 1, 2021. http://archivomariaeugenia.bibna.gub.uy/omeka/files/show/1333.

———. "F. 9r. Cartas de Alberto Nin Frías." Fundación Vaz Ferreira-Raimondi, Biblioteca Nacional de Uruguay, accessed June 1, 2021. http://archivomariaeugenia.bibna.gub.uy/omeka/files/show/1873.

———. "F. 12r. Cartas a Alberto Nin Frías." Fundación Vaz Ferreira-Raimondi, Biblioteca Nacional de Uruguay, accessed June 1, 2021. http://archivomariaeugenia.bibna.gub.uy/omeka/files/show/1342.

———. "F. 17r. Cartas a Alberto Nin Frías." Fundación Vaz Ferreira-Raimondi, Biblioteca Nacional de Uruguay, accessed June 1, 2021. http://archivomariaeugenia.bibna.gub.uy/omeka/files/show/1351.

———. "F. 21r. Cartas a Alberto Nin Frías." Fundación Vaz Ferreira-Raimondi, Biblioteca Nacional de Uruguay, accessed June 1, 2021. http://archivomariaeugenia.bibna.gub.uy/omeka/files/show/1357.

———. *Poesías completas*. Edited by Hugo J. Verani. Colección Poesías. Montevideo, Uruguay: Ediciones de la Plaza, 1986.

Vicens, María. "Clorinda Matto de Turner en Buenos Aires: Redes culturales y estrategias de (auto)legitimación de una escritora en el exilio." *Mora*, no. 19 (2013): 43–60. http://revistascientificas.filo.uba.ar/index.php/mora/article/view/445.

———. "La fantasía porteña: Escritoras peruanas en la Buenos Aires de entresiglos." *Revista del Instituto Riva-Agüero* 3, no. 1 (December 12, 2018): 77–111.

———. "Lectoras de patria grande: Escritoras sudamericanas en la prensa porteña finisecular." *Revista de Crítica Literaria Latinoamericana* 41, no. 82 (2015): 193–219.

———. "Por una tradición propia: Genealogías y legitimación en las escritoras transhispánicas de entresiglos." *Revista de Estudios Hispánicos* 53, no. 1 (March 2019): 371–95.

Vilella, Olga. "Of Bayaderas, Congais, and Fumerias: 'Virtual' Collecting in De Marsella á Tokio: Sensaciones de Egipto, La India, La China y El Japón, by Enrique Gómez Carrillo." In *Collecting from the Margins: Material Culture in a Latin American Context*, edited by María Mercedes Andrade, 49–74. Lewisburg, PA: Bucknell University Press, 2016.

Visca, Arturo Sergio. *Antología de poetas modernistas menores*. Montevideo: Biblioteca Artigas, 1971.

Visca, Pedro. "Ángel C. Maggiolo (1877–1948)." *Sindicato Médico del Uruguay*, n.d. https://www.smu.org.uy/publicaciones/libros/ejemplares/maggiolo.pdf

Ward, Thomas. "Introducción." In *La rosa muerta*, by Aurora Cáceres, vii–xxix. Buenos Aires: Stock Cero, 2007.

Wasem, Marcos. *El amor libre en Montevideo: Roberto de las Carreras y la irrupción del anarquismo erótico en el novecientos*. Uruguay: Ediciones de la Banda Oriental, 2015.

Weiss, Jason. *The Lights of Home: A Century of Latin American Writers in Paris*. New York: Routledge, 2003.

Wilson, Emilia Serrano, Baronesa de. *El mundo literario americano: Escritores contemporáneos, semblanzas, poesías, apreciaciones, pinceladas*. Barcelona: Maucci, 1903. http://bdh.bne.es/bnesearch/detalle/bdh0000010160.

Wolf, Christa Middleton. *The Quest for Christa T*. New York, Farrar, Straus & Giroux, 1971.

ZAC. "Al paso del tren de Rosario." *Búcaro Americano: Periódico de las Familias* 2, no. 9 (February 15, 1897), 175–76.

———. "Al paso del tren de Rosario." *Búcaro Americano: Periódico de las Familias* 2, no. 10 (March 15, 1897), 189–90.

Zanetti, Susana E. "*Búcaro Americano*: Clorinda Matto de Turner en la escena femenina porteña." In *Mujeres y cultura en la Argentina del siglo XIX*, edited by Lea Fletcher, 264–75. Buenos Aires: Feminaria Editora, 1994.

INDEX

"A una golondrina" (To a Swallow) (Vaz Ferreira), 105
Achugar, Hugo, 105, 116
Adam, Paul, 7, 66
afrancesamiento, 19–20. See also Francophilia
Águila, Rocío del, 89
Agustini, Delmira
    critique of Modernismo by, 1–6, 17, 157
    Darío and, 2–3, 7, 21
    divorce and murder of, 5, 124
    intellectual networks and, 127–28
    misreading of, 4–6, 104, 133
    Vaz Ferreira and, 105, 106–7, 117, 120–21, 129–30, 131
Aínsa, Fernando, 124
"Al pie de la escalera" (At the foot of the stairs) (Gutiérrez Nájera), 33–34, 36, 44–45
La Alborada (The Dawn) (magazine), 4
Álbum personal (Cáceres), 94, 134–36, 139–42, 150–55, 160
El alma encantadora de París (The Charming Soul of Paris) (Gómez Carrillo), 60–61
El alma japonesa (The Japanese Soul) (Gómez Carrillo), 60
"El alma sublime de París" (The Sublime Soul of Paris), 62
Almas y cerebros (Souls and Brains) (Gómez Carrillo), 60
La amada inmóvil (The Immobile Beloved) (Nervo), 37
Andrade, María Mercedes, 187n25x
Arguedas, Alcides, 52
Armando Vasseur, Álvaro, 120
Los arrecifes de coral (The Coral Reefs) (Quiroga), 184n102
Art Nouveau, 33
article parisiense, 62–63. See also Paris
"¡Artistas!" (Artists!) (Agustini), 182n64
"Aspectos del modernismo" (Aspects of Modernismo) (Quiroga), 126
Asunción Silva, José, 11
Ateneo de Buenos Aires, 76–78, 80–85, 159
Autobiografía (Autobiography) (Darío), 80, 82
Auza, Néstor Tomás, 82
Aves sin nido (Birds without a Nest) (Matto de Turner), 76, 78, 79
Azul... (Blue...) (Darío), 17–18, 19–20, 23–25, 80, 120

El Bachiller (The Graduate) (Nervo), 37
Baires, Carlos, 175n30
Barra, Eduardo de la, 17–18, 19, 23, 25
Bastos, María Luisa, 61, 74
Batlle y Ordóñez, José, 104, 123–25, 182n62, 184n108
Baudrillard, Jean, 150
"Bautismo" (Baptism) (Matto de Turner), 91–92
Belín Sarmiento, Eugenia, 175n23
Benjamin, Walter, 51, 152–53
Benlliure, Mariano, 140
"La berceuse" (Vaz Ferreira), 111–13, 114, 119
Berman, Marshall, 34
La Biblioteca (The Library) (magazine), 174n12
Blanca Sol (Cabello de Carbonera), 96
Blanco-Fombona, Rufino, 48–49, 52
Blixen, Carina, 104, 106–7, 129, 130, 131
bohemianism, 14, 29–30, 60, 80–84, 104, 124
Bois, Jules, 141, 142
Bonafoux, Luis, 148, 186n11
Bornay, Erika, 64
Borrero, Juana, 21, 165n20
Bourdieu, Pierre, 13
Braddock, Jeremy, 189n79
Brignole, Alberto, 126–27
Bronfen, Elisabeth, 90
Bryce Echenique, Alfredo, 145, 147
Búcaro Americano: Periódico de las Familias (American Vase: Periodical of Families) (magazine)
  Ateneo de Buenos Aires and, 83–85, 159
  "Bautismo" (Baptism) in, 91–92
  Cáceres and, 92–95, 136
  "Despedida" (Farewell) in, 100
  goals and success of, 79–80, 101
  Larrosa de Ansaldo's eulogy in, 86–91, 94
  "La mujer en el Ateneo argentino" in, 81
  "Las obreras del pensamiento en la

Búcaro Americano (continued)
  América del Sur" in, 86, 89, 91, 94
  professionalism vs. frivolity in, 95–100
  "Social" column in, 92
Buckler, Patricia P., 151–52
Buenos Aires
  Gómez Carrillo and, 68–73
  intellectual networks in, 76–78, 79–86, 159
  See also Matto de Turner, Clorinda
"El bulevar día a día" (The Boulevard Day by Day) (Gómez Carrillo), 63–64

Cabello de Carbonera, Mercedes, 96, 177n73
Cabello Hutt, Claudia, 3, 4
Cáceres, Andrés Avelino, 78, 93, 136
Cáceres, Rosa Amelia, 136
Cáceres, Zoila Aurora
  Álbum personal as personal archive of, 134–36, 139–42, 150–55, 160
  Gómez Carrillo and, 46–47, 65, 135, 137, 142–46, 148–49, 164n6
  intellectual networks and, 135, 137–38, 140–43, 146–47, 150–51, 160
  life and career of, 134–38
  Matto de Turner and, 92–95, 101–2, 136
  Modernista contemporaries on, 21, 147–50
  recuperation of, 160–61
  women's rights and, 134, 137–39
Caetani Lovatelli, Ersilia, 140
Cairns, Kathleen, 190n89
Los cálices vacíos (The empty chalices) (Agustini), 5, 164n9
"Las calles de la City" (The Streets of the City) (Gómez Carrillo), 69
La campaña de la Breña, memorias del mariscal del Perú, D. Andrés A. Cáceres (Cáceres and Cáceres), 137
Los cantos de la mañana (Songs of the Morning) (Agustini), 5

INDEX

capital, 13
Caras y Caretas (magazine), 181n54, 185n110
Cárdenas, Mónica, 146
Cardwell, Richard, 19
Carreras, Roberto de las, 124, 128, 129
"Cartas de mujeres" (Letters from women) (Nervo), 37, 39–41, 42, 44, 45
Carvallo, Fernando, 147
Casal, Julián del, 11, 12
Castell, Dorila and Adela, 175n30
Castro, Eugenio de, 7, 175n33
cenáculos (coteries), 104, 125–28
Centro Social de Señoras (Ladies' Social Center), 137–38
Cero, Stock, 137
Cien años de raros (One Hundred Years of Eccentrics) (Rama), 103
La ciudad del sol (City of the Sun) (Cáceres), 137, 148–49
Clayton, Michelle, 155
El Cojo Ilustrado (magazine), 50
Colman de Blanco, María, 177n65
Colombi, Beatriz, 51–52, 56–57, 60, 62–63, 142
Cometti, Margarita V. de, 177n65
Consistorio del Gay Saber (Consistory of Gay Wisdom), 14, 104, 125–28, 159
Conway, Christopher, 38–39
Cornejo Polar, Antonio, 160–61
Cortón, Antonio, 60–61
Crispo Acosta, Osvaldo, 105–6, 107–8
crónica de París, 62–63. See also Paris
cultural capital, 13, 101
Curie, Marie, 55–56

Dailliez, Ana Cecilia Luisa, 37
Darío, Rubén
  Agustini and, 2–3, 7, 21
  Cáceres and, 21, 148
  erotic feminine as metapoetics for, 17–20, 23–28, 30, 44
  Gutiérrez Nájera and, 34
  on individual style, 133
  intellectual networks and, 10, 12, 36–37, 79, 80–82, 146
  on journalistic work, 34–35
  Matto de Turner and, 84, 95, 100
  Nervo and, 36–37
  on Paris and feminine modernity, 50, 52–59, 60–61, 62–63, 74, 158
  rareza (strangeness) and, 7–8, 9, 103. See also *Los raros* (The Strange Ones) (Darío)
  Vaz Ferreira and, 117–18, 120
  on women writers, 21, 148
  See also specific works
"De invierno" (In winter) (Darío), 24–25, 44
De Marsella a Tokio (From Marseille to Tokyo) (Gómez Carrillo), 60
De sobremesa (After-Dinner Conversation) (Silva), 21, 151, 154
Decadentism, 7, 40, 103–4
Delgado, Asdrúbal, 126–27
Denegri, Francesca, 89, 160–61
Derrida, Jacques, 90–91
"Despedida" (Farewell) (Matto de Turner), 100
"Los desterrados" (The Banished) (Vaz Ferreira), 114–16
destierro (banishment, exile), 113–14
El Día (newspaper), 105
Diario de viaje a París (Travel Diary to Paris) (Quiroga), 183n92, 184n102
Díaz, Porfirio, 28–29
Díaz Dufóo, Carlos, 32–33
Díaz Romero, Eugenio, 174n12, 182n62
Díaz-Marcos, Ana María, 172n78
Dijkstra, Bram, 64
"Divagación" (Divagation) (Darío), 66, 182n57
divorce, 124

El donador de almas (The Donor of Souls) (Nervo), 38–39
"La Duquesa Job" (The Duchess Job) (Gutiérrez Nájera), 29–31, 32, 36, 44–45

Eccleston, Sara, 175n30
Echevarría, Sara and Cristina, 182n63
Ehrick, Christine, 124
Ehrlicher, Hanno, 171n50, 172n102
Elegancias (Elegances), 18
"La emancipación de la mujer" (The Emancipation of Woman) (Cáceres), 93, 136, 138, 154
En voz baja (In a Quiet Voice) (Nervo), 40
El encanto de Buenos Aires (The Charm of Buenos Aires) (Gómez Carrillo), 68–72
enferma (sick woman), 21. *See also* illness
enfrentismo, 19
ensueño (reverie), 6–7, 25, 52–59
Entre encajes (Among lace) (Gómez Carrillo), 60
"Entre flores y sonrisas" (Among Flowers and Smiles) (Gómez Carrillo), 71
La Equitativa (The Equitable), 78
"Era un aire suave" (There Was a Soft Air) (Darío), 107–8
Escaja, Tina, 21
"escritura femenina" (feminine writing), 13
Escuela Comercial de Mujeres (Women's Commercial School), 79, 99
Escuela Normal de Profesoras (Normal School of Women Professors), 79
"La eterna canción" (The Eternal Song) (Vaz Ferreira), 105
"La exposición: Los hispanoamericanos" (The Exposition: the Spanish-Americans) (Darío), 170n35

Exposition Universelle (Paris, 1900), 36–37, 52, 54–55

Fabbri, Carlos, 139
Felski, Rita, 166n6
femininity and feminine style
  Búcaro Americano and, 92
  critique of Modernismo by Agustini and, 1–6, 17
  Darío and, 17–20, 23–28, 30, 44–45
  discourses of, 5–7, 8–11, 17–21, 154
  Gutiérrez Nájera and, 18–19, 20–21, 22–23, 28–36, 44–45
  modernity and, 73–74. *See also* Paris
  Nervo and, 18–19, 20, 22–23, 36–45
El feminismo en Berlín (Feminism in Berlin) (Cáceres), 136–37
Feminismo Peruano (Peruvian Feminism) (association), 94, 137–38
feminist scholarship, 3
femmes fatales, 21, 64
Fernández Bravo, Álvaro, 14
Fernández Saldaña, José María, 126–27
Ferrando, Federico, 126–27
field, 13–14
Fombona, Jacinto, 51
Fornaro Bordolli, Marita, 110–11
Foucault, Michel, 184n94
Fox Lockert, Lucía, 188n52
Francophilia, 19–20, 50–52, 99–100. *See also* Paris
Freire, Julio, 105
Freud, Sigmund, 167n40
Freyre, Carolina, 174n21
frivolity
  Gómez Carrillo and, 47–50, 61–69, 74–75
  Matto de Turner and, 95–100
  Vaz Ferreira and, 106
Fuego y mármol (Fire and Marble) (Vaz Ferreira), 111, 179n10
Fuller, Löie, 61

García Calderón, Francisco, 52
García Calderón, Ventura, 47–49, 52

Garet, Leonardo, 179n5, 183n91
Gautier, Théophile, 29
Gavidia, Francisco, 23
The Gay Science (Nietzsche), 179n5
Generación del 98 (Generation of 1898), 19, 73
Generación del 900 (Generation of 1900), 103–4, 124–29, 159–60
Giaudrone, Carla, 124–25, 129, 130–31, 184n94
Giusti, Roberto Fernando, 82, 175n23
Gómez Carrillo, Enrique
  on Buenos Aires, 68–73
  Cáceres and, 46–47, 65, 135, 137, 142–46, 148–49, 164n6
  frivolity and, 47–50, 61–69, 74–75
  intellectual networks and, 10, 36–37, 60
  mainstream newspapers and, 50, 141, 155
  on Paris and feminine modernity, 46–50, 52, 57–69, 71–73, 74–75, 158–59
González, Aníbal, 61
González de Fanning, Teresa, 177n73
Gorriti, Juana Manuela, 87, 89, 91, 94, 101–2, 177n73
La Grecia eterna (Eternal Greece) (Gómez Carrillo), 60
Grigsby, Carlos F., 163n2
Groussac, Paul, 174n12
Guido y Spano, Carlos, 81, 83–84
Guimarães, Luís, 120–21
Gutiérrez, Federico A., 151
Gutiérrez Girardot, Rafael, 13
Gutiérrez Nájera, Manuel
  feminine style and, 18–19, 20–21, 22–23, 28–36, 44–45
  intellectual networks and, 12
  Revista Azul and, 29, 32–36, 39, 44–45

Helfand, Jessica, 151
Herrera y Obes, Julio, 184n108
Herrera y Reissig, Julio, 120, 128
"Hija del Aire" (Daughter of the Air) (Gutiérrez Nájera), 21
"Historia de un sobretodo" (Story of an Overcoat) (Darío), 171n50
"Holocausto" (Holocaust) (Vaz Ferreira), 116–17, 132
homoeroticism, 124
homosociality, 48, 77–78, 82–83, 85, 149–50
Hugo, Victor, 19–20, 51
Huyssen, Andreas, 190n83
hysteria, 34

Ibarbourou, Juana de, 107
Ibsen, Henrik, 7
illness
  enferma (sick woman) and, 21
  Vaz Ferreira and, 107, 110–11, 113–14, 125, 159
El Imparcial (newspaper), 50, 52
indigenismo (Indigenism), 76, 78, 79
intellectual networks
  concept of, 11–14
  in Buenos Aires, 76–78, 79–86
  Cáceres and, 135, 137–38, 140–43, 146–47, 150–51, 160
  Darío and, 10, 12, 36–37, 79, 80–82, 146
  exclusion of women from, 14–15, 22, 82–83, 104, 127–28, 130–31, 146–47
  Gómez Carrillo and, 10, 36–37, 60
  Matto de Turner and, 76–78, 82–95, 101, 159
  Montevideo's Generation of 1900 and, 104, 125–28, 159
  Vaz Ferreira and, 120–24
  women and, 14–15, 88–95, 100–102, 137–38, 159
  See also *veladas* (evening events)
Irwin, Robert McKee, 37
La isla de los cánticos (The Island of Chants) (Vaz Ferreira), 111, 114
"Ite Missa Est" (Darío), 26–28, 44

Jacovkis, Vera Helena, 67
Jaimes, Julio Lucas, 174n21

Jaimes Freyre, Ricardo, 174n12, 174n21, 175n30
Jauretche, Julio J., 126–27

Kahn, Gustave and Rachel, 141
Kanost, Laura, 21, 149, 189n72
Kirkpatrick, Gwen, 21
Kirkpatrick, Susan, 65
Kock, Paul de, 29–30
Kurz, Andreas, 39–40

Labor de armonía interamericana en los Estados Unidos de Norteamérica, 1940-1945 (Labor of Interamerican Harmony in the United States of North America, 1940-1945) (Cáceres), 138
Lange, Helene, 140
Larrosa de Ansaldo, Lola, 86–91, 94
Lavrín, Asunción, 183n81
Leconte de Lisle, 7
Leguizamón, Martiniano, 175n30
"Lettres de femmes" (Letters From Women) (Prévost), 39
El Liberal (newspaper), 50, 141, 150–51, 155
El libro blanco (Frágil) (The White Book [Fragile]) (Agustini), 4–5, 7, 129
El libro de las mujeres (The Book of Women) (Gómez Carrillo), 48, 60, 171n72
Link, Daniel, 163n2
literary field, 13–14
Litvan, Valentina, 103
logic of exclusion, 14–15
Lugones, Leopoldo, 95, 100, 120

Maggiolo, Ángel Carlos, 122
Maíz, Claudio, 14
Malosetti Costa, Laura, 81
Manso, Juana, 87
Mapes, Erwin Kempton, 23
Márquez Acevedo, Sergio, 40

Martí, José, 7, 11, 12, 19, 73, 168n51, 172n101
Martínez, Elia M., 97
Martínez, José María, 17, 22, 37–38, 40
Martinoli, Fanny de, 175n23
masculinity and masculine modernity, 19, 73–74
Matamoros, Mercedes, 165n20
Matthews, Samantha, 153
Matto de Turner, Clorinda
 Cáceres and, 92–95, 101–2, 136
 frivolity and, 95–100
 intellectual networks and, 76–78, 82–95, 101, 159
 Larrosa de Ansaldo and, 86–91, 94
 life and career of, 76–80, 89–90, 164n6, 187n24
 recuperation of, 160–61
 women's rights and education and, 74, 76–77, 79
 See also *Búcaro Americano: Periódico de las Familias* (American Vase: Periodical of Families) (magazine)
Mazzucchelli, Aldo, 126, 128
Medina Betancourt, Manuel, 4
Méndez de Cuenca, Laura, 96, 175n30
El Mercurio de América (The Mercury of America) (magazine), 174n12, 182n62
Mexican Revolution, 28–29
Mi vida con Enrique Gómez Carrillo (My Life with Enrique Gómez Carrillo) (Cáceres), 137, 143–44, 149
Migoya García, Julio, 84
"Mis enlutadas" (My mournful ladies) (Gutiérrez Nájera), 31–32, 36
Miseres, Vanesa, 99–100, 135–36, 143, 146–47, 179n97
Mistral, Gabriela, 107, 131
Modernismo
 female readership of, 17–18, 22–23, 33–34, 37–38

Modernismo (*continued*)
   queer reading of, 3–4, 157
   specific definition of, 11–12
   women's roles and representation in, 1–7, 17–23
   See also femininity and feminine style
El modernismo (Modernismo) (Gómez Carrillo), 60
"El modernismo" (Modernismo) (Nervo), 41–42
Molloy, Sylvia, 6, 21–22, 28, 38, 63, 104, 169n83
"Monólogo" (Monologue) (Vaz Ferreira), 105, 108–9, 111, 121
Las montañas del oro (The Mountains of Gold) (Lugones), 95
Montero Bustamante, Raúl, 105
Moréas, Jean, 7, 145
Moreno de Moreno, Julia, 177n65
Moreno Leyva, Antonia, 136
"La mujer en el Ateneo argentino" (Woman in the Argentine Ateneo) (Matto de Turner), 81
"La mujer moderna" (Modern Woman) (Matto de Turner), 97–98
"La mujer trabajadora" (The Working Woman) (Matto de Turner), 99
Mujeres de ayer y de hoy (Women of Yesterday and of Today) (Cáceres), 137, 148
Mundial Magazine (Worldwide Magazine), 18
El Mundo (newspaper), 36, 168n67
El mundo literario americano (The American Literary World) (Serrano), 140–41
Museo de Bellas Artes (Fine Arts Museum) (Buenos Aires), 174n16
Musset, Alfred de, 29

La Nación (newspaper), 7, 50, 52, 80
El Nacional (newspaper), 36

Naturalism, 21
Nervo, Amado
   Cáceres and, 148
   feminine style and, 18–19, 20, 22–23, 36–45
   Gómez Carrillo and, 47, 48
   Matto de Turner and, 100
   Paris and, 52
neurasthenia, 34
Nietzsche, Friedrich, 179n5
Nin Frías, Alberto
   homoeroticism and, 124
   Vaz Ferreira and, 105, 109–10, 114, 121, 128, 133
"Nuestras miniaturas" (Our miniatures) (Matto de Turner), 84

Oasis de arte (Oasis of Art) (Cáceres), 137, 148
Obligado, Pedro Miguel, 81, 120–21
"Las obreras del pensamiento en la América del Sur" (Matto de Turner), 76–77, 86, 89, 91, 94
"El oro del Perú" (The Gold of Peru) (Cáceres), 136–37
La otra isla de los cánticos (The Other Island of Chants) (Vaz Ferreira), 111
Ott, Katherine, 151–52
Oyuela, Calixto, 81

Pachas Maceda, Sofía, 145, 147, 185n1
"El pájaro azul" (The blue bird) (Darío), 18
"Palabras liminares" (Liminal Words) (Darío), 25–26, 34, 44
Palacios, Alfredo, 140, 150–51
Palma, Ricardo, 78, 83
Pardo Bazán, Emilia, 14, 85
Paris
   Cáceres and, 46–47, 139, 141–42, 143, 147, 160
   Darío and, 50, 52–59, 60–61, 62–63, 74, 158

Paris (*continued*)
  Exposition Universelle (1900) in, 36–37, 52, 54–55
  Gómez Carrillo and, 46–50, 52, 57–69, 71–73, 74–75, 158–59
  as myth, 50–52
  "París y los escritores extranjeros" (Paris and foreign writers) (Darío), 57
Passicot, María Emilia, 88, 176n44
Paul-Margueritte, Lucie, 141
Payró, Roberto, 81
Paz, Octavio, 28
Peluffo, Ana, 21, 27, 86, 89, 149–50, 160–61, 177n73
Pera, Cristóbal, 51
Percovich Bosch, Aída, 183n74
Los Peregrinos (The Pilgrims) (Vaz Ferreira), 105
Pérez, Darío, 141, 150–51
Las perlas de Rosa (The Pearls of Rosa) (Cáceres), 137, 146
El Perú Ilustrado (Illustrated Peru) (magazine), 78, 187n24
The Picture of Dorian Gray (Wilde), 39–40
La piedra filosofal (The Philosophical Stone) (Vaz Ferreira), 105
Pierce, Joseph M., 4, 163n5
Piérola, Nicolás de, 78, 93, 136
Pineda Franco, Adela Eugenia, 37
Piñeiro, Norberto, 175n30
Pleitez Vela, Tania, 106, 130, 131, 180n15
En plena bohemia (In Full Bohemia) (Gómez Carrillo), 61–62
Poe, Edgar Allan, 7
Poesías completas (Complete Poems) (Vaz Ferreira), 111, 118, 131
"El poeta y la ilusión" (The poet and illusion) (Agustini), 1–3, 4–5, 17, 157
Posadas, Sofía, 175n23
Pougy, Liane de, 55–56
Práxedes Muñoz, Margarita, 175n24

Premio de Poesía José Lezama Lima, 164n11
Premio Miguel de Cervantes, 164n11
Premio Reina Sofía de Poesía Iberoamericana, 164n11
Premio Rómulo Gallegos, 164n11
Prévost, Marcel, 39
Price, Leah, 135
La princesa Suma Tica (The Princess Suma Tica) (Cáceres), 137, 155
"Prólogo al poema del Niágara" (Martí), 168n51
Prosas profanas y otros poemas (Profane Proses and Other Poems) (Darío), 7, 17, 25–27, 34, 44, 79, 95, 120. See also "Sonatina" (Darío)
prostitution, 55–56, 64
Psicología de la moda femenina (Psychology of Feminine Fashion) (Gómez Carrillo), 65–66

queer studies, 3–4, 157
Quesada, Ernesto, 175n30
Quiroga, Horacio, 126–27

Rachilde (Marguerite Vallette-Eymery), 8
Rama, Ángel, 13, 103
rareza (strangeness)
  Darío and, 7–8, 9, 103
  intellectual networks and, 12
  Uruguayan culture and, 125. See also Generación del 900 (Generation of 1900)
  women and, 7–15. See also Cáceres, Zoila Aurora; Matto de Turner, Clorinda; Vaz Ferreira, María Eugenia
Los raros (The Strange Ones) (Darío), 7–8, 9, 79, 95, 103
La Razón (newspaper), 50, 105
Real Academia Española (Royal Spanish Academy), 14, 85, 164n11

Resurrexit: Idilio Medioeval (Resurrexit: Medieval Idyll) (Vaz Ferreira), 105
Revista Azul (Azure Magazine) (magazine), 29, 32–36, 39, 44–45
Revista de América (Magazine of America) (magazine), 174n12
Revista del Salto (magazine), 183n92
Revista Moderna de México (magazine), 37
Reyes, Enrique Job, 5, 124, 180n19
Reyes Spíndola, Rafael, 168n67
Reynolds, Andrew, 50, 66
Ribeiro, León, 105
Ribeiro Freire, Belén, 108–10
"La rima vacua" (The Hollow Rhyme) (Vaz Ferreira), 119–20
Rodó, José Enrique, 11, 73, 120–21
Rodríguez Monegal, Emir, 104–5
Rodríguez Ortiz, Óscar, 61
Romanticism, 21, 22, 29
La rosa muerta (A Dead Rose) (Cáceres), 137, 138, 146, 148, 154
El rosario de Eros (The Rosary of Eros) (Agustini), 5

Said, Edward, 177n57
Sánchez Prado, Ignacio, 37
Santa Ana, Arturo, 120, 122
Sanz Álvarez, Arancha, 142
Sarmiento, Domingo Faustino, 51, 74
Schwartz, Marcy, 51
scrapbooks
 Álbum personal (Cáceres) as, 94, 134–36, 139–42, 150–55, 160
 characteristics and scholarship on, 134, 150–54
Secret, Timothy, 90–91
Sensaciones de París y de Madrid (Sensations of Paris and Madrid) (Gómez Carrillo), 60
"El ser neutro" (The Neutral Being) (Nervo), 42–44

Serrano, Emilia, 140–41
Silva, José Asunción, 21, 151, 154
Silverman, Eliane, 190n89
Simeto, Cloris, 122
Simeto, Mario, 122–23
Sindicato de Telefonistas del Perú (Syndicate of Telephone-Operators of Peru), 137–38
"La sirena" (The Mermaid) (Vaz Ferreira), 105
Siskind, Mariano, 52
Skinner, Lee, 166n21
Sobre feminismo (On Feminism) (C. Vaz Ferreira), 124
social capital, 13, 76, 101. *See also* intellectual networks
Sociedad Proteccionista Intelectual (Intellectual Protectionist Society), 78, 87
"Sonatina" (Darío)
 Agustini and, 17
 luxurious and cluttered spaces in, 151
 sadness in, 154
 translations of, 163n2
 Vaz Ferreira and, 118
 woman as metaphor for poetry in, 26, 30
 woman as passive and mute in, 26, 27–28, 44
Sternbach, Nancy Saporta, 21
Stewart, Susan, 153
Streckert, Jens, 51, 52
symbolic capital, 13, 19
Symbolism, 7, 29

Tauzin Castellanos, Isabel, 89
"La tempestad" (The Tempest) (Vaz Ferreira), 131–32
Torre de los Panoramas (Tower of Panoramas), 104, 128, 159
"Los torrentes" (The Torrents) (Vaz Ferreira), 118–19
Tórtola Valencia, Carmen, 154–55
Tucker, Susan, 151–52

Ugarte, Manuel, 36–37, 52, 56, 62, 67, 149, 170n42
Unamuno, Miguel de, 58, 148
Unión Católica de Señoras de Lima (Catholic Union of Ladies of Lima), 137–38
Unión Literaria de los Países Latinos (Literary Union of Latin Countries), 137–38
United States, 74
Universidad de Mujeres (Women's University), 108, 122, 123, 124
"Unpacking My Library" (Benjamin), 152–53
Unruh, Vicky, 176n52
Uriarte, Javier, 103

Valenzuela, José, 37
Valera, Juan, 19–20
Valis, Noël, 23
Vallejo, Catharina, 165n20
vanguardias (avant-gardes), 8, 152
Vasseur, Álvaro Armando, 121–22
Vaz Ferreira, Carlos, 104–5, 108, 111, 121, 122, 124
Vaz Ferreira, María Eugenia
  Agustini and, 105, 106–7, 117, 120–21, 129–30, 131
  archival materials on, 120–24, 159
  eccentricity and illness of, 105–11, 125, 130–33, 159–60
  intellectual networks and, 127–28
  life and career of, 104–5, 164n6
  Modernismo and, 117–19
  reception and collective memory of, 105–7
  recuperation of, 160–61
  on woman as poet, 104, 111–20
Vega Belgrano, Carlos, 81, 82, 84
veladas (evening events)
  Ateneo de Buenos Aires and, 81
  women and, 88–91, 101–2

"El velo de la reina Mab" (The veil of Queen Mab) (Darío), 18
Verani, Hugo J., 111, 181n54
Verlaine, Paul, 7, 28
Viaje de recreo (Recreational Trip) (Matto de Turner), 99–100
Viajes por África, Europa y América (Travels through Africa, Europe, and America) (Sarmiento), 51, 74
Vicens, María, 85, 87–88, 175n24
"La vida artificial" (The artificial life) (Gutiérrez Nájera), 34–36
Vida Moderna (magazine), 181n54
La vida parisiense (Parisian life) (Gómez Carrillo), 60
Vida Social (magazine), 151
"El viejo París" (Old Paris) (Darío), 54–55
Visca, Arturo Sergio, 125, 126
Vistas de Europa (Views of Europe) (Gómez Carrillo), 60, 62

Ward, Thomas, 22, 137, 149
Wasem, Marcos, 129
Weiss, Jason, 52
Wilde, Oscar, 39–40
Wolf, Christa, 150
women's education and professionalization
  Batllismo and, 123–25
  Cáceres and, 93, 134, 135, 136–39
  Matto de Turner and, 76–77, 79, 98–100, 159
  Vaz Ferreira and, 104–5, 108, 159

Xenes, Nieves, 165n20

Zanetti, Susana, 95–96
Zeballos, Estanislao, 175n30